THE NEW FOLGER LIBRARY SHAKESPEARE

Designed to make Shakespeare's great plays available to all readers, the New Folger Library edition of Shakespeare's plays provides accurate texts in modern spelling and punctuation, as well as scene-by-scene action summaries, full explanatory notes, many pictures clarifying Shakespeare's language, and notes recording all significant departures from the early printed versions. Each play is prefaced by a brief introduction, by a guide to reading Shakespeare's language, and by accounts of his life and theater. Each play is followed by an annotated list of further readings and by a "Modern Perspective" written by an expert on that particular play.

Barbara A. Mowat is Director of Academic Programs at the Folger Shakespeare Library, Executive Editor of *Shakespeare Quarterly,* Chair of the Folger Institute, and author of *The Dramaturgy of Shakespeare's Romances* and of essays on Shakespeare's plays and on the editing of the plays.

Paul Werstine is Professor of English at the Graduate School and at King's University College at the University of Western Ontario. He is general editor of the New Variorum Shakespeare and author of many papers and articles on the printing and editing of Shakespeare's plays.

The Folger Shakespeare Library

The Folger Shakespeare Library in Washington, D.C., a privately funded research library dedicated to Shakespeare and the civilization of early modern Europe, was founded in 1932 by Henry Clay and Emily Jordan Folger. In addition to its role as the world's preeminent Shakespeare collection and its emergence as a leading center for Renaissance studies, the Folger Library offers a wide array of cultural and educational programs and services for the general public.

EDITORS

BARBARA A. MOWAT
Director of Academic Programs
Folger Shakespeare Library

PAUL WERSTINE
Professor of English
King's University College at the University of
Western Ontario, Canada

FOLGER SHAKESPEARE LIBRARY

The Tragedy of

King Lear

By
WILLIAM SHAKESPEARE

EDITED BY BARBARA A. MOWAT
AND PAUL WERSTINE

Simon & Schuster Paperbacks
NEW YORK LONDON TORONTO SYDNEY

Simon & Schuster Paperbacks
A Division of Simon & Schuster, Inc.
1230 Avenue of the Americas
New York, NY 10020

First Washington Square Press New Folger Trade Paperback
Edition August 2005
This Simon & Schuster paperback edition October 2009

SIMON & SCHUSTER PAPERBACKS and colophon are
registered trademarks of Simon & Schuster, Inc.

For information regarding special discounts for bulk purchases,
please contact Simon & Schuster Special Sales at
1-866-506-1949 or business@simonandschuster.com.

The Simon & Schuster Speakers Bureau can bring
authors to your live event. For more information or
to book an event, contact the Simon & Schuster Speakers
Bureau at 1-866-248-3049 or visit our website at
www.simonspeakers.com.

Manufactured in the United States of America

10 9 8 7 6 5

ISBN 978-0-7434-8495-4

From the Director of the Library

For over four decades, the Folger Library General Reader's Shakespeare provided accurate and accessible texts of the plays and poems to students, teachers, and millions of other interested readers. Today, in an age often impatient with the past, the passion for Shakespeare continues to grow. No author speaks more powerfully to the human condition, in all its variety, than this actor/playwright from a minor sixteenth-century English village.

Over the years vast changes have occurred in the way Shakespeare's works are edited, performed, studied, and taught. The New Folger Library Shakespeare replaces the earlier versions, bringing to bear the best and most current thinking concerning both the texts and their interpretation. Here is an edition which makes the plays and poems fully understandable for modern readers using uncompromising scholarship. Professors Barbara Mowat and Paul Werstine are uniquely qualified to produce this New Folger Shakespeare for a new generation of readers. The Library is grateful for the learning, clarity, and imagination they have brought to this ambitious project.

Werner Gundersheimer,
Director of the Folger Shakespeare Library
from 1984 to 2002

Contents

Editors' Preface

In recent years, ways of dealing with Shakespeare's texts and with the interpretation of his plays have been undergoing significant change. This edition, while retaining many of the features that have always made the Folger Shakespeare so attractive to the general reader, at the same time reflects these current ways of thinking about Shakespeare. For example, modern readers, actors, and teachers have become interested in the differences between, on the one hand, the early forms in which Shakespeare's plays were first published and, on the other hand, the forms in which editors through the centuries have presented them. In response to this interest, we have based our edition on what we consider the best early printed version of a particular play (explaining our rationale in a section called "An Introduction to This Text") and have marked our changes in the text—unobtrusively, we hope, but in such a way that the curious reader can be aware that a change has been made and can consult the "Textual Notes" to discover what appeared in the early printed version.

Current ways of looking at the plays are reflected in our brief introductions, in many of the commentary notes, in the annotated lists of "Further Reading," and especially in each play's "Modern Perspective," an essay written by an outstanding scholar who brings to the reader his or her fresh assessment of the play in the light of today's interests and concerns.

As in the Folger Library General Reader's Shakespeare, which this edition replaces, we include explanatory notes designed to help make Shakespeare's language clearer to a modern reader, and we place the notes on the page facing the text that they explain. We also follow the earlier edition in including illustrations —of objects, of clothing, of mythological figures—from books and manuscripts in the Folger Library collection. We provide fresh accounts of the life of Shakespeare, of the publishing of his plays, and of the theaters in which his plays were performed, as well as an introduction to the text itself. We also include a section called "Reading Shakespeare's Language," in which we try to help readers learn to "break the code" of Elizabethan poetic language.

For each section of each volume, we are indebted to a host of generous experts and fellow scholars. The "Reading Shakespeare's Language" sections, for example, could not have been written had not Arthur King, of Brigham Young University, and Randal Robinson, author of *Unlocking Shakespeare's Language,* led the way in untangling Shakespearean language puzzles and shared their insights and methodologies generously with us. "Shakespeare's Life" profited by the careful reading given it by S. Schoenbaum, "Shakespeare's Theater" was read and strengthened by Andrew Gurr and John Astington, and "The Publication of Shakespeare's Plays" is indebted to the comments of Peter W. M. Blayney. We, as editors, take sole responsibility for any errors in our editions.

We are grateful to the authors of the "Modern Perspectives," to Leeds Barroll and David Bevington for their generous encouragement, to the Huntington and Newberry Libraries for fellowship support, to King's College for the grants it has provided to Paul Werstine, to the Social Sciences and Humanities Research Council of Canada, which provided him with a Research Time Stipend for 1990–91, and to the Folger Institute's Center for Shakespeare Studies for its fortuitous sponsorship of a workshop on "Shakespeare's Texts for Students and

Teachers" (funded by the National Endowment for the Humanities and led by Richard Knowles of the University of Wisconsin), a workshop from which we learned an enormous amount about what is wanted by college and high-school teachers of Shakespeare today.

Our biggest debt is to the Folger Shakespeare Library: to Werner Gundersheimer, Director of the Library, who has made possible our edition; to Jean Miller, the Library's Art Curator, who combed the Library holdings for illustrations, and to Julie Ainsworth, Head of the Photography Department, who carefully photographed them; to Peggy O'Brien, Director of Education, who gave us expert advice about the needs being expressed by Shakespeare teachers and students (and to Martha Christian and other "master teachers" who used our texts in manuscript in their classrooms); to the staff of the Academic Programs Division, especially Paul Menzer (who drafted "Further Reading" material), Mary Tonkinson, Lena Cowen Orlin, Molly Haws, and Jessica Hymowitz; and, finally, to the staff of the Library Reading Room, whose patience and support have been invaluable.

Special thanks are due Richard Knowles, who allowed us to see his commentary on Acts 1 and 2 for his forthcoming New Variorum edition of *King Lear.*

Barbara A. Mowat and Paul Werstine

Shakespeare's *King Lear*

So great is the suffering depicted in Shakespeare's *King Lear* that one has trouble finding the words to write about it. It is a play that relentlessly challenges its readers and theater audiences with the magnitude, intensity, and sheer duration of the pain that it represents. While other tragedies, including many of Shakespeare's, depict their characters experiencing a measure of joy and satisfaction before the onset of their misery, *King Lear* offers us no such relief. From beginning to end, all of its figures suffer, and all attempt various strategies to escape their suffering—some hardening their hearts, others engaging in orgies of violence, many devoting themselves to alleviating the suffering of others, Lear himself raging against his own pain until his sanity cracks. In this play only death seems to provide escape from "the rack of this tough world."

What, then, keeps bringing us back to *King Lear*? There is, of course, the power of the language. Once one has absorbed this play, one can articulate one's own suffering; one can put language to one's horror in the face of human cruelty and poverty; one has words to express the depths of grief that follow on extreme loss. But the fact that *King Lear* is almost equally powerful when translated (for example, into Japanese), converted to film, and set in lands far different from ancient Britain, makes it likely that it is the story told in *Lear* that, in large part, draws us to the play. Within *Lear* are stories of two families, each caught up in a struggle between greed and cruelty,

on the one hand, and support and consolation on
the other. Each family is centered in an aging father, one an imperious near-tyrant, the other a gullible
sensualist, each of whom sees his children through
a distorted lens and, turning against the child who
truly loves him, unleashes in his other child (or, in
Lear's case, children) enormous greed, lust, and ambition.

This double story draws us because it tells us about
families—about fathers and daughters, fathers and
sons, sisters and their husbands and lovers, brothers
natural and unnatural. In this play, ordinary jealous-
ies, demands for love, sibling rivalries, desire for money and power, petty cruelties are all taken to the extreme; we can see ourselves and our small vices
magnified to gigantic proportions. Also in this play we
can see the end of our lives, with old age portrayed in
all its vulnerability, helplessness, pride, and, finally, perhaps, wisdom. Lear had envisioned a world in
which old men would continue to be respected
even after giving away their money and their power,
a world in which everyone would behave as Kent
does, continuing to admire and obey because of
the authority that inheres in Lear himself. Lear
learns that once time and age have weakened one,
without money and power one is almost helpless
against the ravages of greed and power-hunger—but
his final speech to Cordelia suggests that he also
learns that, finally, greed and power-hunger do
not really matter. Lear moves out of the world of the
young and the middle-aged and into an old-age
world of letting go. This play's special understanding of
old age explains in part why this most devastating of
Shakespeare's tragedies is also perhaps his most moving.

For a "Modern Perspective" on *King Lear*, we invite you, after you have read the play, to read the essay by Professor Susan Snyder of Swarthmore College, printed at the back of this book.

Reading Shakespeare's Language

For many people today, reading Shakespeare's language is not easy. For those who have studied Latin (or even French or German or Spanish) and those who are used to reading poetry, understanding the language of Shakespeare's poetic drama is not a big problem. Others, though, need to develop the skills of untangling unusual sentence structures and of recognizing and understanding poetic compressions, omissions, and wordplay. And even those skilled in reading unusual sentence structures may have occasional trouble with Shakespeare's words. Four hundred years of "static" intervene between his speaking and our hearing. Most of his immense vocabulary is still in use, but a few of his words are not, and, worse, some of his words now have meanings quite different from those they had in the sixteenth century. In the theater, most of these difficulties are solved for us by actors who study the language and articulate it for us so that the essential meaning is heard—or, when combined with stage action, is at least *felt*. When reading on one's own, one must do what each actor does: go over the lines (often with a dictionary close at hand) until the puzzles are solved and the lines yield up their poetry and the characters speak in words and phrases that are, suddenly, rewarding and wonderfully memorable.

Shakespeare's Words

As you begin to read the opening scenes of a play by Shakespeare, you may notice occasional unfamiliar words. Some are unfamiliar simply because we no longer use them. In the opening scenes of *King Lear*, for example, we find such words as *haply* (i.e., perchance, perhaps), *sith* (i.e., since), and *sirrah* (a term of address that shows the speaker's position of authority). Words of this kind are explained in notes to the text and will become familiar the more of Shakespeare's plays you read.

In *King Lear*, as in all of Shakespeare's writing, more problematic than discarded words are words that we still use but that we use with a different meaning. In the opening line of *King Lear*, the word *affected* is used where we would say "been partial to." Later in the first scene, we find *several* where we would use "particular," *addition* where we would use "title," *owes* where we would use "owns," and *plighted* where we would use "pleated" or "folded." In the play's second scene, *character* means "handwriting," *closet* means "private room," and *practices* means "plots." Again, such words will be explained in the notes to this text, but they, too, will become familiar as you continue to read Shakespeare's language.

Some words are strange not because of the "static" introduced by changes in language over the past centuries but because these are words that Shakespeare is using to build a dramatic world that has its own space, time, history, and background mythology. *King Lear* is a particularly interesting example of this practice, in that, in this play, Shakespeare creates two worlds separated by centuries of time but that seem to exist simultaneously. One of these worlds is that of the Britain inhabited by the legendary King Leir, who, in the histories of Shakespeare's time, came to power "in the year of the world 3105"—i.e., in 845 B.C., many years before the founding of Rome. This world is created through references to "the mysteries of Hecate," to "Scythians" and other barbaric peoples who "make their generations messes [i.e., eat their own young]," to "Apollo" and "Jupiter" (both of whom play important parts in the stories of early Britain). This world is recalled throughout the play in references to "Sarum Plain" (the prehistoric name for Salisbury Plain) and "Camelot," in repeated references to "the gods," and in dialogue about astrology (reportedly of wide influence in the early days of Britain), including such terms as "sectary astronomical," "the operations of the orbs," and "under the Dragon's tail."

At the same time, the early scenes of the play create a court and a political world that linguistically reflect Shakespeare's own time. This is a world of "dukes," "princes," "kings"; it is a world of courtly phrases ("My services to your lordship," "I must love you and sue to know you better," "I shall study deserving") and of formal courtly orders ("Attend the lords of Burgundy and France," "To thine and Albany's issue be this perpetual"). The two worlds of the play are linked through words that describe the land of Britain— "shadowy forests," "wide-skirted meads," "champains riched with plenteous rivers"—words that could describe both ancient and seventeenth-century Britain. It is possible that, in part, *King Lear*'s seeming timelessness is a function of this double world created by the play's diction.

Shakespeare's Sentences

In an English sentence, meaning is quite dependent on the place given each word. "The dog bit the boy" and "The boy bit the dog" mean very different things, even though the individual words are the same. Because English places such importance on the positions of words in sentences, on the way words are arranged, unusual arrangements can puzzle a reader. Shakespeare frequently shifts his sentences away from "normal" English arrangements—often in order to create the rhythm he seeks, sometimes in order to use a line's poetic rhythm to emphasize a particular word, sometimes to give a character his or her own speech patterns or to allow the character to speak in a special way. Again, when we attend a good performance of the play, the actors will have worked out the sentence structures and will articulate the sentences so that the meaning is clear. In reading for yourself, do as the actor does. That is, when you become puzzled by a character's speech, check to see if words are being presented in an unusual sequence.

Look first for the placement of subject and verb. Shakespeare often places the verb before the subject or places the subject between the two parts of a verb (i.e., instead of "He goes" we find "Goes he," and instead of "He does go" we find "Does he go"). In the opening scene of *King Lear*, when Gloucester says "yet was his mother fair" (instead of "yet his mother was fair"), he is using such a construction; in the second scene, when he says "Why so earnestly *seek you* to put up that letter?," he again places the subject and verb in an unusual order. (The normal order would be "do you seek.") Such inversions rarely cause much confusion. More problematic is Shakespeare's frequent placing of the object before the subject and verb (i.e., instead of "I hit him," we might find "Him I hit"). When Lear says "That we our largest bounty may extend," he is using such an inverted construction (the normal order would be "that we may extend our largest bounty"). Lear uses another such inversion later in the same scene when he says "Ourself . . . shall our abode / Make with you," and again with "Five days we do allot thee for provision." The king of France uses a similar inversion when he says to Cordelia "Thee and thy virtues here I seize upon." *King Lear* is among those plays of Shakespeare that make frequent use of this more complicated kind of inversion. In this play, in fact, Shakespeare sometimes complicates his sentences yet further by combining subject/verb/object inversions with subject/verb inversions—as in Goneril's remark to Regan: "Such unconstant starts are we like to have from him" (where the normal order would be "We are like [i.e., likely] to have such unconstant starts from him").

Inversions are not the only unusual sentence structures in Shakespeare's language. Often in his sentences words that would normally appear together are separated from each other. (Again, this is often done to create a particular rhythm or to stress a particular word.) In Lear's command to his daughters in the opening scene, "Tell me, my daughters— / Since now we will divest us both of rule, / Interest of territory, cares of state— / Which of you shall we say doth love us most," the phrase "tell me . . . which" is interrupted by Lear's explanation of why he is giving this command. Later in the scene he separates subject from verb when he says "Ourself by monthly course, / With reservation of an hundred knights / By you to be sustained, shall our abode /

Make with you by due turn," where "ourself [i.e.,
I] . . . shall our abode / Make" is interrupted by a series
of phrases, and the verb and its object, as noted above,
are themselves inverted. In order to create for yourself
sentences that seem more like the English of everyday
speech, you may wish to rearrange the words, putting
together the word clusters and placing the remaining
words in their more normal order. You will usually find
that the sentence will gain in clarity but will lose its
rhythm or shift its emphasis. You can then see for
yourself why Shakespeare chose his own unusual ar-
rangement.

Locating and, if necessary, rearranging words that
"belong together" is especially necessary in passages
that separate subjects from verbs and verbs from objects
by long delaying or expanding interruptions—a structure that is used frequently in *King Lear*. For example,
when Lear asks Burgundy whether he wants to marry
the now dowerless Cordelia, he uses such an interrupted
construction:

Will you, with those infirmities she owes,
Unfriended, new-adopted to our hate,
Dowered with our curse and strangered with our oath,
Take her or leave her?   (1.1.231–35)

The king of France answers Lear's charges against
Cordelia with a speech containing a similarly interrupted clause:

                            This is most strange,
That *she* whom even but now was your best object,
The argument of your praise, balm of your age,

The best, the dearest, *should* in this trice of time
Commit a thing so monstrous to dismantle
So many folds of favor.   (1.1.245–51)

Cordelia herself responds to France's speech with a plea to Lear built around an interrupted structure:

                    I yet *beseech your Majesty*—
If for I want that glib and oily art
To speak and purpose not, since what I well intend
I'll do 't before I speak—*that you make known*
It is no vicious blot, murder, or foulness,
No unchaste action or dishonored step
That hath deprived me of your grace and favor. . . .
                    (1.1.257–64)

In each of these cases—and similar constructions occur throughout the play—the interruption of the main sentence elements serves to heighten emotional intensity. The separation of the basic sentence elements— "will you . . . take her or leave her," "she . . . should . . . commit," "I beseech your Majesty . . . that you make known"—forces the audience to attend to the characters' accusations and explanations, and to feel the power of emotion conveyed in the interrupting material, while waiting for the basic sentence elements to come together.

Occasionally, rather than separating basic sentence elements, Shakespeare simply holds them back, delaying them until much subordinate material has already been given. Again, emotional intensity is heightened for an audience as it listens and waits for the sentence's subject and verb. Lear uses such a delaying structure when he says to Cordelia, at 1.1.121–28:

> For by the sacred radiance of the sun,
> The mysteries of Hecate and the night,
> By all the operation of the orbs
> From whom we do exist and cease to be,
> Here *I disclaim all my paternal care,*
> *Propinquity, and property of blood,*
> *And as a stranger* to my heart and me
> *Hold thee* from this forever.

Again, in his speech banishing Kent, Lear uses a similar delaying structure:

> That [i.e., because] thou hast sought to make us
>   break our vows—
> Which we durst never yet—and with strained pride
> To come betwixt our sentence and our power,
> Which nor our nature nor our place can bear,
> Our potency made good, *take thy reward.* . . .
>   (1.1.192–96)

Shakespeare's sentences are sometimes complicated not because of unusual structures or interruptions or delays but because of the omission of words and parts of words that English sentences normally require. (In conversation, we, too, often omit words. We say "Heard from him yet?" and our hearer supplies the missing "Have you.") Frequent reading of Shakespeare —and of other poets—trains us to supply such missing words. In plays written five or ten years earlier than *King Lear*, omissions seem to be used primarily for rhythmic effects. In *King Lear*, however, Shakespeare uses omissions—of verbs, of nouns, of prepositions, of parts of words—as an integral part of the language world he is creating. Oftentimes the omission is uncomplicated, as in Kent's "My life I never held but as a pawn / To wage against thine enemies, nor fear to lose it," where "nor do I fear" becomes "nor fear." A similarly uncomplicated omission is found in Lear's "Therefore beseech you" (1.1.241), a compression of "therefore I beseech you," as well as in France's "Commit a thing so monstrous to dismantle" (1.1.250), where one needs to supply an "as" before "to dismantle."

Many times in *Lear*, however, omissions are coupled with inversions or other dislocations of language. When Cordelia says, at line 317, "But yet, alas, *stood I* within his grace," the word "if" has been omitted and the subject and verb inverted. When Regan replies to her, at line 320, *"Prescribe not us* our duty," omission has again been combined with subject/verb inversion. (The normal structure would be "Do not prescribe our duty to us.") Gloucester's "Why so earnestly seek you to put up that letter?" (1.2.29–30) combines two inversions and an omission. (The normal order would be "Why do you seek to put up . . . ?") Since these omissions and inversions occur as often in prose as they do in verse, they seem to be used not only for rhythmic effects but also to create a language world of unusually complicated syntax.

Shakespearean Wordplay

Shakespeare plays with language so routinely and so variously that entire books are written on the topic. His wordplay in *King Lear* is particularly interesting in the way it varies Shakespeare's usual use of puns and figurative language. A pun is a play on words that sound the same but that have different meanings. In many of

Shakespeare's plays (*Romeo and Juliet* and *Taming of the Shrew* are good examples), puns are used frequently. In *King Lear* they are used less often; when they are used, they carry interesting ambiguities, often conveying what may be sophisticated courtly wit or may be somewhat crass *double entendre*. For example, in the opening lines of the play, Gloucester responds to Kent's question "Is not this your son, my lord?" with the statement "His breeding, sir, hath been at my charge," a sentence that plays on two meanings of "breeding" and two meanings of "at my charge," so that Gloucester can be heard to say, simultaneously, "I have been accused of begetting him" and "I have had to pay for his education." In response to Kent's "I cannot conceive you" (in which *cannot conceive* means "do not understand"), Gloucester replies "Sir, this young fellow's mother could," pretending to understand *conceive* to mean "conceive a child." When Gloucester asks Kent "Do you smell a fault?" Kent replies "I cannot wish the fault undone, the issue of it being so proper," playing with *issue* as meaning both "results" and "offspring" and with *proper* as meaning both "appropriate, fitting" and "handsome," so that Kent's words say both that the outcome is fitting and the offspring attractive. In a more serious passage near the end of the same scene, Cordelia leaves her sisters with the statement "Time shall unfold what plighted cunning hides," where *plighted* has the primary meaning of "pleated, folded," and *unfold* is a pun on "unpleat" and "discover"; the statement carries an additional resonance in that *plighted* can also be used in reference to someone who has pledged her word or her honesty, so that Cordelia can be heard to say that her sisters, who have outwardly plighted their truth and love to Lear, have actually pledged instead their cunning.

Not only are puns used rarely and complexly in *King Lear,* but figurative language is also shifted away from Shakespeare's customary use of metaphors (i.e., plays on words in which one object or idea is expressed as if it were something else, something with which it shares common features). Occasionally one does find straightforward metaphoric language. For example, as the characters' suffering intensifies near the end of the play, their anguish is expressed through metaphors about instruments of torture. Lear says to Cordelia, for instance, near the end of Act 4, "I am bound / Upon a wheel of fire, that mine own tears / Do scald like molten lead"; a similar metaphor of torture is used at the end of the play when Kent urges Edgar to let Lear die: "O, let him pass! He hates him / That would upon the rack of this tough world / Stretch him out longer."

These straightforward metaphors are, however, relatively rare in *King Lear.* More often the metaphors are either displaced or are placed slightly beneath the surface of the language. Most of the Fool's speeches can be seen as examples of displaced and extended metaphor—as analogies in which the listener must provide the sometimes difficult connections between Lear's situation and the Fool's seemingly random comments. To take only two of many examples: In Act 1, scene 4, Goneril addresses Lear as if he were her dependent, threatening him with "censure" and "redresses":

I had thought by making this well known unto you
To have found a safe redress, but now grow fearful,
By what yourself too late have spoke and done,
That you protect this course and put it on
By your allowance; which if you should, the fault

Would not 'scape censure, nor the redresses sleep
Which in the tender of a wholesome weal
Might in their working do you that offense,
Which else were shame, that then necessity
Will call discreet proceeding.   (1.4.210–19)

In response to this speech, the Fool comments:

The hedge-sparrow fed the cuckoo so long,
    That it's had it head bit off by it young.
So out went the candle, and we were left darkling.
                                        (1.4.221–23)

Metaphorically, according to the Fool, Lear is a hedge-
sparrow, Goneril the bird that the sparrow has fed,
thinking it his; like the sparrow, Lear is now being
attacked by his young. As Goneril continues her attack,
the Fool comments: "May not an ass know when the
cart draws the horse?" Metaphorically, Lear and Goneril are a horse and cart whose functions have gotten
reversed.

Often the play's language contains metaphors that do
not lie clearly on the surface of the play but, when
discovered, make the characters' speeches much more
vivid. When Edmund says, in the play's second scene,
"This is the excellent foppery of the world, that when
we are sick in fortune (often the surfeits of our own
behavior) we make guilty of our disasters the sun, the
moon, and stars," just under the surface of his language
is a metaphor in which bad luck is imaged as a sickness caused by our own "surfeits"—i.e., overindul-
gences. (These lines also contain an amusing play on
the word *disasters,* a word of astrological origin meaning, literally, "from the stars.") In the opening scene,

Lear's "'tis our fast intent / To shake all cares and business from our age, / Conferring them on younger strengths, while we / Unburdened crawl toward death" (1.1.40–43) carries within it a metaphor in which man is pictured as a pack-animal that, in its old age, shakes off its heavy load. Later in the same scene, within Lear's "I do invest you jointly with my power, / Preeminence, and all the large effects / That troop with majesty" (1.1.146–48), the word *troop* metaphorically makes "power" and "preeminence" and other "large effects" into companions that march along with "majesty."

In this final example we see not only a metaphor (in which the attributes of kingship are likened to the king's traveling companions); we see also personification, a kind of figurative language used with unusual frequency and power in *King Lear*. In personification, abstract qualities or natural objects are given human characteristics (so that "power" is allowed to "troop"). Kent uses personification when he says to Lear:

> Think'st thou that duty shall have dread to speak
> When power to flattery bows? To plainness honor's
>   bound
> When majesty falls to folly.   (1.1.164–67)

In these lines, *duty, power, flattery, honor,* and *majesty* are given the ability to speak, to feel dread, to fall, to bow, to receive bows, to remain loyal.

Some of the most powerful scenes in *King Lear* depend heavily on personification. Lear responds to Goneril's initial attack on him with his personification of "ingratitude":

> Ingratitude, thou marble-hearted fiend,
> More hideous when thou show'st thee in a child
> Than the sea monster!   (1.4.270–72)

His powerful speeches in Act 4, scene 6, on "how this world goes" depend heavily on the personification of such abstractions as *vices*, *sin*, and *justice*, to which he attributes the ability to wear clothing and to be dressed in gold-plated armor:

> Through tattered clothes small vices do appear.
> Robes and furred gowns hide all. Plate sin with gold,
> And the strong lance of justice hurtless breaks.
> Arm it in rags, a pygmy's straw does pierce it.
>   (4.6.180–84)

Most importantly, his speeches in the storm scenes of Act 3 are built around personifications in which wind, rain, lightning, and thunder are given cheeks that can crack, emotions that can rage; the elements, in these speeches, experience "horrible pleasures" and become "servile ministers" who have joined with Goneril and Regan to destroy him.

Implied Stage Action

In reading Shakespeare's plays we should always remember that what we are reading is a performance script. The dialogue is written to be spoken by actors who, at the same time, are moving, gesturing, picking up objects, weeping, shaking their fists. Some stage action is described in what are called "stage directions";

some is suggested within the dialogue itself. We must learn to be alert to such signals as we stage the play in our imaginations. When, in the second scene of *King Lear*, Gloucester says to Edmund "Why so earnestly seek you to put up that letter?" it is clear that Edmund puts away the piece of paper he has been holding; Gloucester's following question, "What . . . needed that terrible dispatch of it into your pocket?" lets us know that Edmund's putting away of the letter was done obtrusively and that he put it in his pocket, not on a shelf or in a book. When, in Act 2, scene 4, Goneril enters and Lear says "O, Regan, will you take her by the hand?" the stage action is obvious. It is less obvious, in Act 2, scene 1, exactly how we are to imagine Edmund's actions when he says "Some blood drawn on me would beget opinion / Of my more fierce endeavor. I have seen drunkards / Do more than this in sport." Since a few lines later he says to his father "Look, sir, I bleed," he has clearly wounded himself in some fashion, but the director and the actor (and the reader, in imagination) must decide on his precise action. Which weapon he uses and how and where he wounds himself will be answered variously from production to production. Learning to read the language of stage action repays one many times over when one reaches a crucial scene like that of the blinding of Gloucester (3.7) or the play's final scene with its sequence of duels, exits, entrances, and deaths, in both of which scenes implied stage action vitally affects our response to the play.

It is immensely rewarding to work carefully with Shakespeare's language so that the words, the sentences, the wordplay, and the implied stage action all become clear—as readers for the past four centuries have discovered. It may be more pleasurable to attend a good performance of a play—though not everyone has thought so. But the joy of being able to stage one of Shakespeare's plays in one's imagination, to return to passages that continue to yield further meanings (or further questions) the more one reads them—these are pleasures that, for many, rival (or at least augment) those of the performed text, and certainly make it worth considerable effort to "break the code" of Elizabethan poetic drama and let free the remarkable language that makes up a Shakespeare text.

Shakespeare's Life

Surviving documents that give us glimpses into the life of William Shakespeare show us a playwright, poet, and actor who grew up in the market town of Stratford-upon-Avon, spent his professional life in London, and returned to Stratford a wealthy landowner. He was born in April 1564, died in April 1616, and is buried inside the chancel of Holy Trinity Church in Stratford.

We wish we could know more about the life of the world's greatest dramatist. His plays and poems are testaments to his wide reading—especially to his knowledge of Virgil, Ovid, Plutarch, Holinshed's *Chronicles*, and the Bible—and to his mastery of the English language, but we can only speculate about his education. We know that the King's New School in Stratford-upon-Avon was considered excellent. The school was one of the English "grammar schools" established to educate young men, primarily in Latin grammar and literature. As in other schools of the time, students began their studies at the age of four or five in the attached "petty school," and there learned to read and write in English, studying primarily the catechism from the Book of Common Prayer. After two years in the petty school, students entered the lower form (grade) of the grammar school, where they began the serious study of Latin grammar and Latin texts that would occupy most of the remainder of their school days. (Several Latin texts that Shakespeare used repeatedly in writing his plays and poems were texts that schoolboys memorized and recited.) Latin comedies were introduced early in the lower form; in the upper form, which the boys entered at age ten or eleven, students wrote their own Latin orations and declamations, studied Latin historians and rhetoricians, and began the study of Greek using the Greek New Testament.

Since the records of the Stratford "grammar school" do not survive, we cannot prove that William Shakespeare attended the school; however, every indication (his father's position as an alderman and bailiff of Stratford, the playwright's own knowledge of the Latin classics, scenes in the plays that recall grammar-school experiences—for example, *The Merry Wives of Windsor*, 4.1) suggests that he did. We also lack generally accepted documentation about Shakespeare's life after his schooling ended and his professional life in London began. His marriage in 1582 (at age eighteen) to Anne Hathaway and the subsequent births of his daughter Susanna (1583) and the twins Judith and Hamnet (1585) are recorded, but how he supported himself and where he lived are not known. Nor do we know when and why he left Stratford for the London

CATECHISMVS

paruus pueris primùm Latinè
qui ediscatur, proponendus
in Scholis.

LONDINI
Apud Iohannem Dayum Typo-
graphum. An. 1573.

Cum Priuilegio Regiæ Maieſtatis.

An Elizabethan schoolroom.
Title page of *Catechismus paruus pueris primum
Latine* . . . (1573).

theatrical world, nor how he rose to be the important figure in that world that he had become by the early 1590s.

We do know that by 1592 he had achieved some prominence in London as both an actor and a playwright. In that year was published a book by the playwright Robert Greene attacking an actor who had the audacity to write blank-verse drama and who was "in his own conceit [i.e., opinion] the only Shake-scene in a country." Since Greene's attack includes a parody of a line from one of Shakespeare's early plays, there is little doubt that it is Shakespeare to whom he refers, a "Shake-scene" who had aroused Greene's fury by successfully competing with university-educated dramatists like Greene himself. It was in 1593 that Shakespeare became a published poet. In that year he published his long narrative poem *Venus and Adonis;* in 1594, he followed it with *The Rape of Lucrece.* Both poems were dedicated to the young earl of Southampton (Henry Wriothesley), who may have become Shakespeare's patron.

It seems no coincidence that Shakespeare wrote these narrative poems at a time when the theaters were closed because of the plague, a contagious epidemic disease that devastated the population of London. When the theaters reopened in 1594, Shakespeare apparently resumed his double career of actor and playwright and began his long (and seemingly profitable) service as an acting-company shareholder. Records for December of 1594 show him to be a leading member of the Lord Chamberlain's Men. It was this company of actors, later named the King's Men, for whom he would be a principal actor, dramatist, and shareholder for the rest of his career.

So far as we can tell, that career spanned about twenty

The Globe theater.
From Visscher's *Londinum Florentissima Britanniae Urbs*
(c. 1625).

years. In the 1590s, he wrote his plays on English history as well as several comedies and at least two tragedies (*Titus Andronicus* and *Romeo and Juliet*). These histories, comedies, and tragedies are the plays credited to him in 1598 in a work, *Palladis Tamia,* that in one chapter compares English writers with "Greek, Latin, and Italian Poets." There the author, Francis Meres, claims that Shakespeare is comparable to the Latin dramatists Seneca for tragedy and Plautus for comedy, and calls him "the most excellent in both kinds for the stage." He also names him "mellifluous and honey-tongued Shakespeare": "I say," writes Meres, "that the Muses would speak with Shakespeare's fine filed phrase, if they would speak English." Since Meres also mentions Shakespeare's "sugared sonnets among his private friends," it is assumed that many of Shakespeare's sonnets (not published until 1609) were also written in the 1590s.

In 1599, Shakespeare's company built a theater for themselves across the river from London, naming it the Globe. The plays that are considered by many to be Shakespeare's major tragedies (*Hamlet, Othello, King Lear,* and *Macbeth*) were written while the company was resident in this theater, as were such comedies as *Twelfth Night* and *Measure for Measure*. Many of Shakespeare's plays were performed at court (both for Queen Elizabeth I and, after her death in 1603, for King James I), some were presented at the Inns of Court (the residences of London's legal societies), and some were doubtless performed in other towns, at the universities, and at great houses when the King's Men went on tour; otherwise, his plays from 1599 to 1608 were, so far as we know, performed only at the Globe. Between 1608 and 1612, Shakespeare wrote several plays—among them *The Winter's Tale* and *The Tempest*—presuma-

Ptolemaic universe.
From Marcus Manilius, *The sphere of . . .* (1675).

bly for the company's new indoor Blackfriars theater, though the plays seem to have been performed also at the Globe and at court. Surviving documents describe a performance of *The Winter's Tale* in 1611 at the Globe, for example, and performances of *The Tempest* in 1611 and 1613 at the royal palace of Whitehall.

Shakespeare wrote very little after 1612, the year in which he probably wrote *King Henry VIII*. (It was at a performance of *Henry VIII* in 1613 that the Globe caught fire and burned to the ground.) Sometime between 1610 and 1613 he seems to have returned to live in Stratford-upon-Avon, where he owned a large house and considerable property, and where his wife and his two daughters and their husbands lived. (His son Hamnet had died in 1596.) During his professional years in London, Shakespeare had presumably derived income from the acting company's profits as well as from his own career as an actor, from the sale of his play manuscripts to the acting company, and, after 1599, from his shares as an owner of the Globe. It was presumably that income, carefully invested in land and other property, that made him the wealthy man that surviving documents show him to have become. It is also assumed that William Shakespeare's growing wealth and reputation played some part in inclining the crown, in 1596, to grant John Shakespeare, William's father, the coat of arms that he had so long sought. William Shakespeare died in Stratford on April 23, 1616 (according to the epitaph carved under his bust in Holy Trinity Church) and was buried on April 25. Seven years after his death, his collected plays were published as *Mr. William Shakespeares Comedies, Histories, & Tragedies* (the work now known as the First Folio).

The years in which Shakespeare wrote were among the most exciting in English history. Intellectually, the discovery, translation, and printing of Greek and Roman classics were making available a set of works and worldviews that interacted complexly with Christian texts and beliefs. The result was a questioning, a vital intellectual ferment, that provided energy for the period's amazing dramatic and literary output and that fed directly into Shakespeare's plays. The Ghost in *Hamlet,* for example, is wonderfully complicated in part because he is a figure from Roman tragedy—the spirit of the dead returning to seek revenge—who at the same time inhabits a Christian hell (or purgatory); Hamlet's description of humankind reflects at one moment the Neoplatonic wonderment at mankind ("What a piece of work is a man!") and, at the next, the Christian disparagement of human sinners ("And yet, to me, what is this quintessence of dust?").

As intellectual horizons expanded, so also did geographical and cosmological horizons. New worlds—both North and South America—were explored, and in them were found human beings who lived and worshiped in ways radically different from those of Renaissance Europeans and Englishmen. The universe during these years also seemed to shift and expand. Copernicus had earlier theorized that the earth was not the center of the cosmos but revolved as a planet around the sun. Galileo's telescope, created in 1609, allowed scientists to see that Copernicus had been correct: the universe was not organized with the earth at the center, nor was it so nicely circumscribed as people had, until that time, thought. In terms of expanding horizons, the impact of these discoveries on people's beliefs—religious, scientific, and philosophical—cannot be overstated.

London, too, rapidly expanded and changed during the years (from the early 1590s to around 1610) that Shakespeare lived there. London—the center of England's government, its economy, its royal court, its overseas trade—was, during these years, becoming an exciting metropolis, drawing to it thousands of new citizens every year. Troubled by overcrowding, by poverty, by recurring epidemics of the plague, London was also a mecca for the wealthy and the aristocratic, and for those who sought advancement at court, or power in government or finance or trade. One hears in Shakespeare's plays the voices of London—the struggles for power, the fear of venereal disease, the language of buying and selling. One hears as well the voices of Stratford-upon-Avon—references to the nearby Forest of Arden, to sheep herding, to small-town gossip, to village fairs and markets. Part of the richness of Shakespeare's work is the influence felt there of the various worlds in which he lived: the world of metropolitan London, the world of small-town and rural England, the world of the theater, and the worlds of craftsmen and shepherds.

That Shakespeare inhabited such worlds we know from surviving London and Stratford documents, as well as from the evidence of the plays and poems themselves. From such records we can sketch the dramatist's life. We know from his works that he was a voracious reader. We know from legal and business documents that he was a multifaceted theater man who became a wealthy landowner. We know a bit about his family life and a fair amount about his legal and financial dealings. Most scholars today depend upon such evidence as they draw their picture of the world's greatest playwright. Such, how-

ever, has not always been the case. Until the late eighteenth century, the William Shakespeare who lived
in most biographies was the creation of legend and
tradition. This was the Shakespeare who was supposedly caught poaching deer at Charlecote, the estate of Sir Thomas Lucy close by Stratford; this was
the Shakespeare who fled from Sir Thomas's vengeance and made his way in London by taking care
of horses outside a playhouse; this was the Shakespeare who reportedly could barely read, but whose
natural gifts were extraordinary, whose father was
a butcher who allowed his gifted son sometimes to
help in the butcher shop, where William supposedly
killed calves "in a high style," making a speech for the
occasion. It was this legendary William Shakespeare
whose Falstaff (in *1* and *2 Henry IV*) so pleased Queen
Elizabeth that she demanded a play about Falstaff in
love, and demanded that it be written in fourteen days
(hence the existence of *The Merry Wives of Windsor*). It
was this legendary Shakespeare who reached the top
of his acting career in the roles of the Ghost in *Hamlet*
and old Adam in *As You Like It*—and who died of
a fever contracted by drinking too hard at "a merry
meeting" with the poets Michael Drayton and Ben
Jonson. This legendary Shakespeare is a rambunc-
tious, undisciplined man, as attractively "wild" as his
plays were seen by earlier generations to be. Unfortunately, there is no trace of evidence to support these
wonderful stories.

   Perhaps in response to the disreputable Shakespeare of legend—or perhaps in response to the frag-
mentary and, for some, all-too-ordinary Shakespeare
documented by surviving records—some people
since the mid-nineteenth century have argued that
William Shakespeare could not have written the

plays that bear his name. These persons have put forward some dozen names as more likely authors, among them Queen Elizabeth, Sir Francis Bacon, Edward de Vere (earl of Oxford), and Christopher Marlowe. Such attempts to find what for these people is a more believable author of the plays is a tribute to the regard in which the plays are held. Unfortunately for their claims, the documents that exist that provide evidence for the facts of Shakespeare's life tie him inextricably to the body of plays and poems that bear his name. Unlikely as it seems to those who want the works to have been written by an aristocrat, a university graduate, or an "important" person, the plays and poems seem clearly to have been produced by a man from Stratford-upon-Avon with a very good "grammar-school" education and a life of experience in London and in the world of the London theater. How this particular man produced the works that dominate the cultures of much of the world almost four hundred years after his death is one of life's mysteries—and one that will continue to tease our imaginations as we continue to delight in his plays and poems.

Shakespeare's Theater

The actors of Shakespeare's time are known to have performed plays in a great variety of locations. They played at court (that is, in the great halls of such royal residences as Whitehall, Hampton Court, and Greenwich); they played in halls at the universities of Oxford and Cambridge, and at the Inns of Court (the residences in London of the legal societies); and they also played in the private houses of great lords and civic officials. Sometimes acting companies went on tour from London into the provinces, often (but not only) when outbreaks of bubonic plague in the capital forced the closing of theaters to reduce the possibility of contagion in crowded audiences. In the provinces the actors usually staged their plays in churches (until around 1600) or in guildhalls. While surviving records show only a handful of occasions when actors played at inns while on tour, London inns were important playing places up until the 1590s.

The building of theaters in London had begun only shortly before Shakespeare wrote his first plays in the 1590s. These theaters were of two kinds: outdoor or public playhouses that could accommodate large numbers of playgoers, and indoor or private theaters for much smaller audiences. What is usually regarded as the first London outdoor public playhouse was called simply the Theatre. James Burbage —the father of Richard Burbage, who was perhaps the most famous actor in Shakespeare's company— built it in 1576 in an area north of the city of London called Shoreditch. Among the more famous of the other public playhouses that capitalized on the new fashion were the Curtain and the Fortune (both also built north of the city), the Rose, the Swan, the Globe, and the Hope (all located on the Bankside, a region just across the Thames south of the city of London). All these playhouses had to be built outside the jurisdiction of the city of London because many civic officials were hostile to the performance of drama and repeatedly petitioned the royal council to abolish it.

The theaters erected on the Bankside (a region under the authority of the Church of England, whose head was the monarch) shared the neighborhood with houses of prostitution and with the Paris Garden, where the blood sports of bearbaiting and bullbaiting were carried on. There may have been no clear distinction between playhouses and buildings for such sports, for we know that the Hope was used for both plays and baiting and that Philip Henslowe, owner of the Rose and, later, partner in the ownership of the Fortune, was also a partner in a monopoly on baiting. All these forms of entertainment were easily accessible to Londoners by boat across the Thames or over London Bridge.

Evidently Shakespeare's company prospered on the Bankside. They moved there in 1599. Threatened by difficulties in renewing the lease on the land where their first theater (the Theatre) had been built, Shakespeare's company took advantage of the Christmas holiday in 1598 to dismantle the Theatre and transport its timbers across the Thames to the Bankside, where, in 1599, these timbers were used in the building of the Globe. The weather in late December 1598 is recorded as having been especially harsh. It was so cold that the Thames was "nigh [nearly] frozen," and there was heavy snow. Perhaps the weather aided Shakespeare's company in eluding their landlord, the snow hiding their activity and the freezing of the Thames allowing them to slide the timbers across to the Bankside without paying tolls for repeated trips over London Bridge. Attractive as this narrative is, it remains just as likely that the heavy snow hampered transport of the timbers in wagons through the London streets to the river. It also must be remembered that the Thames was, according to report,

From the frontispiece of William Alabaster, *Roxana*
(1632).

only "nigh frozen" and therefore as impassable as it ever was. Whatever the precise circumstances of this fascinating event in English theater history, Shakespeare's company was able to begin playing at their new Globe theater on the Bankside in 1599. After the first Globe burned down in 1613 during the staging of Shakespeare's *Henry VIII* (its thatch roof was set alight by cannon fire called for by the performance), Shakespeare's company immediately rebuilt on the same location. The second Globe seems to have been a grander structure than its predecessor. It remained in use until the beginning of the English Civil War in 1642, when Parliament officially closed the theaters. Soon thereafter it was pulled down.

The public theaters of Shakespeare's time were very different buildings from our theaters today. First of all, they were open-air playhouses. As recent excavations of the Rose and the Globe confirm, some were polygonal or roughly circular in shape; the Fortune, however, was square. The most recent estimates of their size put the diameter of these buildings at 72 feet (the Rose) to 100 feet (the Globe), but we know that they held vast audiences of two or three thousand, who must have been squeezed together quite tightly. Some of these spectators paid extra to sit or stand in the two or three levels of roofed galleries that extended, on the upper levels, all the way around the theater and surrounded an open space. In this space were the stage and, perhaps, the tiring house (what we would call dressing rooms), as well as the so-called yard. In the yard stood the spectators who chose to pay less, the ones whom Hamlet contemptuously called "groundlings." For a roof they had only the sky, and so they were exposed to all kinds of weather. They stood on a floor that was sometimes made of mortar and sometimes of ash mixed with the shells of hazelnuts. The latter provided a porous and therefore dry footing for the crowd, and the shells may have been more comfortable to stand on because they were not as hard as mortar. Availability of shells may not have been a problem if hazelnuts were a favorite food for Shakespeare's audiences to munch on as they watched his plays. Archaeologists who are today unearthing the remains of theaters from this period have discovered quantities of these nutshells on theater sites.

Unlike the yard, the stage itself was covered by a roof. Its ceiling, called "the heavens," is thought to have been elaborately painted to depict the sun, moon, stars, and planets. Just how big the stage was remains hard to determine. We have a single sketch of part of the interior of the Swan. A Dutchman named Johannes de Witt visited this theater around 1596 and sent a sketch of it back to his friend, Arend van Buchel. Because van Buchel found de Witt's letter and sketch of interest, he copied both into a book. It is van Buchel's copy, adapted, it seems, to the shape and size of the page in his book, that survives. In this sketch, the stage appears to be a large rectangular platform that thrusts far out into the yard, perhaps even as far as the center of the circle formed by the surrounding galleries. This drawing, combined with the specifications for the size of the stage in the building contract for the Fortune, has led scholars to conjecture that the stage on which Shakespeare's plays were performed must have measured approximately 43 feet in width and 27 feet in depth, a vast acting area. But the digging up of a large part of the Rose by archaeologists has provided evidence of a quite different stage design. The Rose stage was a platform tapered at the corners and much shallower than what seems to be depicted in the van Buchel sketch. Indeed, its measurements seem to be about 37.5 feet across at its widest point and only 15.5 feet deep. Because the surviving indications of stage size and design differ from each other so much, it is possible that the stages in other theaters, like the Theatre, the Curtain, and the Globe (the outdoor playhouses where we know that Shakespeare's plays were performed), were different from those at both the Swan and the Rose.

After about 1608 Shakespeare's plays were staged not only at the Globe but also at an indoor or private playhouse in Blackfriars. This theater had been constructed in 1596 by James Burbage in an upper hall of a former Dominican priory or monastic house. Although Henry VIII had dissolved all English monasteries in the 1530s (shortly after he had founded the Church of England), the area remained under church, rather than hostile civic, control. The hall that Burbage had purchased and renovated was a large one in which Parliament had once met. In the private theater that he constructed, the stage, lit by candles, was built across the narrow end of the hall, with boxes flanking it. The rest of the hall offered seating room only. Because there was no provision for standing room, the largest audience it could hold was less than a thousand, or about a quarter of what the Globe could accommodate. Admission to Blackfriars was correspondingly more expensive. Instead of a penny to stand in the yard at the Globe, it cost a minimum of sixpence to get into Blackfriars. The best seats at the Globe (in the Lords' Room in the gallery above and behind the stage) cost sixpence; but the boxes flanking the stage at Blackfriars were half a crown, or five times sixpence. Some spectators who were particularly interested in displaying themselves paid even more to sit on stools on the Blackfriars stage.

Whether in the outdoor or indoor playhouses, the stages of Shakespeare's time were different from ours. They were not separated from the audience by the dropping of a curtain between acts and scenes. Therefore the playwrights of the time had to find other ways of signaling to the audience that one scene (to be imagined as occurring in one location at a given time) had ended and the next (to be imagined at perhaps a different location at a later time) had begun. The customary way used by Shakespeare and many of his contemporaries was to have everyone on stage exit at the end of one scene and have one or more different characters enter to begin the next. In a few cases, where characters remain onstage from one scene to another, the dialogue or stage action makes the change of location clear, and the characters are generally to be imagined as having moved from one place to another. For example, in *Romeo and Juliet*, Romeo and his friends remain onstage in Act 1 from scene 4 to scene 5, but they are represented as having moved between scenes from the street that leads to Capulet's house into Capulet's house itself. The new location is signaled in part by the appearance onstage of Capulet's servingmen carrying napkins, something they would not take into the streets. Playwrights had to be quite resourceful in the use of hand properties, like the napkin, or in the use of dialogue to specify where the action was taking place in their plays because, in contrast to most of today's theaters, the playhouses of Shakespeare's time did not use movable scenery to dress the stage and make the setting precise. As another consequence of this difference, however, the playwrights of Shakespeare's time did not have to specify exactly where the action of their plays was set when they did not choose to do so, and much of the action of their plays is tied to no specific place.

Usually Shakespeare's stage is referred to as a "bare stage," to distinguish it from the stages of the last two or three centuries with their elaborate sets. But the stage in Shakespeare's time was not completely bare. Philip Henslowe, owner of the Rose, lists in his inventory of stage properties a rock, three tombs, and two mossy banks. Stage directions in plays of the time also call for such things as thrones (or "states"), banquets (presumably tables with plaster replicas of food on them), and beds and tombs to be pushed onto the stage. Thus the stage often held more than the actors.

The actors did not limit their performing to the stage alone. Occasionally they went beneath the stage, as the Ghost appears to do in the first act of *Hamlet*. From there they could emerge onto the stage through a trapdoor. They could retire behind the hangings across the back of the stage (or the front of the tiring house), as, for example, the actor playing Polonius does when he hides behind the arras. Sometimes the hangings could be drawn back during a performance to "discover" one or more actors behind them. When performance required that an actor appear "above," as when Juliet is imagined to stand at the window of her chamber in the famous and misnamed "balcony scene," then the actor probably climbed the stairs to the gallery over the back of the stage and temporarily shared it with some of the spectators. The stage was also provided with ropes and winches so that actors could descend from, and reascend to, the "heavens."

Perhaps the greatest difference between dramatic performances in Shakespeare's time and ours was that in Shakespeare's England the roles of women were played by boys. (Some of these boys grew up to take male roles in their maturity.) There were no women in the acting companies, only in the audience. It had not always been so in the history of the English stage. There are records of women on English stages in the thirteenth and fourteenth centuries, two hundred years before Shakespeare's plays were performed. After the accession of James I in 1603, the queen of England and her ladies took part in entertainments at court called masques, and with the reopening of the theaters in 1660 at the restoration of Charles II, women again took their place on the public stage.

The chief competitors for the companies of adult actors such as the one to which Shakespeare belonged and for which he wrote were companies of exclusively boy actors. The competition was most intense in the early 1600s. There were then two principal children's companies: the Children of Paul's (the choirboys from St. Paul's Cathedral, whose private playhouse was near the cathedral); and the Children of the Chapel Royal (the choirboys from the monarch's private chapel, who performed at the Blackfriars theater built by Burbage in 1596, which Shakespeare's company had been stopped from using by local residents who objected to crowds). In *Hamlet* Shakespeare writes of "an aerie [nest] of children, little eyases [hawks], that cry out on the top of question and are most tyrannically clapped for 't. These are now the fashion and . . . berattle the common stages [attack the public theaters]." In the long run, the adult actors prevailed. The Children of Paul's dissolved around 1606. By about

1608 the Children of the Chapel Royal had been forced to stop playing at the Blackfriars theater, which was then taken over by the King's Men, Shakespeare's own troupe.

Acting companies and theaters of Shakespeare's time were organized in different ways. For example, Philip Henslowe owned the Rose and leased it to companies of actors, who paid him from their takings. Henslowe would act as manager of these companies, initially paying playwrights for their plays and buying properties, recovering his outlay from the actors. Shakespeare's company, however, managed itself, with the principal actors, Shakespeare among them, having the status of "sharers" and the right to a share in the takings, as well as the responsibility for a part of the expenses. Five of the sharers themselves, Shakespeare among them, owned the Globe. As actor, as sharer in an acting company and in ownership of theaters, and as playwright, Shakespeare was about as involved in the theatrical industry as one could imagine. Although Shakespeare and his fellows prospered, their status under the law was conditional upon the protection of powerful patrons. "Common players"—those who did not have patrons or masters—were classed in the language of the law with "vagabonds and sturdy beggars." So the actors had to secure for themselves the official rank of servants of patrons. Among the patrons under whose protection Shakespeare's company worked were the lord chamberlain and, after the accession of King James in 1603, the king himself.

We are now perhaps on the verge of learning a great deal more about the theaters in which Shakespeare and his contemporaries performed—or at least of opening up new questions about them. Already about 70 percent of the Rose has been excavated, as has about 10 percent of the second Globe, the one built in 1614. It is to be hoped that soon more will be available for study. These are exciting times for students of Shakespeare's stage.

The Publication of Shakespeare's Plays

Eighteen of Shakespeare's plays found their way into print during the playwright's lifetime, but there is nothing to suggest that he took any interest in their publication. These eighteen appeared separately in editions called quartos. Their pages were not much larger than the one you are now reading, and these little books were sold unbound for a few pence. The earliest of the quartos that still survive were printed in 1594, the year that both *Titus Andronicus* and a version of the play now called *2 King Henry VI* became available. While almost every one of these early quartos displays on its title page the name of the acting company that performed the play, only about half provide the name of the playwright, Shakespeare. The first quarto edition to bear the name Shakespeare on its title page is *Love's Labor's Lost* of 1598. A few of these quartos were popular with the book-buying public of Shakespeare's lifetime; for example, quarto *Richard II* went through five editions between 1597 and 1615. But most of the quartos were far from best-sellers; *Love's Labor's Lost* (1598), for instance, was not reprinted in quarto until 1631. After

Shakespeare's death, two more of his plays appeared in quarto format: *Othello* in 1622 and *The Two Noble Kinsmen*, coauthored with John Fletcher, in 1634.

In 1623, seven years after Shakespeare's death, *Mr. William Shakespeares Comedies, Histories, & Tragedies* was published. This printing offered readers in a single book thirty-six of the thirty-eight plays now thought to have been written by Shakespeare, including eighteen that had never been printed before. And it offered them in a style that was then reserved for serious literature and scholarship. The plays were arranged in double columns on pages nearly a foot high. This large page size is called "folio," as opposed to the smaller "quarto," and the 1623 volume is usually called the Shakespeare First Folio. It is reputed to have sold for the lordly price of a pound. (One copy at the Folger Library is marked fifteen shillings—that is, three-quarters of a pound.)

In a preface to the First Folio entitled "To the great Variety of Readers," two of Shakespeare's former fellow actors in the King's Men, John Heminge and Henry Condell, wrote that they themselves had collected their dead companion's plays. They suggested that they had seen his own papers: "we have scarce received from him a blot in his papers." The title page of the Folio declared that the plays within it had been printed "according to the True Original Copies." Comparing the Folio to the quartos, Heminge and Condell disparaged the quartos, advising their readers that "before you were abused with divers stolen and surreptitious copies, maimed, and deformed by the frauds and stealths of injurious impostors." Many Shakespeareans of the eighteenth and nineteenth centuries believed Heminge and Condell and regarded the Folio plays as superior to anything in the quartos.

Once we begin to examine the Folio plays in detail, it becomes less easy to take at face value the word of Heminge and Condell about the superiority of the Folio texts. For example, of the first nine plays in the Folio (one quarter of the entire collection), four were essentially reprinted from earlier quarto printings that Heminge and Condell had disparaged; and four have now been identified as printed from copies written in the hand of a professional scribe of the 1620s named Ralph Crane; the ninth, *The Comedy of Errors,* was apparently also printed from a manuscript, but one whose origin cannot be readily identified. Evidently then, eight of the first nine plays in the First Folio were not printed, in spite of what the Folio title page announces, "according to the True Original Copies," or Shakespeare's own papers, and the source of the ninth is unknown. Since today's editors have been forced to treat Heminge and Condell's pronouncements with skepticism, they must choose whether to base their own editions upon quartos or the Folio on grounds other than Heminge and Condell's story of where the quarto and Folio versions originated.

Editors have often fashioned their own narratives to explain what lies behind the quartos and Folio. They have said that Heminge and Condell meant to criticize only a few of the early quartos, the ones that offer much shorter and sometimes quite different, often garbled, versions of plays. Among the examples of these are the 1600 quarto of *Henry V* (the Folio offers a much fuller version) or the 1603 *Hamlet* quarto (in 1604 a different, much longer form of the play got into print as a quarto). Early in this century editors speculated that these questionable texts were produced when someone in the audience took notes from the plays' dialogue during performances and then employed "hack poets" to fill out the notes. The poor results were then sold to a publisher and presented in print as Shakespeare's plays. More recently this story has given way to another in which the shorter versions are said to be recreations from memory of Shakespeare's plays by actors who wanted to stage them in the provinces but lacked manuscript copies. Most of the quartos offer much better texts than these so-called bad quartos. Indeed, in most of the quartos we find texts that are at least equal to or better than what is printed in the Folio. Many of this century's Shakespeare enthusiasts have persuaded themselves that most of the quartos were set into type directly from Shakespeare's own papers, although there is nothing on which to base this conclusion except the desire for it to be true. Thus speculation continues about how the Shakespeare plays got to be printed. All that we have are the printed texts.

The book collector who was most successful in bringing together copies of the quartos and the First Folio was Henry Clay Folger, founder of the Folger Shakespeare Library in Washington, D.C. While it is estimated that there survive around the world only about 230 copies of the First Folio, Mr. Folger was able to acquire more than seventy-five copies, as well as a large number of fragments, for the library that bears his name. He also amassed a substantial number of quartos. For example, only fourteen copies of the First Quarto of *Love's Labor's Lost* are known to exist, and three are at the Folger Shakespeare Library. As a consequence of Mr. Folger's labors, twentieth-

century scholars visiting the Folger Library have
been able to learn a great deal about sixteenth-
and seventeenth-century printing and, particularly,
about the printing of Shakespeare's plays. And Mr.
Folger did not stop at the First Folio, but collected
many copies of later editions of Shakespeare, beginning with the Second Folio (1632), the Third (1663–
64), and the Fourth (1685). Each of these later folios
was based on its immediate predecessor and was
edited anonymously. The first editor of Shakespeare
whose name we know was Nicholas Rowe, whose
first edition came out in 1709. Mr. Folger collected
this edition and many, many more by Rowe's suc-
cessors.

An Introduction to This Text

The play we call *King Lear* was printed in two different
versions in the first quarter of the seventeenth century.

In 1608 appeared *M. William Shak-speare: His True
Chronicle Historie of the life and death of King Lear and
his three Daughters. With the vnfortunate life of Edgar,
sonne and heire to the Earle of Gloster, and his sullen and
assumed humor of Tom of Bedlam.* This printing was
a quarto or pocket-size book known today as "Q1."
It is remarkable among early printed Shakespeare
plays for its hundreds of lines of verse that are either er-
roneously divided or set as prose; in addition, some
of its prose is set as verse. As Q1 was going through
the press, it was extensively corrected; thus different
copies of its pages contain different readings. Sometimes the correction appears to be competent; at oth-

er times, however, it is better called "miscorrection." (In 1619 appeared a second quarto printing of the play ["Q2"]. It was, for the most part, simply a reprint of Q1, but it contained many corrections [as well as new errors] and changes, especially in the lining of verse in the last scene or so of Act 4 and in Act 5. This second printing had exactly the same title as Q1; it even fraudulently retained on its title page the 1608 date of Q1; the true date of Q2's printing [1619] was not discovered until early in the twentieth century.)

The second version to see print is found in the First Folio of Shakespeare's plays, published in 1623 ("F"). Entitled simply *The Tragedie of King Lear*, F contains over 100 lines that are not in Q1; at the same time F lacks about 300 lines (including a whole scene, 4.3) that are present in Q1. Many of the lines unique to Q1 or to F cluster together in quite extensive passages. The Q1 and F versions also differ from each other in their readings of over 800 words. In spite of the wide differences between the quarto and Folio printings, there is, nevertheless, such close agreement in punctuation between Q2 and F on some pages that the suspicion arises that F was printed from an annotated copy of Q2 (supplemented with the additional passages unique to F) or from a manuscript that had been prepared with some reference to Q2. Thus when F agrees with Q2 against Q1, editors sometimes suspect that F may have been led into error by Q2 (see, for example, in the textual notes 1.4.32, 141; 2.1.141; 2.2.165; 4.2.74, 96; 4.6.298; 4.7.68; 5.3.186). In other cases, however, F agrees with Q2 in the correction of obvious (or nearly obvious) errors in Q1 (see, for example, in the textual notes 1.1.163; 1.4.327; 1.5.8; 2.1.13, 63; 2.2.98, 152, 163, 171; 2.4.122, 187, 247; 3.3.3; 3.7.90; 4.1.10; 4.2.18; 4.4.30;

M. William Shak-speare:

HIS
True Chronicle Historie of the life and
death of King L E A R and his three
Daughters.

With the vnfortunate life of Edgar, *sonne*
and heire to the Earle of Gloster, and his
sullen and assumed humor of
T O M of Bedlam :

As it was played before the Kings Maieſtie at Whitehall vpon
S. Stephans *night in Chriſtmas Hollidayes.*

By his Maiesties seruants playing vsually at the Gloabe
on the Bancke-side.

LONDON,
Printed for *Nathaniel Butter*, and are to be sold at his shop in *Pauls*
Church-yard at the signe of the Pide Bull neere
S^t. *Auſtins* Gate. 1 6 0 8

Title page of the First Quarto of *King Lear,* 1608 (facsimile).

THE TRAGEDIE OF
KING LEAR.

Actus Primus. Scœna Prima.

Enter Kent, Gloucester, and Edmond.

Kent.

I Thought the King had more affected the
Duke of *Albany*, then *Cornwall*.

Glou. It did alwayes feeme fo to vs : But
now in the diuifion of the Kingdome, it ap-
peares not which of the Dukes hee valewes
moft, for qualities are fo weigh'd, that curiofity in neither, can make choife of eithers moity.

Kent. Is not this your Son, my Lord?

Glou. His breeding Sir,hath bin at my charge. I haue
fo often bluth'd to acknowledge him, that now I am
braz'd too't.

Kent. I cannot conceiue you.

Glou. Sir,this yong Fellowes mother could ; where-
vpon fhe grew round womb'd, and had indeede (Sir) a
Sonne for her Cradle, ere fhe had a husband for her bed.
Do you fmell a fault?

Kent. I cannot wifh the fault vndone, the iffue of it,
being fo proper.

Glou. But I haue a Sonne, Sir, by order of Law,fome
yeere elder then this ; who, yet is no deerer in my account, though this Knaue came fomthing fawcily to the
world before he was fent for : yet was his Mother fayre,
there was good fport at his making, and the horfon muft
be acknowledged. Doe you know this Noble Gentleman, *Edmond?*

Edm. No, my Lord.

Glou. My Lord of Kent :
Remember him heereafter,as my Honourable Friend.

Edm. My feruices to your Lordfhip.

Kent. I muft loue you, and fue to know you better.

Edm. Sir,I fhall ftudy deferuing.

Glou. He hath bin out nine yeares, and away he fhall
againe. The King is comming.

Sennet. Enter King Lear, Cornwall, Albany,Gonerill, Re-
gan, Cordelia,and attendants.

Lear. Attend the Lords of France & Burgundy ,Glofter.

Glou. I fhall,my Lord.   *Exit.*

Lear. Meane time we fhal expreffe our darker purpofe.
Giue me the Map there. Know, that we haue diuided
In three our Kingdome : and 'tis our faft intent,
To fhake all Cares and Bufineffe from our Age,
Conferring them on yonger ftrengths, while we
Vnburthen'd crawle toward death. Our fon of *Cornwal*,
And you our no leffe louing Sonne of *Albany*,

We haue this houre a conftant will to publifh
Our daughters feuerall Dowers, that future ftrife
May be preuented now. The Princes ,*France* & *Burgundy*,
Great Riuals in our yongeft daughters loue,
Long in our Court, haue made their amorous foiourne,
And heere are to be anfwer'd. Tell me my daughters
(since now we will diueft vs both of Rule,
Intereft of Territory, Cares of State)
Which of you fhall we fay doth loue vs moft,
That we, our largeft bountie may extend
Where Nature doth with merit challenge. *Gonerill,*
Our eldeft borne, fpeake firft.

Gon. Sir, I loue you more then word can weild § matter,
Deerer then eye-fight, fpace, and libertie,
Beyond what can be valewed, rich or rare,
No leffe then life, with grace, health,beauty, honor :
As much as Childe ere lou'd, or Father found.
A loue that makes breath poore,and fpeech vnable,
Beyond all manner of fo much I loue you.

Cor. What fhall *Cordelia* fpeake? Loue,and be filent.

Lear. Of all thefe bounds euen from this Line,to this,
With fhadowie Forrefts,and with Champains rich'd
With plenteous Riuers,and wide-skirted Meades
We make thee Lady. To thine and *Albanies* iffues
Be this perpetuall. What fayes our fecond Daughter?
Our deereft *Regan*, wife of *Cornwall* ?

Reg. I am made of that felfe-mettle as my Sifter,
And prize me at her worth. In my true heart,
I finde fhe names my very deede of loue :
Onely fhe comes too fhort, that I profeffe
My felfe an enemy to all other ioyes,
Which the moft precious fquare of fenfe profeffes,
And finde I am alone felicitate
In your deere Highneffe loue.

Cor. Then poore *Cordelia,*
And yet not fo, fince I am fure my loue's
More ponderous then my tongue.

Lear. To thee,and thine hereditarie euer,
Remaine this ample third of our faire Kingdome,
No leffe in fpace, validitie, and pleafure
Then that confeir'd on *Gonerill*. Now our Ioy,
Although our laft and leaft : to whofe yong loue,
The Vines of France, and Milke of Burgundie,
Striue to be intereft. What can you fay, to draw
A third, more opilent then your Sifters? fpeake.

Cor. Nothing my Lord.

Lear. Nothing?

Cor.

From the 1623 First Folio.
(Copy 54 in the Folger Library collection.)

4.5.8; 4.6.49, 53, 85, 100, 127, 286; 5.1.63; 5.2.5; 5.3.30, 365, 370).

Since early in the eighteenth century, editors have combined Q1 and F to produce what is termed a "conflated text." But it is impossible in any edition to combine the whole of the two versions because they often provide alternative readings that are mutually exclusive, as, for example, when Q1 has the earl of Gloucester in his first speech refer to Lear's planned "division of the kingdoms," the Folio prints the singular "kingdom." In such cases (and there are a great many such cases), editors must choose whether to be guided by Q1 or by F in selecting what to print.

Twentieth-century editors of Shakespeare have made the decision about which version of *King Lear* to prefer according to their theories about the origins of the early printed texts. For the greater part of the century, editors have preferred F to Q1 in the belief that the Q1 text originated either in a shorthand transcription of a performance or in a reconstruction of the play by actors who depended on their memories of their parts. On the other hand, the F text was believed to have come down to us without the intervention of shorthand or memorial reconstruction. In the last decade or so, however, Q1 has found more favor with some editors according to a theory that it was printed directly from Shakespeare's own manuscript and that F was set into type from a version of the play that had been rehandled by another dramatist after Shakespeare's retirement from the theater. This second theory is today in competition with yet a third theory that holds that Q1 and F are distinct, independent Shakespearean versions of the play that ought never to be combined with each other in an edition. Those who hold this third theory think that Q1 was printed from Shakespeare's own manuscript, but they also think that the F text is the product of a revision of the play by Shakespeare after the printing of Q1. Nevertheless, as scholars reexamine all such narratives about the origins of the printed texts, we discover that the evidence upon which they are based is questionable, and we become more skeptical about ever identifying with any certainty how the play assumed the forms in which it was printed.

The present edition is based upon a fresh examination of the early printed texts rather than upon any modern edition.* It offers its readers the Folio printing of *King Lear*.** But it offers an *edition* of the Folio because it prints such Q1 readings and such later editorial emendations as are, in the editors' judgments, necessary to repair what may be errors and deficiencies in the Folio. Furthermore, the present edition also offers its readers all the passages and a number of the words that are to be found only in Q1 (and not in F), marking them as such (see below).

Q1 words are *added* when their omission seems to leave a gap in our text. For example, in the first scene of

---

*We have also consulted a computerized text of the First Folio provided by the Text Archive of the Oxford University Computing Centre, to which we are grateful. Also of great value was Michael Warren's *The Complete King Lear* (Berkeley: University of California Press, 1989).

**We choose F not because we believe that it stands in closer relation to Shakespeare than Q1 (we do not think it possible to establish which of Q1 or F is closer to the historical figure Shakespeare) but because F is a "better" text than Q1 in that it requires an editor to make fewer changes to its line division and wording than an editor must make to Q1.

the play, a speech of Cordelia's concludes in F with the line "Sure I shall never marry like my sisters"—without specifying the respect in which her marriage will differ from theirs. Q1 alone provides the required specification with an additional half-line, "To love my father all," and we include Q1's half-line in our text. (For similar additions, see 1.1.49, 75, 175, 246, 335; 1.2.140–41; 1.3.29; 1.4.195, 267–68, 321; 2.2.29; 3.2.85; 3.4.51, 52, 122, 143; 4.1.48; 4.5.43; 4.6.298; 4.7.28, 67; 5.1.20; 5.3.54. In a number of these cases the Q1 word or words are added to fill out short [and metrically deficient] lines in F.) We also add an oath from Q1 ("Fut," 1.2.138) that may have been removed from the F text through censorship. However, when F lacks Q1 words that appear to add nothing of significance, we do not add these words to our text. For example, Q1 adds the word "attire" to the end of Lear's statement to Edgar, "I do not like the fashion of your garments. You will say they are Persian" (3.6.83–85). Here the Q1 word "attire" seems a mere repetition of the earlier "garments." (Compare, among many instances, Q1 additions not included in our text [words that are sometimes needless, sometimes superfluous] listed in the text notes at 1.1.60; 2.4.266; 3.6.83; 3.7.66, 68; 4.6.297.)

Sometimes Q1 readings are *substituted* for F words when a word in F is unintelligible (i.e., not a word) or is incorrect according to the standards of that time for acceptable grammar, rhetoric, idiom, or usage, and Q1 provides an intelligible and acceptable word. Examples of such substitutions are Q1's "fathers" (modernized to "father's") for F's "Farhers" (1.2.18), Q1's "your" for F's "yout" (2.1.122), Q1's "possesses" for F's "professes" (1.1.82), or Q1's "panting" for F's "painting" when Oswald is referred to as "half breathless, ⟨panting⟩"

(2.4.36). (Compare substitutions from Q1 at 1.1.5, 73, 176, 259; 1.4.1, 51, 164, 182, 203; 2.1.2, 61, 80, 92, 101–2, 144; 2.2.0 SD, 23, 82, 83, 131, 141, 166, 187; 2.3.4, 18, 19; 2.4.8, 12, 36, 39, 65, 82, 145, 147, 213; 3.2.3; 3.4.12, 51, 56, 57, 97, 123; 3.5.26; 3.6.73; 4.1.65; 4.2.91; 4.4.3, 12, 20; 4.6.22, 77, 102, 180, 300; 4.7.0, 15; 5.1.52, 55; 5.3.82, 99, 101, 118, 160, 163, 177, 308.) We recognize that our understanding of what was acceptable in Shakespeare's time is to some extent inevitably based upon reading others' editions of *King Lear,* but it is also based on reading other writing from the period and on historical dictionaries and studies of Shakespeare's grammar.

Finally we print a word from Q1 rather than from F when a word in F seems at odds with the story that the play tells and Q1 supplies a word that coheres with the story. For example, when Lear enters at the beginning of 2.4 he wonders, in F, why Cornwall and Regan did "not send back my Messengers." But, as far as we know, Lear has sent only a single messenger (Kent) to Cornwall and Regan. Therefore, like most other editors, we print Q1's "messenger" for F's "Messengers." (Compare 1.1.214 and 5.3.193.) Because we rarely substitute Q1 words for F's, our edition is closer to F than are most other editions of the play available today.

In order to enable its readers to tell the difference between the F and Q1 versions, the present edition uses a variety of signals:

(1) All the words in this edition that are printed only in the First Quarto but not in the Folio appear in pointed brackets (⟨ ⟩).

(2) All full lines that are found only in the Folio and not in the First Quarto are printed in brackets ([ ]).

(3) Sometimes neither the Folio nor the First Quarto

seems to offer a satisfactory reading, and it is necessary to print a word different from what is offered by either. Such words (called "emendations" by editors) are printed within half-brackets (⌐ ⌐).

In this edition, whenever we change the wording of the Folio or add anything to its stage directions, we mark the change. We want our readers to be immediately aware when we have intervened. (Only when we correct an obvious typographical error in the First Quarto or Folio does the change not get marked in our text.) Whenever we change the Folio or Quarto's wording or change its punctuation so that meaning is changed, we list the change in the textual notes at the back of the book. Those who wish to find the Quarto's alternatives to the Folio's readings will be able to find these also in the textual notes.

For the convenience of the reader, we have modernized the punctuation and the spelling of both the Folio and the First Quarto. Thus, for example, our text supplies the modern standard spelling "father's" for the Quarto's spelling "fathers" (quoted above). Sometimes we go so far as to modernize certain old forms of words; for example, when *a* means "he," we change it to *he;* we change *mo* to *more* and *ye* to *you.* But it is not our practice in editing any of the plays to modernize some words that sound distinctly different from modern forms. For example, when the early printed texts read *sith* or *apricocks* or *porpentine,* we have not modernized to *since, apricots, porcupine.* When the forms *an, and,* or *and if* appear instead of the modern form *if,* we have reduced *and* to *an* but have not changed any of these forms to their modern equivalent, *if.* We also modernize and, where necessary, correct passages in foreign languages, unless an error in the early printed text can be reasonably explained as a joke.

We correct or regularize a number of the proper names, as is the usual practice in editions of the play. For example, the Folio's spellings "Gloster" and "Burgundie" are changed to the familiar "Gloucester" and "Burgundy"; and there are a number of other comparable adjustments in the names.

This edition differs from many earlier ones in its efforts to aid the reader in imagining the play as a performance rather than as a series of fictional events. Thus stage directions are written with reference to the stage. For example, in 1.2 Edmund is represented in the dialogue and in the fiction of the play as putting a letter in his pocket. On the stage this letter would, however, be represented by a piece of paper. Thus the present edition reads *"He puts a paper in his pocket"* rather than "a letter." Whenever it is reasonably certain, in our view, that a speech is accompanied by a particular action, we provide a stage direction describing the action. (Occasional exceptions to this rule occur when the action is so obvious that to add a stage direction would insult the reader.) Stage directions for the entrance of characters in mid-scene are, with rare exceptions, placed so that they immediately precede the characters' participation in the scene, even though these entrances may appear somewhat earlier in the early printed texts. Whenever we move a stage direction, we record this change in the textual notes. Latin stage directions (e.g., *Exeunt*) are translated into English (e.g., *They exit*).

We expand the often severely abbreviated forms of names used as speech headings in early printed texts into the full names of the characters. We also regularize the speakers' names in speech headings, using only a single designation for each character, even though the early printed texts sometimes use a variety of designations. Variations in the speech headings of the early printed texts are recorded in the textual notes.

In the present edition, as well, we mark with a dash any change of address within a speech, unless a stage direction intervenes. When the *-ed* ending of a word is to be pronounced, we mark it with an accent.

Like editors for the last two centuries, we print metrically linked lines in the following way:

LEAR
  Mak'st thou this shame thy pastime?
KENT   No, my lord.

However, when there are a number of short verse lines that can be linked in more than one way, we do not, with rare exceptions, indent any of them.

The Explanatory Notes

The notes that appear on the pages facing the text are designed to provide readers with the help that they may need to enjoy the play. Whenever the meaning of a word in the text is not readily accessible in a good contemporary dictionary, we offer the meaning in a note. Sometimes we provide a note even when the relevant meaning is to be found in the dictionary but when the word has acquired since Shakespeare's time other potentially confusing meanings. In our notes, we try to offer modern synonyms for Shakespeare's words. We also try to indicate to the reader the connection between the word in the play and the modern synonym. For example, Shakespeare sometimes uses the word *head* to mean "source," but, for modern readers, there may be no connection evident between these two words. We provide the connection by explaining Shakespeare's usage as follows: **"head:** fountainhead, source." On some occasions, a whole phrase or clause needs explanation. Then, when space allows, we rephrase in our own words the difficult passage, and add at the end synonyms for individual words in the passage. When scholars have been unable to determine the meaning of a word or phrase, we acknowledge the uncertainty.

The Tragedy of

KING LEAR

Characters in the Play

LEAR, king of Britain

GONERIL, Lear's eldest daughter
DUKE OF ALBANY, her husband
OSWALD, her steward

REGAN, Lear's second daughter
DUKE OF CORNWALL, her husband

CORDELIA, Lear's youngest daughter
KING OF FRANCE, her suitor and then husband
DUKE OF BURGUNDY, her suitor

EARL OF KENT

FOOL

EARL OF GLOUCESTER
EDGAR, his elder son
EDMUND, his younger and illegitimate son
CURAN, gentleman of Gloucester's household
OLD MAN, a tenant of Gloucester's

KNIGHT, serving Lear
GENTLEMEN
Three SERVANTS
MESSENGERS
DOCTOR
CAPTAINS
HERALD

Knights in Lear's train, Servants, Officers, Soldiers,
   Attendants, Gentlemen

3

The Tragedy of

KING LEAR

ACT 1

1.1 King Lear, intending to divide his power and kingdom among his three daughters, demands public professions of their love. His youngest daughter, Cordelia, refuses. Lear strips her of her dowry, divides the kingdom between his two other daughters, and then banishes the Earl of Kent, who has protested against Lear's rash actions. The King of France, one of Cordelia's suitors, chooses to marry her despite her father's casting her away. Lear tells his daughters Goneril and Regan that they and their husbands should divide his powers and revenues; he himself will keep a hundred knights and will live with Goneril and Regan by turns.

---

1. **more affected:** been more partial to
5–7. **equalities . . . moiety:** i.e., the equal portions (of the divided kingdom awarded by Lear to the dukes) are so balanced that the most minute examination of either can find no difference between their shares **moiety:** share, portion
9–10. **breeding . . . charge:** (1) upbringing has been at my expense; (2) parentage has been imputed to me
11. **brazed:** hardened (like brass)
12. **conceive:** understand
15. **ere:** before
16. **fault:** misdeed
17. **issue:** (1) result; (2) offspring, child
18. **proper:** attractive
19. **a son . . . law:** i.e., a legitimate son
20. **some year:** i.e., a year or so
20–21. **dearer . . . account:** (1) more loved by me; (2) more valuable in my assessment

(continued)

ACT 1

Scene 1
Enter Kent, Gloucester, and Edmund.

KENT I thought the King had more affected the Duke of Albany than Cornwall.

GLOUCESTER It did always seem so to us, but now in the division of the kingdom, it appears not which of the dukes he values most, for ⟨equalities⟩ are so weighed that curiosity in neither can make choice of either's moiety. 5

KENT Is not this your son, my lord?

GLOUCESTER His breeding, sir, hath been at my charge. I have so often blushed to acknowledge him that now I am brazed to 't. 10

KENT I cannot conceive you.

GLOUCESTER Sir, this young fellow's mother could, whereupon she grew round-wombed and had indeed, sir, a son for her cradle ere she had a husband for her bed. Do you smell a fault? 15

KENT I cannot wish the fault undone, the issue of it being so proper.

GLOUCESTER But I have a son, sir, by order of law, some year elder than this, who yet is no dearer in my account. Though this knave came something saucily to the world before he was sent for, yet was his mother fair, there was good sport at his making, 20

7

21. **this knave:** i.e., Edmund, the illegitimate son (The word **knave** meant "boy" or "fellow," but was also a term for a servant, a sense playfully continued by Gloucester in "came something saucily . . . before he was sent for," as if he were an impudent servant who intrudes before he is summoned.); **something:** somewhat

22. **saucily:** (1) impudently; (2) bawdily

23. **fair:** beautiful

24. **whoreson:** bastard (here used affectionately)

24–25. **Do . . . Edmund:** It is possible that Edmund does not hear the conversation until this point.

29. **services:** respects (a courtly term)

30. **sue:** beg, entreat

31. **study deserving:** strive to deserve (your acquaintance)

32. **He:** i.e., Edmund; **out:** i.e., away

33 SD. **Sennet:** trumpets announcing an approach

34. **Attend:** escort (to the king)

37. **we:** i.e., I (the royal "we," which continues in the lines that follow)

40. **fast:** firm

43. **son:** i.e., son-in-law

46. **constant will:** firm intention; **publish:** make public

47. **several:** separate, particular; **dowers:** i.e., inheritances, legacies (Only Cordelia's portion would have been an actual dowry.)

and the whoreson must be acknowledged.—Do you
know this noble gentleman, Edmund?   25
EDMUND   No, my lord.
GLOUCESTER   My lord of Kent. Remember him here-
after as my honorable friend.
EDMUND   My services to your Lordship.
KENT   I must love you and sue to know you better.   30
EDMUND   Sir, I shall study deserving.
GLOUCESTER   He hath been out nine years, and away he
shall again. (*Sennet.*) The King is coming.

Enter King Lear, Cornwall, Albany, Goneril, Regan,
Cordelia, and Attendants.

LEAR
Attend the lords of France and Burgundy,
Gloucester.   35
GLOUCESTER   I shall, my lord.   *He exits.*
LEAR
Meantime we shall express our darker purpose.—
Give me the map there.   ⌐*He is handed a map.*⌐
                          Know that we have divided
In three our kingdom, and 'tis our fast intent   40
To shake all cares and business from our age,
Conferring them on younger strengths, [while we
Unburdened crawl toward death. Our son of
    Cornwall
And you, our no less loving son of Albany,   45
We have this hour a constant will to publish
Our daughters' several dowers, that future strife
May be prevented now.]
The ⟨two great⟩ princes, France and Burgundy,
Great rivals in our youngest daughter's love,   50
Long in our court have made their amorous sojourn
And here are to be answered. Tell me, my
    daughters—
[Since now we will divest us both of rule,

55. **Interest of:** claim or title to

58. **Where nature . . . challenge:** i.e., to her whose merit, along with Lear's natural affection, lays claim to it (i.e., to Lear's **largest bounty**)

60–61. **wield the matter:** express the substance (of her love)

63. **valued:** estimated, appraised

65. **found:** i.e., found himself to be loved

66. **breath:** voice; **unable:** unequal to the task

69. **these bounds:** i.e., the lands within these boundaries

70. **shadowy:** shady; **champains riched:** i.e., rich plains

71. **wide-skirted meads:** broad meadows

72. **issue:** descendants

76. **self:** same; **mettle:** (1) temperament; (2) metal

77. **prize:** esteem, value (with a secondary sense of "price")

78. **my . . . love:** i.e., my love exactly

79. **that:** i.e., in that

81. **square of sense:** No satisfactory explanation of these words has been found. Among the possible meanings of **square** are (1) area; (2) measure (i.e., carpenter's square); (3) perfection.

83. **felicitate:** made happy

87. **More ponderous:** weightier (and therefore more significant)

Interest of territory, cares of state—]   55
Which of you shall we say doth love us most,
That we our largest bounty may extend
Where nature doth with merit challenge. Goneril,
Our eldest born, speak first.
GONERIL
  Sir, I love you more than word can wield the   60
    matter,
  Dearer than eyesight, space, and liberty,
  Beyond what can be valued, rich or rare,
  No less than life, with grace, health, beauty, honor;
  As much as child e'er loved, or father found;   65
  A love that makes breath poor, and speech unable.
  Beyond all manner of so much I love you.
CORDELIA, ⌐*aside*¬
  What shall Cordelia speak? Love, and be silent.
LEAR, ⌐*pointing to the map*¬
  Of all these bounds, even from this line to this,
  With shadowy forests [and with champains riched,   70
  With plenteous rivers] and wide-skirted meads,
  We make thee lady. To thine and Albany's ⟨issue⟩
  Be this perpetual.—What says our second
    daughter,
  Our dearest Regan, wife of Cornwall? ⟨Speak.⟩   75
REGAN
  I am made of that self mettle as my sister
  And prize me at her worth. In my true heart
  I find she names my very deed of love;
  Only she comes too short, that I profess
  Myself an enemy to all other joys   80
  Which the most precious square of sense
    ⟨possesses,⟩
  And find I am alone felicitate
  In your dear Highness' love.
CORDELIA, ⌐*aside*¬   Then poor Cordelia!   85
  And yet not so, since I am sure my love's
  More ponderous than my tongue.

90. **validity:** value
93. **vines:** i.e., vineyards; **milk:** i.e., pastures
94. **to be interessed:** (1) to have a right or share; (2) to be closely connected; **draw:** gain
99. **Nothing . . . nothing:** proverbial
102. **bond:** duty or obligation (of child to father)
106. **bred me:** educated me, brought me up
107. **right fit:** fitting, appropriate
110. **Haply:** perchance, perhaps
111. **must take my plight:** will receive my vow or pledge

LEAR
  To thee and thine hereditary ever
  Remain this ample third of our fair kingdom,
  No less in space, validity, and pleasure   90
  Than that conferred on Goneril.—Now, our joy,
  Although our last and least, to whose young love
  [The vines of France and milk of Burgundy
  Strive to be interessed,] what can you say to draw
  A third more opulent than your sisters'? Speak.   95
CORDELIA Nothing, my lord.
[LEAR   Nothing?
CORDELIA Nothing.]
LEAR
  Nothing will come of nothing. Speak again.
CORDELIA
  Unhappy that I am, I cannot heave   100
  My heart into my mouth. I love your Majesty
  According to my bond, no more nor less.
LEAR
  How, how, Cordelia? Mend your speech a little,
  Lest you may mar your fortunes.
CORDELIA   Good my lord,   105
  You have begot me, bred me, loved me.
  I return those duties back as are right fit:
  Obey you, love you, and most honor you.
  Why have my sisters husbands if they say
  They love you all? Haply, when I shall wed,   110
  That lord whose hand must take my plight shall
       carry
  Half my love with him, half my care and duty.
  Sure I shall never marry like my sisters,
  ⟨To love my father all.⟩   115
LEAR   But goes thy heart with this?
CORDELIA Ay, my good lord.
LEAR   So young and so untender?
CORDELIA So young, my lord, and true.

122. **mysteries:** secret rites; **Hecate:** goddess of witchcraft and of the moon. (Her name, in Shakespeare, is pronounced as a two-syllable word.)

123–24. **operation . . . be:** i.e., influence of the planets that govern human life and death

126. **Propinquity . . . blood:** kinship

127–28. **as . . . this:** i.e., consider you a stranger from this moment

129. **Scythian:** member of a tribe noted in classical literature for savagery (See page 22.)

130. **makes . . . messes:** eats his own offspring (See page 18.)

132. **well neighbored:** closely placed; **relieved:** helped in distress

133. **sometime:** former

137–38. **thought . . . nursery:** i.e., expected to commit myself entirely to her loving care **set my rest:** venture everything (The term is from the card game of primero.)

140. **So . . . as:** i.e., as I hope to rest in peace in my grave

141. **France:** i.e., the king of France; **Who stirs?:** an impatient outburst: "Does no one move?"

144. **digest the third:** i.e., absorb what was to be Cordelia's dowry

145. **plainness:** plain-speaking, frankness; **marry her:** i.e., get her a husband

146. **invest:** endow; clothe

147–48. **large effects . . . majesty:** i.e., considerable signs (of power), or splendid shows, that are associated with rulership

148. **Ourself:** the royal "we"; **by monthly course:** i.e., a month at a time

(continued)

LEAR
Let it be so. Thy truth, then, be thy dower, 120
For by the sacred radiance of the sun,
The ⌜mysteries⌝ of Hecate and the night,
By all the operation of the orbs
From whom we do exist and cease to be,
Here I disclaim all my paternal care, 125
Propinquity, and property of blood,
And as a stranger to my heart and me
Hold thee from this forever. The barbarous
	Scythian,
Or he that makes his generation messes 130
To gorge his appetite, shall to my bosom
Be as well neighbored, pitied, and relieved
As thou my sometime daughter.
KENT   Good my liege—
LEAR   Peace, Kent. 135
Come not between the dragon and his wrath.
I loved her most and thought to set my rest
On her kind nursery. ⌜*To Cordelia.*⌝ Hence and avoid
	my sight!—
So be my grave my peace, as here I give 140
Her father's heart from her.—Call France. Who stirs?
Call Burgundy. ⌜*An Attendant exits.*⌝ Cornwall and
	Albany,
With my two daughters' dowers digest the third.
Let pride, which she calls plainness, marry her. 145
I do invest you jointly with my power,
Preeminence, and all the large effects
That troop with majesty. Ourself by monthly course,
With reservation of an hundred knights
By you to be sustained, shall our abode 150
Make with you by due turn. Only we shall retain
The name and all th' addition to a king.
The sway, revenue, execution of the rest,

149. **With reservation of:** i.e., reserving for myself

150. **sustained:** provided for

152. **addition to:** titles of

153. **revenue:** accent on second syllable; **execution:** carrying out, performance; **rest:** i.e., everything else associated with kingship

160. **Make . . . shaft:** get out of the way of the arrow

161. **fork:** forked arrowhead

165–66. **To plainness . . . bound:** i.e., honor obliges one to speak bluntly

167. **Reserve thy state:** keep your power

168. **in . . . consideration:** i.e., by pausing for reflection; **check:** stop

169–70. **Answer . . . judgment:** i.e., I will bet my life on the truth of my opinion that

172–73. **those . . . hollowness:** Proverbial: "Empty vessels have the loudest sounds."

175. **pawn:** (1) something to be set at risk; (2) chess piece of least value

176. **wage:** (1) wager, bet; (2) risk in warfare

178. **motive:** i.e., my reason for acting

181. **blank:** white bull's eye in the center of a target (See page 26.)

182. **Apollo:** god of the sun

185. **vassal:** slave; **Miscreant:** misbeliever; villain

Belovèd sons, be yours, which to confirm,
This coronet part between you.   155
KENT   Royal Lear,
  Whom I have ever honored as my king,
  Loved as my father, as my master followed,
  As my great patron thought on in my prayers—
LEAR
  The bow is bent and drawn. Make from the shaft.   160
KENT
  Let it fall rather, though the fork invade
  The region of my heart. Be Kent unmannerly
  When Lear is mad. What wouldst thou do, old man?
  Think'st thou that duty shall have dread to speak
  When power to flattery bows? To plainness honor's   165
    bound
  When majesty falls to folly. Reserve thy state,
  And in thy best consideration check
  This hideous rashness. Answer my life my
    judgment,   170
  Thy youngest daughter does not love thee least,
  Nor are those empty-hearted whose low sounds
  Reverb no hollowness.
LEAR   Kent, on thy life, no more.
KENT
  My life I never held but as ⟨a⟩ pawn   175
  To wage against thine enemies, ⟨nor⟩ fear to lose
    it,
  Thy safety being motive.
LEAR   Out of my sight!
KENT
  See better, Lear, and let me still remain   180
  The true blank of thine eye.
LEAR Now, by Apollo—
KENT Now, by Apollo, king,
  Thou swear'st thy gods in vain.
LEAR O vassal! Miscreant!   185

191. **recreant:** traitor
192. **That:** i.e., in that
193. **strained:** excessive
194. **our sentence:** my statement of condemnation, my judgment
195. **nor . . . nor:** neither . . . nor; **place:** position as king
196. **Our . . . good:** i.e., with my power put into effect
201. **trunk:** i.e., body
202. **Jupiter:** king of the Roman gods
204. **Sith:** since
205. **hence:** elsewhere, away from here
209–10. **your . . . approve:** i.e., may your actions fulfill your grand expressions (of love)
211. **effects:** results, i.e., deeds

"He that makes his generation messes." (1.1.130)
From Bauern-praktik, *Bauren Practica, odder Wetterbuchlin* . . . (1555).

[ALBANY/CORNWALL   Dear sir, forbear.]
KENT
Kill thy physician, and thy fee bestow
Upon the foul disease. Revoke thy gift,
Or whilst I can vent clamor from my throat,
I'll tell thee thou dost evil.   190
LEAR
Hear me, recreant; on thine allegiance, hear me!
That thou hast sought to make us break our vows—
Which we durst never yet—and with strained pride
To come betwixt our sentence and our power,
Which nor our nature nor our place can bear,   195
Our potency made good, take thy reward:
Five days we do allot thee for provision
To shield thee from disasters of the world,
And on the sixth to turn thy hated back
Upon our kingdom. If on the tenth day following   200
Thy banished trunk be found in our dominions,
The moment is thy death. Away! By Jupiter,
This shall not be revoked.
KENT
Fare thee well, king. Sith thus thou wilt appear,
Freedom lives hence, and banishment is here.   205
⌜*To Cordelia.*⌝ The gods to their dear shelter take
thee, maid,
That justly think'st and hast most rightly said.
⌜*To Goneril and Regan.*⌝ And your large speeches
may your deeds approve,   210
That good effects may spring from words of love.—
Thus Kent, O princes, bids you all adieu.
He'll shape his old course in a country new.
                                                        He exits.

Flourish. Enter Gloucester with France, and Burgundy,
                    ⌜*and*⌝ *Attendants.*

⟨GLOUCESTER⟩
Here's France and Burgundy, my noble lord.

216. **We . . . address:** i.e., I . . . address myself

217. **rivaled:** competed

218. **in . . . her:** i.e., as her immediate (or available) dowry

222. **tender:** offer

224. **so:** i.e., dear, precious

226. **aught:** anything; **little seeming substance:** This dismissive reference to Cordelia may allude to her stature, her manners, or her monetary worth.

227. **pieced:** added, joined to it

228. **fitly:** suitably; **like:** please

231. **infirmities:** imperfections; **owes:** owns

233. **strangered with:** made a stranger to me by

237. **Election . . . conditions:** i.e., choice is not possible on such terms

239. **tell:** (1) describe for you; (2) count up for you; **For:** i.e., as for

240. **make . . . stray:** stray so much

241. **To:** as to; **match:** marry; **beseech:** i.e., I beseech

242. **avert:** turn

246–47. **best object:** dearest object of your love

248. **argument:** subject

LEAR My lord of Burgundy,   215
    We first address toward you, who with this king
    Hath rivaled for our daughter. What in the least
    Will you require in present dower with her,
    Or cease your quest of love?
BURGUNDY   Most royal Majesty,   220
    I crave no more than hath your Highness offered,
    Nor will you tender less.
LEAR   Right noble Burgundy,
    When she was dear to us, we did hold her so,
    But now her price is fallen. Sir, there she stands.   225
    If aught within that little seeming substance,
    Or all of it, with our displeasure pieced
    And nothing more, may fitly like your Grace,
    She's there, and she is yours.
BURGUNDY   I know no answer.   230
LEAR
    Will you, with those infirmities she owes,
    Unfriended, new-adopted to our hate,
    Dowered with our curse and strangered with our
        oath,
    Take her or leave her?   235
BURGUNDY   Pardon me, royal sir,
    Election makes not up in such conditions.
LEAR
    Then leave her, sir, for by the power that made me
    I tell you all her wealth.—For you, great king,
    I would not from your love make such a stray   240
    To match you where I hate. Therefore beseech you
    T' avert your liking a more worthier way
    Than on a wretch whom Nature is ashamed
    Almost t' acknowledge hers.
FRANCE   This is most strange,   245
    That she whom even but now was your ⟨best⟩
        object,
    The argument of your praise, balm of your age,

250–51. **to dismantle . . . favor:** i.e., as to strip away the mantle of your goodwill

253. **That monsters it:** i.e., that makes it monstrous or hideous

253–54. **or . . . taint:** or else your hitherto professed love must now appear tainted (blemished, stained)

254. **which:** referring back to Cordelia's **offense**

256. **Should:** i.e., could

258. **for I want:** because I do not have

259. **speak and purpose not:** i.e., say things that I do not intend to do

265. **for which:** i.e., for wanting (lacking)

266. **still-soliciting:** always begging or enticing

272. **tardiness in nature:** natural reserve

273. **leaves . . . unspoke:** does not tell the story

276. **regards:** considerations

276–77. **stands / Aloof from:** i.e., are irrelevant to

"The barbarous Scythian." (1.1.128–29)
From Conrad Lycosthenes, *Prodigiorum* . . . (1557).

The best, the dearest, should in this trice of time
Commit a thing so monstrous to dismantle   250
So many folds of favor. Sure her offense
Must be of such unnatural degree
That monsters it, or your forevouched affection
Fall into taint; which to believe of her
Must be a faith that reason without miracle   255
Should never plant in me.
CORDELIA, ⌜*to Lear*⌝ I yet beseech your Majesty—
If for I want that glib and oily art
To speak and purpose not, since what I ⟨well⟩
        intend   260
I'll do 't before I speak—that you make known
It is no vicious blot, murder, or foulness,
No unchaste action or dishonored step
That hath deprived me of your grace and favor,
But even for want of that for which I am richer: 265
A still-soliciting eye and such a tongue
That I am glad I have not, though not to have it
Hath lost me in your liking.
LEAR   Better thou
Hadst not been born than not t' have pleased me   270
        better.
FRANCE
Is it but this—a tardiness in nature
Which often leaves the history unspoke
That it intends to do?—My lord of Burgundy,
What say you to the lady? Love's not love   275
When it is mingled with regards that stands
Aloof from th' entire point. Will you have her?
She is herself a dowry.
BURGUNDY, ⌜*to Lear*⌝   Royal king,
Give but that portion which yourself proposed,   280
And here I take Cordelia by the hand,
Duchess of Burgundy.
LEAR
Nothing. I have sworn. I am firm.

286. **Peace be with:** a phrase usually used as a greeting, but used here as a farewell

288. **respect and fortunes:** i.e., mercenary considerations (Many editors print the First Quarto's reading "respects of fortune," which also means considerations of wealth.)

293. **Be it lawful:** i.e., if it be lawful that

298. **chance:** lot, fortune, fate

300. **wat'rish:** filled with rivers; also, thin, poor, weak (i.e., water as opposed to Burgundy's wine)

301. **unprized:** unvalued

302. **though unkind:** i.e., though they are (1) unnatural, (2) unaffectionate

303. **here:** i.e., this place; **where:** i.e., place

308. **benison:** blessing

311. **The:** i.e., you, who are the; **washed:** i.e., tear-filled

312. **what:** i.e., for what

313. **like a sister:** i.e., because I am your sister

BURGUNDY, ⌈*to Cordelia*⌉
  I am sorry, then, you have so lost a father
  That you must lose a husband.   285
CORDELIA   Peace be with
  Burgundy.
  Since that respect and fortunes are his love,
  I shall not be his wife.
FRANCE
  Fairest Cordelia, that art most rich being poor;   290
  Most choice, forsaken; and most loved, despised,
  Thee and thy virtues here I seize upon,
  Be it lawful I take up what's cast away.
  Gods, gods! 'Tis strange that from their cold'st
    neglect   295
  My love should kindle to enflamed respect.—
  Thy dowerless daughter, king, thrown to my
    chance,
  Is queen of us, of ours, and our fair France.
  Not all the dukes of wat'rish Burgundy   300
  Can buy this unprized precious maid of me.—
  Bid them farewell, Cordelia, though unkind.
  Thou losest here a better where to find.
LEAR
  Thou hast her, France. Let her be thine, for we
  Have no such daughter, nor shall ever see   305
  That face of hers again. ⌈*To Cordelia.*⌉ Therefore
    begone
  Without our grace, our love, our benison.—
  Come, noble Burgundy.
                   Flourish. ⌈*All but France, Cordelia,*
                         Goneril, and Regan⌉ *exit.*
FRANCE   Bid farewell to your sisters.   310
CORDELIA
  The jewels of our father, with washed eyes
  Cordelia leaves you. I know you what you are,
  And like a sister am most loath to call

314. **as they are named:** by their proper names

316. **professèd bosoms:** i.e., publicly proclaimed love

318. **prefer:** recommend

323. **At Fortune's alms:** i.e., as a charity donation from Fortune; **scanted:** withheld, begrudged

324. **are . . . wanted:** i.e., deserve to be deprived as you deprived (your father)

325. **plighted:** pleated, folded

326. **Who . . . derides:** i.e., **Time**, who at first covers faults, but who at last uncovers and derides them

330. **appertains:** pertains, concerns

334. **changes:** changefulness, fickleness

338. **grossly:** obviously

341. **best . . . time:** i.e., prime of his life

342. **but rash:** i.e., completely hotheaded, overhasty

343–44. **of . . . condition:** i.e., firmly embedded in his character

344. **therewithal:** together with them; i.e., also

Aiming at "the blank." (1.1.181)
From Gilles Corrozet, *Hecatongraphie* . . . (1543).

Your faults as they are named. Love well our
   father.   315
To your professèd bosoms I commit him;
But yet, alas, stood I within his grace,
I would prefer him to a better place.
So farewell to you both.
REGAN
Prescribe not us our duty.   320
GONERIL   Let your study
Be to content your lord, who hath received you
At Fortune's alms. You have obedience scanted
And well are worth the want that you have wanted.
CORDELIA
Time shall unfold what plighted cunning hides,   325
Who covers faults at last with shame derides.
Well may you prosper.
FRANCE   Come, my fair Cordelia.
                                      France and Cordelia exit.
GONERIL   Sister, it is not little I have to say of what
   most nearly appertains to us both. I think our   330
   father will hence tonight.
REGAN   That's most certain, and with you; next month
   with us.
GONERIL   You see how full of changes his age is; the
   observation we have made of it hath ⟨not⟩ been   335
   little. He always loved our sister most, and with
   what poor judgment he hath now cast her off
   appears too grossly.
REGAN   'Tis the infirmity of his age. Yet he hath ever
   but slenderly known himself.   340
GONERIL   The best and soundest of his time hath been
   but rash. Then must we look from his age to
   receive not alone the imperfections of long-en-
   graffed condition, but therewithal the unruly way-
   wardness that infirm and choleric years bring with   345
   them.

347. **unconstant starts:** i.e., abrupt fits or outbursts; **like:** i.e., likely

349. **compliment:** ceremony

350. **sit:** take counsel

352. **last surrender:** i.e., recent surrender of the kingdom

355. **i' th' heat:** Compare the proverb, "Strike while the iron is hot."

1.2 Edmund, the Earl of Gloucester's illegitimate son, plots to displace his legitimate brother, Edgar, as Gloucester's heir by turning Gloucester against Edgar. He tricks Gloucester into thinking Edgar seeks Gloucester's life.

---

1. **Nature:** i.e., that which is natural, as opposed to spiritual or social

3. **Stand in . . . custom:** i.e., be exposed to the evil of a social convention (by which the elder—and legitimate—son will inherit everything)

4. **curiosity of nations:** i.e., elaborate legal or social distinctions

5. **For that:** because; **moonshines:** months

6. **Lag of:** lagging behind (in birth); younger than; **base:** (1) base-born; illegitimate; (2) inferior

7. **compact:** compacted, put together

8. **generous:** noble, courageous; **true:** proper

9. **honest . . . issue:** the child of a legally married woman **honest:** chaste

13. **More . . . quality:** i.e., a stronger constitution and more energy

15. **fops:** fools

(continued)

REGAN Such unconstant starts are we like to have
from him as this of Kent's banishment.

GONERIL There is further compliment of leave-taking
between France and him. Pray you, let us sit   350
together. If our father carry authority with such
disposition as he bears, this last surrender of his will
but offend us.

REGAN We shall further think of it.

GONERIL We must do something, and i' th' heat.   355

They exit.

Scene 2
Enter ⌐Edmund, the⌐ Bastard.

EDMUND

Thou, Nature, art my goddess. To thy law
My services are bound. Wherefore should I
Stand in the plague of custom, and permit
The curiosity of nations to deprive me
For that I am some twelve or fourteen moonshines   5
Lag of a brother? Why "bastard"? Wherefore "base,"
When my dimensions are as well compact,
My mind as generous and my shape as true
As honest madam's issue? Why brand they us
With "base," with "baseness," "bastardy," "base,"   10
    "base,"
Who, in the lusty stealth of nature, take
More composition and fierce quality
Than doth within a dull, stale, tired bed
Go to th' creating a whole tribe of fops   15
Got 'tween asleep and wake? Well then,
Legitimate Edgar, I must have your land.
Our father's love is to the bastard Edmund
As to th' legitimate. Fine word, "legitimate."
Well, my legitimate, if this letter speed   20

16. **Got:** begotten, conceived
17. **your land:** i.e., the land you are to inherit
20. **speed:** prove successful
21. **invention:** inventiveness; or, plot, scheme
24. **choler:** anger; **parted:** departed
25. **tonight:** i.e., last night; **prescribed his power:** i.e., told how much power he retains
26. **Confined to exhibition:** restricted to an allowance
27. **Upon the gad:** i.e., on a sudden impulse **gad:** goad, spur
29. **put up:** i.e., put away
34. **terrible:** frightened
34–35. **dispatch:** putting away
35. **quality:** nature
40–41. **for . . . o'erlooking:** i.e., for you to read
44–45. **to blame:** blameworthy, deserving rebuke
48. **essay or taste:** test
49. **policy . . . age:** i.e., this policy of reverencing the aged
50. **the best . . . times:** the prime of our lives

And my invention thrive, Edmund the base
Shall ⌜top⌝ th' legitimate. I grow, I prosper.
Now, gods, stand up for bastards!

Enter Gloucester.

GLOUCESTER
Kent banished thus? And France in choler parted?
And the King gone tonight, prescribed his power,   25
Confined to exhibition? All this done
Upon the gad?—Edmund, how now? What news?
EDMUND   So please your Lordship, none. ⌜*He puts a
paper in his pocket.*⌝
GLOUCESTER   Why so earnestly seek you to put up that
letter?   30
EDMUND   I know no news, my lord.
GLOUCESTER   What paper were you reading?
EDMUND   Nothing, my lord.
GLOUCESTER   No? What needed then that terrible dis-
patch of it into your pocket? The quality of nothing   35
hath not such need to hide itself. Let's see. Come, if
it be nothing, I shall not need spectacles.
EDMUND   I beseech you, sir, pardon me. It is a letter
from my brother that I have not all o'erread; and
for so much as I have perused, I find it not fit for   40
your o'erlooking.
GLOUCESTER   Give me the letter, sir.
EDMUND   I shall offend either to detain or give it. The
contents, as in part I understand them, are to
blame.   45
GLOUCESTER   Let's see, let's see.
⌜*Edmund gives him the paper.*⌝
EDMUND   I hope, for my brother's justification, he
wrote this but as an essay or taste of my virtue.
GLOUCESTER (*reads*) *This policy and reverence of age
makes the world bitter to the best of our times, keeps*   50
our fortunes from us till our oldness cannot relish

52. **idle and fond:** silly and foolish
53. **who sways:** which rules
54. **suffered:** allowed, tolerated
64. **closet:** private room
65. **character:** handwriting
67. **matter:** i.e., subject matter
68. **in respect of that:** i.e., considering the contents
69. **fain:** gladly
73. **sounded:** i.e., questioned, probed
76. **fit:** fitting, appropriate; **at perfect age:** i.e., fully grown
77. **declined:** i.e., in decline, or failing in vigor; **ward:** one legally placed under the protection of a guardian
80. **Abhorred:** abhorrent; **detested:** detestable
81. **sirrah:** term of address that shows the speaker's position of authority
87. **run . . . course:** i.e., act with certainty; **where:** i.e., whereas

them. I begin to find an idle and fond bondage in the
oppression of aged tyranny, who sways not as it hath
power but as it is suffered. Come to me, that of this I
may speak more. If our father would sleep till I waked 55
him, you should enjoy half his revenue forever and
live the beloved of your brother. Edgar.
Hum? Conspiracy? "Sleep till I wake him, you
should enjoy half his revenue." My son Edgar! Had
he a hand to write this? A heart and brain to breed it 60
in?—When came you to this? Who brought it?

EDMUND It was not brought me, my lord; there's the
cunning of it. I found it thrown in at the casement
of my closet.

GLOUCESTER You know the character to be your 65
brother's?

EDMUND If the matter were good, my lord, I durst
swear it were his; but in respect of that, I would
fain think it were not.

GLOUCESTER It is his. 70

EDMUND It is his hand, my lord, but I hope his heart is
not in the contents.

GLOUCESTER Has he never before sounded you in this
business?

EDMUND Never, my lord. But I have heard him oft 75
maintain it to be fit that, sons at perfect age and
fathers declined, the father should be as ward to the
son, and the son manage his revenue.

GLOUCESTER O villain, villain! His very opinion in the
letter. Abhorred villain! Unnatural, detested, brut- 80
ish villain! Worse than brutish!—Go, sirrah, seek
him. I'll apprehend him.—Abominable villain!—
Where is he?

EDMUND I do not well know, my lord. If it shall please
you to suspend your indignation against my brother 85
till you can derive from him better testimony of his
intent, you should run a certain course; where, if

91. **pawn down:** stake, bet
92. **feel:** test
93. **pretense of danger:** dangerous purpose
95. **meet:** fitting, proper
97. **auricular:** perceived by the ear; **have . . . satisfaction:** i.e., convince yourself
103. **wind me into him:** i.e., for my sake, insinuate yourself into his confidence; **Frame:** manage
104. **after . . . wisdom:** as you judge wise
104–5. **unstate . . . resolution:** i.e., give up my rank and fortune if only I could resolve my doubts
106. **presently:** immediately; **convey:** conduct
108. **withal:** i.e., with what happens
109. **late:** recent
110–11. **the wisdom of nature:** i.e., the study of nature, "natural philosophy" (what we would now call "science")
111. **nature:** i.e., human nature
112. **scourged:** afflicted; **sequent effects:** disasters that follow (the eclipses)
113–14. **mutinies:** riots
116. **prediction:** portent, omen
117. **bias of nature:** natural inclination (In the game of bowls, the **bias** is the curve that brings the ball to the desired point. See page 44.)
120. **disquietly:** unquietly

you violently proceed against him, mistaking his
purpose, it would make a great gap in your own
honor and shake in pieces the heart of his obedi-   90
ence. I dare pawn down my life for him that he hath
writ this to feel my affection to your Honor, and to
no other pretense of danger.

GLOUCESTER   Think you so?

EDMUND   If your Honor judge it meet, I will place you   95
where you shall hear us confer of this, and by an
auricular assurance have your satisfaction, and that
without any further delay than this very evening.

GLOUCESTER   He cannot be such a monster.

⟨EDMUND   Nor is not, sure.⟩   100

GLOUCESTER   To his father, that so tenderly and entirely loves him! Heaven and earth!⟩ Edmund, seek him
out; wind me into him, I pray you. Frame the
business after your own wisdom. I would unstate
myself to be in a due resolution.   105

EDMUND   I will seek him, sir, presently, convey the
business as I shall find means, and acquaint you
withal.

GLOUCESTER   These late eclipses in the sun and moon
portend no good to us. Though the wisdom of   110
nature can reason it thus and thus, yet nature finds
itself scourged by the sequent effects. Love cools,
friendship falls off, brothers divide; in cities, mutinies; in countries, discord; in palaces, treason; and
the bond cracked 'twixt son and father. [This villain   115
of mine comes under the prediction: there's son
against father. The King falls from bias of nature:
there's father against child. We have seen the best of
our time. Machinations, hollowness, treachery, and
all ruinous disorders follow us disquietly to our   120
graves.]—Find out this villain, Edmund. It shall
lose thee nothing. Do it carefully.—And the noble
and true-hearted Kent banished! His offense, honesty! 'Tis strange.   *He exits.*

125. **foppery:** foolishness

126. **surfeits:** sicknesses caused by intemperance

127–28. **guilty . . . stars:** Edmund here places his father's talk about omens within the larger context of belief in astrology, where the position of the stars, moon, and planets at the moment of one's birth are thought to control one's life. (See page 74.)

129. **on:** by

130. **treachers:** deceivers, traitors; **by spherical predominance:** i.e., through the influence of the celestial spheres (According to Ptolemaic astronomy heavenly bodies were carried around the earth in crystalline spheres. See page xxxvi.)

133. **divine thrusting on:** supernatural incitement

134–35. **lay . . . star:** blame his lecherousness on a star

136. **compounded with:** i.e., had sex with (literally, contracted with, made terms with)

136–37. **under the Dragon's tail:** perhaps, when the constellation Draco was in the ascendant; or, perhaps, while the moon was at the southward node of its orbit

137. **Ursa Major:** the constellation called the Great Bear

138. **rough:** violent, harsh, rude; **Fut:** i.e., 'sfoot, or Christ's foot (a strong oath)

139. **that:** that which; **maidenliest:** i.e., chastest

140. **twinkled . . . bastardizing:** in astrological terms, "been in the ascendant at the moment I was conceived (as a bastard)"

141. **pat:** at exactly the right moment; **catastrophe:** conclusion, winding up

(continued)

EDMUND   This is the excellent foppery of the world, that   125
   when we are sick in fortune (often the surfeits of
   our own behavior) we make guilty of our disasters
   the sun, the moon, and stars, as if we were villains
   on necessity; fools by heavenly compulsion; knaves,
   thieves, and treachers by spherical predominance;   130
   drunkards, liars, and adulterers by an enforced
   obedience of planetary influence; and all that we
   are evil in, by a divine thrusting on. An admirable
   evasion of whoremaster man, to lay his goatish
   disposition on the charge of a star! My father   135
   compounded with my mother under the Dragon's
   tail, and my nativity was under Ursa Major, so that it
   follows I am rough and lecherous. ⟨Fut,⟩ I should
   have been that I am, had the maidenliest star in the
   firmament twinkled on my bastardizing. ⟨Edgar⟩—   140

Enter Edgar.

⟨and⟩ pat he comes like the catastrophe of the old
   comedy. My cue is villainous melancholy, with a
   sigh like Tom o' Bedlam.—O, these eclipses do
   portend these divisions. *Fa, sol, la, mi.*
EDGAR   How now, brother Edmund, what serious con-   145
   templation are you in?
EDMUND   I am thinking, brother, of a prediction I read
   this other day, what should follow these eclipses.
EDGAR   Do you busy yourself with that?
EDMUND   I promise you, the effects he writes of suc-   150
   ceed unhappily, ⟨as of unnaturalness between the
   child and the parent, death, dearth, dissolutions of
   ancient amities, divisions in state, menaces and
   maledictions against king and nobles, needless diffidences, banishment of friends, dissipation of co-   155
   horts, nuptial breaches, and I know not what.
EDGAR   How long have you been a sectary astronomical?

143. **Tom o'Bedlam:** a beggar who has escaped or been discharged from Bedlam (London's Bethlehem Hospital for the insane) or who pretends to be so in order to make people give him money

148. **this:** i.e., the

150–51. **succeed:** follow, turn out

154–55. **diffidences:** distrust

155–56. **dissipation of cohorts:** (perhaps mutinous) disbanding of troops of soldiers

157–58. **sectary astronomical:** believer in astrology

163. **in:** on

164. **countenance:** manner

166. **Bethink yourself:** recollect

167–68. **forbear his presence:** i.e., avoid him

168. **qualified:** reduced

170. **with . . . person:** i.e., even physical harm to you

171. **allay:** calm, assuage

173–74. **have . . . forbearance:** i.e., restrain yourself patiently (Both **continent** and **forbearance** connote self-restraint.)

176. **fitly:** at a convenient time

181. **meaning:** intention

183. **image and horror:** i.e., horrible image

185. **anon:** soon

190. **practices . . . easy:** i.e., plots easily succeed; **the business:** i.e., how to proceed

191. **wit:** cleverness

192. **fashion fit:** i.e., shape to my own ends

EDMUND   Come, come,⟩ when saw you my father last?
EDGAR   The night gone by.   160
EDMUND   Spake you with him?
EDGAR   Ay, two hours together.
EDMUND   Parted you in good terms? Found you no
    displeasure in him by word nor countenance?
EDGAR   None at all.   165
EDMUND   Bethink yourself wherein you may have of-
    fended him, and at my entreaty forbear his pres-
    ence until some little time hath qualified the heat
    of his displeasure, which at this instant so rageth in
    him that with the mischief of your person it would   170
    scarcely allay.
EDGAR   Some villain hath done me wrong.
EDMUND   That's my fear. [I pray you have a continent
    forbearance till the speed of his rage goes slower;
    and, as I say, retire with me to my lodging, from   175
    whence I will fitly bring you to hear my lord speak.
    Pray you go. There's my key. If you do stir abroad,
    go armed.
EDGAR   Armed, brother?]
EDMUND   Brother, I advise you to the best. I am no   180
    honest man if there be any good meaning toward
    you. I have told you what I have seen and heard, but
    faintly, nothing like the image and horror of it. Pray
    you, away.
EDGAR   Shall I hear from you anon?   185
EDMUND   I do serve you in this business.   *Edgar exits.*
    A credulous father and a brother noble,
    Whose nature is so far from doing harms
    That he suspects none; on whose foolish honesty
    My practices ride easy. I see the business.   190
    Let me, if not by birth, have lands by wit.
    All with me's meet that I can fashion fit.
                                              He exits.

1.3 Goneril, with whom Lear has gone to live, expresses her anger at Lear and his knights. She orders her steward, Oswald, to inform Lear that she will not see him and to treat Lear coldly.

---

5. **crime:** offense
10. **come slack:** fall short
11. **answer:** i.e., answer for
14. **to question:** into dispute
15. **distaste:** dislike; **let him:** i.e., let him go
17. **Idle:** silly, useless
18. **authorities:** powers
21–22. **checks . . . abused:** reprimands in place of (or, perhaps, as well as) flattering words, when they (old men) are seen to be deceived
27. **would . . . occasions:** i.e., wish to create opportunities
28. **straight:** straightway, immediately
29. **hold . . . course:** i.e., follow exactly my course of action

"Old fools are babes again." (1.3.20)
From August Casimir Redel, *Apophtegmata symbolica* . . . (n.d.).

Scene 3
Enter Goneril and ⌐Oswald, her⌐ Steward.

GONERIL   Did my father strike my gentleman for chid-
ing of his Fool?
OSWALD   Ay, madam.
GONERIL
By day and night he wrongs me. Every hour
He flashes into one gross crime or other   5
That sets us all at odds. I'll not endure it.
His knights grow riotous, and himself upbraids us
On every trifle. When he returns from hunting,
I will not speak with him. Say I am sick.
If you come slack of former services,   10
You shall do well. The fault of it I'll answer.
OSWALD   He's coming, madam. I hear him.
GONERIL
Put on what weary negligence you please,
You and your fellows. I'd have it come to question.
If he distaste it, let him to my sister,   15
Whose mind and mine I know in that are one,
⟨Not to be overruled. Idle old man
That still would manage those authorities
That he hath given away. Now, by my life,
Old fools are babes again and must be used   20
With checks as flatteries, when they are seen
    abused.⟩
Remember what I have said.
OSWALD   Well, madam.
GONERIL
And let his knights have colder looks among you.   25
What grows of it, no matter. Advise your fellows so.
⟨I would breed from hence occasions, and I shall,
That I may speak.⟩ I'll write straight to my sister
To hold my ⟨very⟩ course. Prepare for dinner.
                    They exit ⌐in different directions.⌐

1.4 The Earl of Kent returns in disguise, offers his services to Lear, and is accepted as one of Lear's followers. Goneril rebukes Lear for his knights' rowdiness and demands he dismiss half of them. After attacking her verbally for her ingratitude, he prepares to leave for Regan's.

1–4. **If . . . likeness:** i.e., if I can disguise my way of speaking as well as I have my appearance, then I may be able fully to carry out my plan **diffuse:** disorder, and thereby disguise **razed:** erased; shaved off **likeness:** outward appearance

5–6. **where . . . condemned:** i.e., in Lear's presence

7. **come:** i.e., happen that

8 SD. **Horns:** i.e., the sound of hunting horns

9. **stay:** wait

12. **What . . . profess?:** What is your trade or calling?

14. **profess to be:** assert that I am

15. **put . . . trust:** i.e., trust me, have confidence in me

16. **honest:** honorable; **converse:** associate

17. **fear judgment:** i.e., fear coming before a judge, either divine or human

17–18. **cannot choose:** i.e., have to fight

18. **eat no fish:** This seems to be a joke, though its meaning is unclear. It may mean "I am a Protestant" or "I eat meat and am therefore manly."

23. **What wouldst thou?:** i.e., what do you want?

29. **fain:** gladly

Scene 4
Enter Kent ⌐in disguise.⌐

KENT
If but as ⟨well⟩ I other accents borrow
That can my speech diffuse, my good intent
May carry through itself to that full issue
For which I razed my likeness. Now, banished Kent,
If thou canst serve where thou dost stand   5
    condemned,
So may it come thy master, whom thou lov'st,
Shall find thee full of labors.

Horns within. Enter Lear, ⌐Knights,⌐ and Attendants.

LEAR   Let me not stay a jot for dinner. Go get it ready.
                                    ⌐An Attendant exits.⌐
How now, what art thou?   10
KENT   A man, sir.
LEAR   What dost thou profess? What wouldst thou with
us?
KENT   I do profess to be no less than I seem, to serve
him truly that will put me in trust, to love him that   15
is honest, to converse with him that is wise and says
little, to fear judgment, to fight when I cannot
choose, and to eat no fish.
LEAR   What art thou?
KENT   A very honest-hearted fellow, and as poor as the   20
King.
LEAR   If thou be'st as poor for a subject as he's for a
king, thou art poor enough. What wouldst thou?
KENT   Service.
LEAR   Who wouldst thou serve?   25
KENT   You.
LEAR   Dost thou know me, fellow?
KENT   No, sir, but you have that in your countenance
which I would fain call master.

33. **keep . . . counsel:** keep honorable secrets; or, perhaps, honestly keep secrets
34. **curious:** elaborate
38. **to love:** i.e., as to love
43. **knave:** boy
47. **clotpole:** blockhead
54. **roundest:** rudest
58. **entertained:** treated
59. **were wont:** i.e., used to be

A game of bowls. (1.2.117)
From *Le centre de l'amour* . . . (1650?).

LEAR What's that? 30
KENT Authority.
LEAR What services canst do?
KENT I can keep honest counsel, ride, run, mar a
curious tale in telling it, and deliver a plain mes-
sage bluntly. That which ordinary men are fit for I 35
am qualified in, and the best of me is diligence.
LEAR How old art thou?
KENT Not so young, sir, to love a woman for singing,
nor so old to dote on her for anything. I have years
on my back forty-eight. 40
LEAR Follow me. Thou shalt serve me—if I like thee
no worse after dinner. I will not part from thee
yet.—Dinner, ho, dinner!—Where's my knave, my
Fool? Go you and call my Fool hither.
⌐*An Attendant exits.*⌐

Enter ⌐*Oswald, the*⌐ *Steward.*

You, you, sirrah, where's my daughter? 45
OSWALD So please you—   *He exits.*
LEAR What says the fellow there? Call the clotpole
back. ⌐*A Knight exits.*⌐ Where's my Fool? Ho! I think
the world's asleep.

⌐*Enter Knight again.*⌐

How now? Where's that mongrel? 50
KNIGHT He says, my lord, your ⟨daughter⟩ is not well.
LEAR Why came not the slave back to me when I
called him?
KNIGHT Sir, he answered me in the roundest manner,
he would not. 55
LEAR He would not?
KNIGHT My lord, I know not what the matter is, but to
my judgment your Highness is not entertained
with that ceremonious affection as you were wont.
There's a great abatement of kindness appears as 60

61. **the . . . dependents:** i.e., all the servants
67. **but remembrest:** only remind
67–68. **conception:** idea, thought
68. **faint neglect:** i.e., unenthusiastic service
69–70. **blamed . . . curiosity:** charged to my own oversensitivity
70. **very pretense:** actual purpose
72. **this:** i.e., these
84. **bandy:** exchange (literally, hit back and forth like a tennis ball)
85. **strucken:** struck
86. **base:** low, inferior
91. **differences:** perhaps, differences in rank
91–92. **measure . . . length:** i.e., be tripped again
lubber: clumsy oaf

Football players. (1.4.87)
From Henry Peacham, *Minerua Britanna* . . . (1612).

46

well in the general dependents as in the Duke
    himself also, and your daughter.
LEAR   Ha? Sayst thou so?
KNIGHT   I beseech you pardon me, my lord, if I be
    mistaken, for my duty cannot be silent when I think   65
    your Highness wronged.
LEAR   Thou but remembrest me of mine own concep-
    tion. I have perceived a most faint neglect of late,
    which I have rather blamed as mine own jealous
    curiosity than as a very pretense and purpose of   70
    unkindness. I will look further into 't. But where's
    my Fool? I have not seen him this two days.
KNIGHT   Since my young lady's going into France, sir,
    the Fool hath much pined away.
LEAR   No more of that. I have noted it well.—Go you   75
    and tell my daughter I would speak with her. ⌐An
    Attendant exits.⌐ Go you call hither my Fool.
                                        ⌐Another exits.⌐

        Enter ⌐Oswald, the⌐ Steward.

    O you, sir, you, come you hither, sir. Who am I, sir?
OSWALD   My lady's father.
LEAR   "My lady's father"? My lord's knave! You whore-   80
    son dog, you slave, you cur!
OSWALD   I am none of these, my lord, I beseech your
    pardon.
LEAR   Do you bandy looks with me, you rascal?
                                ⌐Lear strikes him.⌐
OSWALD   I'll not be strucken, my lord.   85
KENT, ⌐tripping him⌐   Nor tripped neither, you base
    football player?
LEAR   I thank thee, fellow. Thou serv'st me, and I'll
    love thee.
KENT, ⌐to Oswald⌐   Come, sir, arise. Away. I'll teach you   90
    differences. Away, away. If you will measure your
    lubber's length again, tarry. But away. Go to. Have
    you wisdom? So.   ⌐Oswald exits.⌐

94. **knave:** servant

95. **earnest:** a small payment that promises a greater reward to come

97. **coxcomb:** fool's cap (See page 52.)

99. **were best:** had better

103–4. **an . . . sits:** i.e., if you cannot adjust to shifts in power   **an:** i.e., if   **as the wind sits:** in the direction the wind blows

105. **on 's:** i.e., of his

108. **nuncle:** i.e., mine uncle, the Fool's familiar way of addressing Lear

111. **living:** property

115–17. **Truth . . . stink:** perhaps, truth-telling is whipped out of the house while flattery is rewarded (This meaning depends on the traditional symbolic link between flattery and dogs.) **Brach:** bitch-hound

118. **gall:** a painful sore; or, a vexation; or, bile, a bitter secretion of the liver

121. **Mark:** pay attention to, listen to

124. **owest:** own

125. **goest:** walk

126. **trowest:** believe

127. **Set . . . throwest:** bet less than you win throwing dice

LEAR   Now, my friendly knave, I thank thee. There's
   earnest of thy service.   ⌜*He gives Kent a purse.*⌝   95

                     Enter Fool.

FOOL   Let me hire him too. ⌜*To Kent.*⌝ Here's my
   coxcomb.   ⌜*He offers Kent his cap.*⌝
LEAR   How now, my pretty knave, how dost thou?
FOOL, ⌜*to Kent*⌝ Sirrah, you were best take my coxcomb.   100
LEAR   Why, my boy?
FOOL   Why? For taking one's part that's out of favor.
   ⌜*To Kent.*⌝ Nay, an thou canst not smile as the
   wind sits, thou'lt catch cold shortly. There, take my
   coxcomb. Why, this fellow has banished two on 's   105
   daughters and did the third a blessing against his
   will. If thou follow him, thou must needs wear my
   coxcomb.—How now, nuncle? Would I had two
   coxcombs and two daughters.
LEAR   Why, my boy?   110
FOOL   If I gave them all my living, I'd keep my coxcombs myself. There's mine. Beg another of thy
   daughters.
LEAR   Take heed, sirrah—the whip.
FOOL   Truth's a dog must to kennel; he must be   115
   whipped out, when the Lady Brach may stand by th'
   fire and stink.
LEAR   A pestilent gall to me!
FOOL   Sirrah, I'll teach thee a speech.
LEAR   Do.   120
FOOL   Mark it, nuncle:
            Have more than thou showest,
            Speak less than thou knowest,
            Lend less than thou owest,
            Ride more than thou goest,   125
            Learn more than thou trowest,
            Set less than thou throwest;

131. **a score:** twenty

133. **unfee'd:** unpaid (Proverbial: "A lawyer will not plead without a fee.")

140. **bitter:** harsh, cutting

147. **Do . . . stand:** i.e., you stand in his place

149. **presently:** immediately

150. **motley:** the multicolored costume of the professional fool

155. **altogether fool:** i.e., just fooling (The Fool's reply assumes that "altogether fool" means "all the folly that there is.")

156. **let me:** i.e., allow me to monopolize foolishness

157. **on 't:** i.e., of it

162–63. **eat . . . meat:** i.e., eaten up the edible part

"And ladies too . . . they'll be snatching." (1.4.158–59)
From Theodor de Bry, *Emblemata* . . . (1593).

50

Leave thy drink and thy whore
And keep in-a-door,
And thou shalt have more   130
Than two tens to a score.

KENT   This is nothing, Fool.

FOOL   Then 'tis like the breath of an unfee'd lawyer.
You gave me nothing for 't.—Can you make no use
of nothing, nuncle?   135

LEAR   Why no, boy. Nothing can be made out of
nothing.

FOOL, ⌐*to Kent*⌐   Prithee tell him, so much the rent of his
land comes to. He will not believe a Fool.

LEAR   A bitter Fool!   140

FOOL   Dost know the difference, my boy, between a
bitter fool and a sweet one?

LEAR   No, lad, teach me.

FOOL   (That lord that counseled thee
To give away thy land,   145
Come place him here by me;
Do thou for him stand.
The sweet and bitter fool
Will presently appear:
The one in motley here,   150
The other found out there.

LEAR   Dost thou call me "fool," boy?

FOOL   All thy other titles thou hast given away. That
thou wast born with.

KENT   This is not altogether fool, my lord.   155

FOOL   No, faith, lords and great men will not let me. If
I had a monopoly out, they would have part on 't.
And ladies too, they will not let me have all the fool
to myself; they'll be snatching.)—Nuncle, give me
an egg, and I'll give thee two crowns.   160

LEAR   What two crowns shall they be?

FOOL   Why, after I have cut the egg i' th' middle and eat
up the meat, the two crowns of the egg. When thou

165. **bor'st . . . ass:** i.e., carried your donkey
168. **like myself:** i.e., like a fool
170. **grace:** favor
171. **foppish:** foolish
172. **wear:** possess and enjoy as their own
173. **apish:** foolishly imitative
176. **used it:** made it my practice
181. **bo-peep:** a child's game
194. **frontlet:** i.e., frown

"Here's my coxcomb." (1.4.96–97)
From Sebastian Brant, *Stultifera nauis* (1570).

clovest thy ⟨crown⟩ i' th' middle and gav'st away
both parts, thou bor'st thine ass on thy back o'er   165
the dirt. Thou hadst little wit in thy bald crown
when thou gav'st thy golden one away. If I speak
like myself in this, let him be whipped that first
finds it so. ⌜*Sings.*⌝
    Fools had ne'er less grace in a year,   170
      For wise men are grown foppish
    And know not how their wits to wear,
      Their manners are so apish.
LEAR   When were you wont to be so full of songs,
sirrah?   175
FOOL   I have used it, nuncle, e'er since thou mad'st thy
daughters thy mothers. For when thou gav'st them
the rod and put'st down thine own breeches,
⌜*Sings.*⌝
    Then they for sudden joy did weep,
      And I for sorrow sung,   180
    That such a king should play bo-peep
      And go the ⟨fools⟩ among.
Prithee, nuncle, keep a schoolmaster that can teach
thy Fool to lie. I would fain learn to lie.
LEAR   An you lie, sirrah, we'll have you whipped.   185
FOOL   I marvel what kin thou and thy daughters are.
They'll have me whipped for speaking true, thou'lt
have me whipped for lying, and sometimes I am
whipped for holding my peace. I had rather be any
kind o' thing than a Fool. And yet I would not be   190
thee, nuncle. Thou hast pared thy wit o' both sides
and left nothing i' th' middle. Here comes one o' the
parings.

Enter Goneril.

LEAR
How now, daughter? What makes that frontlet on?
⟨Methinks⟩ you are too much of late i' th' frown.   195

197–98. **an O without a figure:** a zero with no number before it (to give it a numerical value)

204. **want:** need

205. **shelled peascod:** an empty pea pod

206. **all-licensed Fool:** i.e., servant who, as Fool, may do whatever he pleases

208. **carp:** (1) find fault; (2) talk noisily

209. **rank:** gross, excessive

211. **a . . . redress:** a sure remedy

212. **yourself too late:** you, all too recently

213. **put it on:** encourage it

214. **allowance:** approval

214–19. **which . . . proceeding:** Goneril's speech becomes much less direct as she begins to threaten Lear, but her general sense is clear: if you continue to encourage your knights' riotous behavior, I will move against them for the general good even if I offend and embarrass you; and I will be thought right to do so.

215. **censure:** blame; **redresses:** remedies

216. **tender . . . weal:** regard for the general good

217. **working:** implementation

218. **else were:** otherwise would be seen as; **shame:** shameful; **necessity:** the obvious need

221–22. **The hedge . . . young:** This couplet offers a nature story: the cuckoo lays its egg in the sparrow's nest, and the sparrow feeds the young cuckoo until it gets so big it kills the sparrow. **it's:** i.e., it has; **it:** i.e., its

223. **darkling:** (1) in the dark; (2) confused

225. **would:** wish

226. **fraught:** filled

227. **dispositions:** (1) inclinations; (2) temperaments

FOOL Thou wast a pretty fellow when thou hadst no
　　need to care for her frowning. Now thou art an O
　　without a figure. I am better than thou art now. I
　　am a Fool. Thou art nothing. ⌈*To Goneril.*⌉ Yes,
　　forsooth, I will hold my tongue. So your face bids　　200
　　me, though you say nothing.
　　　　Mum, mum,
　　　　He that keeps nor crust ⟨nor⟩ crumb,
　　　　Weary of all, shall want some.
　　　　　　　　　　　　　⌈*He points at Lear.*⌉
　　That's a shelled peascod.　　　　　　　　　　　205
GONERIL
　　Not only, sir, this your all-licensed Fool,
　　But other of your insolent retinue
　　Do hourly carp and quarrel, breaking forth
　　In rank and not-to-be-endurèd riots. Sir,
　　I had thought by making this well known unto you　　210
　　To have found a safe redress, but now grow fearful,
　　By what yourself too late have spoke and done,
　　That you protect this course and put it on
　　By your allowance; which if you should, the fault
　　Would not 'scape censure, nor the redresses sleep　　215
　　Which in the tender of a wholesome weal
　　Might in their working do you that offense,
　　Which else were shame, that then necessity
　　Will call discreet proceeding.
FOOL For you know, nuncle,　　　　　　　　　　220
　　　　The hedge-sparrow fed the cuckoo so long,
　　　　That it's had it head bit off by it young.
　　So out went the candle, and we were left darkling.
LEAR Are you our daughter?
GONERIL
　　I would you would make use of your good wisdom,　　225
　　Whereof I know you are fraught, and put away
　　These dispositions which of late transport you
　　From what you rightly are.

230. **Jug:** a nickname for "Joan"

234. **notion:** mind; **discernings:** mental faculties

235. **lethargied:** asleep; **Waking?:** i.e., am I awake?

238–40. **marks . . . reason:** i.e., by the tokens that designate kingship (titles, dress, entourage), and by knowledge and reason

240. **false:** falsely

242. **Which:** i.e., whom

244. **admiration:** pretended amazement

244–45. **much o' th' savor / Of:** i.e., of a kind with

247. **should:** i.e., you should

249. **disordered:** disorderly, unruly

251. **Shows:** looks; **Epicurism:** sensuality; or, gluttony

253. **graced:** honorable, dignified; **speak:** i.e., ask

255. **else:** otherwise

256. **disquantity:** lessen the number of; **train:** attendants

257. **remainders . . . depend:** i.e., those that remain as your dependents

258. **besort:** suit

FOOL May not an ass know when the cart draws the
    horse? Whoop, Jug, I love thee!   230

LEAR
  Does any here know me? This is not Lear.
  Does Lear walk thus, speak thus? Where are his
    eyes?
  Either his notion weakens, his discernings
  Are lethargied—Ha! Waking? 'Tis not so.   235
  Who is it that can tell me who I am?

FOOL Lear's shadow.

⟨LEAR I would learn that, for, by the marks of
    sovereignty,
  Knowledge, and reason, I should be false persuaded   240
  I had daughters.

FOOL Which they will make an obedient father.⟩

LEAR Your name, fair gentlewoman?

GONERIL
  This admiration, sir, is much o' th' savor
  Of other your new pranks. I do beseech you   245
  To understand my purposes aright.
  As you are old and reverend, should be wise.
  Here do you keep a hundred knights and squires,
  Men so disordered, so debauched and bold,
  That this our court, infected with their manners,   250
  Shows like a riotous inn. Epicurism and lust
  Makes it more like a tavern or a brothel
  Than a graced palace. The shame itself doth speak
  For instant remedy. Be then desired,
  By her that else will take the thing she begs,   255
  A little to disquantity your train,
  And the remainders that shall still depend
  To be such men as may besort your age,
  Which know themselves and you.

LEAR   Darkness and   260
    devils!—
  Saddle my horses. Call my train together.
                          ⌜*Some exit.*⌝

267. **Woe that:** i.e., woe to the one who
271. **thou . . . thee:** you reveal yourself
273. **patient:** calm
274. **kite:** vulture
275. **parts:** qualities
277. **in . . . support:** i.e., maintain with precise observance (of their duty)
278. **worships:** honor
280–82. **Which . . . place:** i.e., which distorted, twisted, me away from what I should be (The image of these lines may be of a building [**frame**] dislodged from its foundation [**fixed place**].) **engine:** machine
285. **dear:** precious
287. **moved you:** aroused your feelings

A kite. (1.4.274)
From Konrad Gesner, *Historia animalium* . . . (1585–1604).

Degenerate bastard, I'll not trouble thee.
Yet have I left a daughter.

GONERIL
You strike my people, and your disordered rabble   265
Make servants of their betters.

Enter Albany.

LEAR
Woe that too late repents!—⟨O, sir, are you
    come?⟩
Is it your will? Speak, sir.—Prepare my horses.
                                    ⌈*Some exit.*⌉
Ingratitude, thou marble-hearted fiend,   270
More hideous when thou show'st thee in a child
Than the sea monster!
[ALBANY   Pray, sir, be patient.]
LEAR, ⌈*to Goneril*⌉ Detested kite, thou liest.
My train are men of choice and rarest parts,   275
That all particulars of duty know
And in the most exact regard support
The worships of their name. O most small fault,
How ugly didst thou in Cordelia show,
Which, like an engine, wrenched my frame of   280
    nature
From the fixed place, drew from my heart all love
And added to the gall! O Lear, Lear, Lear!
                          ⌈*He strikes his head.*⌉
Beat at this gate that let thy folly in
And thy dear judgment out. Go, go, my people.   285
                                    ⌈*Some exit.*⌉

ALBANY
My lord, I am guiltless as I am ignorant
[Of what hath moved you.]
LEAR   It may be so, my lord.—
Hear, Nature, hear, dear goddess, hear!
Suspend thy purpose if thou didst intend   290

291. **this creature:** i.e., Goneril

293. **increase:** procreation

294. **derogate:** dishonored

295. **If . . . teem:** i.e., if it is her destiny to bear a child

296. **spleen:** spite, malice

297. **thwart:** perverse; **disnatured:** unnatural

299. **cadent:** falling; **fret:** wear

300. **her . . . benefits:** i.e., Goneril's motherly efforts and kindnesses

306. **disposition:** temperament

307. **As dotage:** i.e., that senility

308. **at a clap:** i.e., at one stroke

315. **Blasts and fogs:** sudden infections and foul (infectious) air

317. **untented woundings:** perhaps, wounds too deep to be probed (A **tent** was a probe used to cleanse a wound.)

318. **fond:** foolish

319. **Beweep . . . again:** i.e., if (you, i.e., eyes) weep again over this matter

To make this creature fruitful.
Into her womb convey sterility.
Dry up in her the organs of increase,
And from her derogate body never spring
A babe to honor her. If she must teem,   295
Create her child of spleen, that it may live
And be a thwart disnatured torment to her.
Let it stamp wrinkles in her brow of youth,
With cadent tears fret channels in her cheeks,
Turn all her mother's pains and benefits   300
To laughter and contempt, that she may feel
How sharper than a serpent's tooth it is
To have a thankless child.—Away, away!
                    ⌜*Lear and the rest of his train*⌝ *exit.*

ALBANY
Now, gods that we adore, whereof comes this?
GONERIL
Never afflict yourself to know more of it,   305
But let his disposition have that scope
As dotage gives it.

                    Enter Lear ⌜*and the Fool.*⌝

LEAR
What, fifty of my followers at a clap?
Within a fortnight?
ALBANY   What's the matter, sir?   310
LEAR
I'll tell thee. ⌜*To Goneril.*⌝ Life and death! I am
    ashamed
That thou hast power to shake my manhood thus,
That these hot tears, which break from me perforce,
Should make thee worth them. Blasts and fogs upon   315
    thee!
Th' untented woundings of a father's curse
Pierce every sense about thee! Old fond eyes,
Beweep this cause again, I'll pluck you out

320. **waters . . . loose:** i.e., tears that you shed
321. **temper:** moisten, soften
323. **comfortable:** comforting
325. **visage:** face
328. **mark:** hear
337. **Should . . . slaughter:** i.e., would certainly be sent to execution
338. **halter:** hangman's rope
342. **politic:** prudent (said sarcastically)
343. **At point:** armed
344–45. **dream, buzz, fancy:** All mean "whim," but **buzz** may also mean "whisper," "rumor."
346. **enguard:** i.e., guard, protect
347. **in mercy:** i.e., at his mercy
348. **too far:** i.e., unreasonably
350. **still take away:** always remove
351. **Not . . . taken:** i.e., rather than always fear being overtaken (by those harms)
354. **unfitness:** unsuitableness

"A tavern or a brothel." (1.4.252)
From *Le centre de l'amour . . .* (1650?).

And cast you, with the waters that you loose,   320
To temper clay. ⟨Yea, is 't come to this?⟩
Ha! Let it be so. I have another daughter
Who, I am sure, is kind and comfortable.
When she shall hear this of thee, with her nails
She'll flay thy wolvish visage. Thou shalt find   325
That I'll resume the shape which thou dost think
I have cast off forever.   *He exits.*
GONERIL   Do you mark that?
ALBANY
    I cannot be so partial, Goneril,
    To the great love I bear you—   330
GONERIL Pray you, content.—What, Oswald, ho!—
    You, sir, more knave than Fool, after your master.
FOOL Nuncle Lear, Nuncle Lear, tarry. Take the Fool
    with thee.
            A fox, when one has caught her,   335
            And such a daughter,
            Should sure to the slaughter,
            If my cap would buy a halter.
            So the Fool follows after.   *He exits.*
[GONERIL
    This man hath had good counsel. A hundred   340
        knights!
    'Tis politic and safe to let him keep
    At point a hundred knights! Yes, that on every
        dream,
    Each buzz, each fancy, each complaint, dislike,   345
    He may enguard his dotage with their powers
    And hold our lives in mercy.—Oswald, I say!
ALBANY Well, you may fear too far.
GONERIL Safer than trust too far.
    Let me still take away the harms I fear,   350
    Not fear still to be taken. I know his heart.
    What he hath uttered I have writ my sister.
    If she sustain him and his hundred knights
    When I have showed th' unfitness—

359. **full:** i.e., fully

361. **compact:** confirm

364. **milky . . . course:** i.e., mild and gentle course

365. **under pardon:** i.e., if you will excuse me

366. **at task:** blamed; **want:** lack

371. **Well . . . event:** perhaps a version of a proverb such as "time will tell" or "the end crowns all"

1.5 Lear, setting out for Regan's with his Fool, sends the disguised Kent ahead with a letter to Regan.

---

1. **Gloucester:** presumably, the town (or county) of that name

1–2. **these letters:** i.e., this letter

3. **demand out of:** questions arising from

8. **in 's:** in his

9. **kibes:** chilblains (i.e., sores resulting from exposure to the cold)

Enter ⌜Oswald, the⌝ Steward.

How now, Oswald?]   355
What, have you writ that letter to my sister?
OSWALD   Ay, madam.
GONERIL
Take you some company and away to horse.
Inform her full of my particular fear,
And thereto add such reasons of your own   360
As may compact it more. Get you gone,
And hasten your return. ⌜*Oswald exits.*⌝ No, no, my
    lord,
This milky gentleness and course of yours,
Though I condemn not, yet, under pardon,   365
⌜You⌝ are much more at task for want of wisdom
Than praised for harmful mildness.
ALBANY
How far your eyes may pierce I cannot tell.
Striving to better, oft we mar what's well.
GONERIL   Nay, then—   370
ALBANY   Well, well, th' event.
                                              They exit.

Scene 5
Enter Lear, Kent ⌜in disguise,⌝ Gentleman, and Fool.

LEAR, ⌜*to Kent*⌝   Go you before to Gloucester with these
    letters. Acquaint my daughter no further with any-
    thing you know than comes from her demand out of
    the letter. If your diligence be not speedy, I shall be
    there afore you.   5
KENT   I will not sleep, my lord, till I have delivered
    your letter.   *He exits.*
FOOL   If a man's brains were in 's heels, were 't not in
    danger of kibes?
LEAR   Ay, boy.   10

11–12. **go slipshod:** i.e., have to wear slippers (The Fool may be suggesting either that Lear has no brains, or that his brains do not lie in his heels, since his are taking him on a senseless journey.)

14. **Shalt:** i.e., thou shalt

15. **this:** i.e., Goneril; **crab:** i.e., crabapple

20. **on 's:** of his

22. **side 's:** i.e., side of his

24. **her:** i.e., Cordelia

34. **gone about 'em:** i.e., getting them ready

35. **seven stars:** i.e., the star cluster known as the Pleiades

39. **perforce:** forcibly

45. **mad:** insane

46. **in temper:** i.e., steady, calm

"The cart draws the horse." (1.4.229–30)
From Edmund W. Ashbee's 1871 reprint from John Taylor, *Mad fashions, od fashions . . .* (1642).

FOOL   Then, I prithee, be merry; thy wit shall not go
slipshod.
LEAR   Ha, ha, ha!
FOOL   Shalt see thy other daughter will use thee kind-
ly, for, though she's as like this as a crab's like an   15
apple, yet I can tell what I can tell.
LEAR   What canst tell, boy?
FOOL   She will taste as like this as a crab does to a crab.
Thou canst tell why one's nose stands i' th' middle
on 's face?   20
LEAR   No.
FOOL   Why, to keep one's eyes of either side 's nose,
that what a man cannot smell out he may spy into.
LEAR   I did her wrong.
FOOL   Canst tell how an oyster makes his shell?   25
LEAR   No.
FOOL   Nor I neither. But I can tell why a snail has a
house.
LEAR   Why?
FOOL   Why, to put 's head in, not to give it away to his   30
daughters and leave his horns without a case.
LEAR   I will forget my nature. So kind a father!—Be
my horses ready?   ⌜*Gentleman exits.*⌝
FOOL   Thy asses are gone about 'em. The reason why
the seven stars are no more than seven is a pretty   35
reason.
LEAR   Because they are not eight.
FOOL   Yes, indeed. Thou wouldst make a good Fool.
LEAR   To take 't again perforce! Monster ingratitude!
FOOL   If thou wert my Fool, nuncle, I'd have thee   40
beaten for being old before thy time.
LEAR   How's that?
FOOL   Thou shouldst not have been old till thou hadst
been wise.
LEAR
O, let me not be mad, not mad, sweet heaven!   45
Keep me in temper. I would not be mad!

⌜*Enter Gentleman.*⌝

How now, are the horses ready?
GENTLEMAN Ready, my lord.
LEAR Come, boy.
FOOL
  She that's a maid now and laughs at my departure,   50
  Shall not be a maid long, unless things be cut
    shorter.
                                        They exit.

The Tragedy of

KING LEAR

ACT 2

2.1 Edmund tricks Edgar into fleeing from Gloucester's castle. After more of Edmund's lies, Gloucester condemns Edgar to death and makes Edmund his heir. Cornwall and Regan arrive at Gloucester's castle, hear the false stories about Edgar, and welcome Edmund into their service.

---

0 SD. **severally:** separately

1. **Save:** i.e., God save (an ordinary greeting)

5. **How . . . that?:** i.e., how did this happen?

7. **abroad:** i.e., going around; **ones, they:** i.e., news (regarded as plural)

8. **ear-kissing:** i.e., barely heard because not yet widely known

10. **toward:** about to happen

13. **do:** i.e., hear

14. **The better, best:** i.e., so much the better—in fact, the best that could happen

15. **perforce:** necessarily

17. **queasy question:** hazardous, uncertain nature

18. **Briefness:** i.e., quick action; **work:** succeed

20. **watches:** perhaps, has ordered that a watch be kept for you

ACT 2

Scene 1

Enter ⌈Edmund, the⌉ Bastard and Curan, severally.

EDMUND   Save thee, Curan.

CURAN   And ⟨you,⟩ sir. I have been with your father and
given him notice that the Duke of Cornwall and
Regan his duchess will be here with him this night.

EDMUND   How comes that?   5

CURAN   Nay, I know not. You have heard of the news
abroad—I mean the whispered ones, for they are
yet but ear-kissing arguments.

EDMUND   Not I. Pray you, what are they?

CURAN   Have you heard of no likely wars toward 'twixt   10
the dukes of Cornwall and Albany?

EDMUND   Not a word.

CURAN   You may do, then, in time. Fare you well, sir.
He exits.

EDMUND
The Duke be here tonight? The better, best.
This weaves itself perforce into my business.   15
My father hath set guard to take my brother,
And I have one thing of a queasy question
Which I must act. Briefness and fortune work!—
Brother, a word. Descend. Brother, I say!

Enter Edgar.

My father watches. O sir, fly this place!   20

73

21. **Intelligence is given:** i.e., information has been given out

24. **i' th' haste:** i.e., in haste

26. **Upon . . . Albany:** perhaps, against Cornwall's side in his dispute with Albany; or, perhaps, on Cornwall's behalf against the duke of Albany

27. **Advise yourself:** i.e., think about it

31. **Draw:** i.e., draw your sword; **quit you:** i.e., acquit yourself

33–35. **Yield . . . farewell:** Edmund alternates between hostile shouts and instructions uttered in a low voice.

36. **drawn on:** i.e., drawn from

36–37. **beget . . . endeavor:** i.e., create a belief that I fought fiercely

38. **in sport:** i.e., as a joke, unseriously

45. **stand:** i.e., stand in support of him as

Astrologers casting a baby's horoscope. (1.2.127–28)
From Jakob Ruff, *De conceptu et generatione hominis* . . . (1580).

Intelligence is given where you are hid.
You have now the good advantage of the night.
Have you not spoken 'gainst the Duke of Cornwall?
He's coming hither, now, i' th' night, i' th' haste,
And Regan with him. Have you nothing said   25
Upon his party 'gainst the Duke of Albany?
Advise yourself.
EDGAR   I am sure on 't, not a word.
EDMUND
I hear my father coming. Pardon me.
In cunning I must draw my sword upon you.   30
Draw. Seem to defend yourself. Now, quit you
   well.   ⌜*They draw.*⌝
Yield! Come before my father! Light, hoa, here!
⌜*Aside to Edgar.*⌝ Fly, brother.—Torches, torches!
—So, farewell.   *Edgar exits.*   35
Some blood drawn on me would beget opinion
Of my more fierce endeavor. I have seen drunkards
Do more than this in sport.   ⌜*He wounds his arm.*⌝
                      Father, father!
Stop, stop! No help?   40

Enter Gloucester, and Servants with torches.

GLOUCESTER   Now, Edmund, where's the
   villain?
EDMUND
Here stood he in the dark, his sharp sword out,
Mumbling of wicked charms, conjuring the moon
To stand auspicious mistress.   45
GLOUCESTER   But where is he?
EDMUND   Look, sir, I bleed
GLOUCESTER   Where is the villain,
   Edmund?
EDMUND
Fled this way, sir, when by no means he could—   50

54. **that:** i.e., when
55. **bend:** direct
56. **Spoke with:** i.e., and when I spoke of
57. **in fine:** in conclusion
58. **how . . . stood:** i.e., with what loathing I opposed
59. **fell motion:** fierce attack
60. **preparèd:** i.e., already drawn; **charges home:** impetuously and effectively attacks
61. **unprovided:** defenseless
62. **best alarumed spirits:** i.e., my best courage aroused by the **alarum** (call to arms)
63. **quarrel's right:** i.e., in the rightness of my cause
64. **ghasted:** aghast, frightened
65. **Full:** very
66. **Let . . . far:** perhaps, "he'd better flee a long way if he hopes to escape me"
68. **dispatch:** i.e., let him be killed
69. **arch and patron:** i.e., archpatron, chief patron
71. **he which finds him:** i.e., whoever finds Edgar
72. **stake:** place of execution
75. **pight:** determined (obsolete form of "pitched"); **curst:** angry
76. **discover:** expose
77. **unpossessing:** i.e., without property (Illegitimate children could not inherit.)
77–80. **dost . . . faithed:** i.e., if I contradicted you, do you think anyone would believe you, or repose in you the trust, virtue, or worth necessary to credit your words?   **faithed:** credited, believed

GLOUCESTER
  Pursue him, ho! Go after. ⌈*Servants exit.*⌉ By no
  means what?
EDMUND
  Persuade me to the murder of your Lordship,
  But that I told him the revenging gods
  'Gainst parricides did all the thunder bend,   55
  Spoke with how manifold and strong a bond
  The child was bound to th' father—sir, in fine,
  Seeing how loathly opposite I stood
  To his unnatural purpose, in fell motion
  With his preparèd sword he charges home   60
  My unprovided body, ⟨lanced⟩ mine arm;
  And when he saw my best alarumed spirits,
  Bold in the quarrel's right, roused to th' encounter,
  Or whether ghasted by the noise I made,
  Full suddenly he fled.   65
GLOUCESTER   Let him fly far!
  Not in this land shall he remain uncaught,
  And found—dispatch. The noble duke my master,
  My worthy arch and patron, comes tonight.
  By his authority I will proclaim it   70
  That he which finds him shall deserve our thanks,
  Bringing the murderous coward to the stake;
  He that conceals him, death.
EDMUND
  When I dissuaded him from his intent
  And found him pight to do it, with curst speech   75
  I threatened to discover him. He replied
  "Thou unpossessing bastard, dost thou think
  If I would stand against thee, would the reposal
  Of any trust, virtue, or worth in thee
  Make thy words faithed? No. What ⟨I should⟩   80
  deny—
  As this I would, though thou didst produce

83. **My very character:** i.e., evidence against me written in my own handwriting

83–84. **turn . . . To:** i.e., make it all appear to be

84. **suggestion:** tempting; **practice:** treachery

85–88. **thou must . . . seek it:** i.e., you must think the world is stupid if you think people would not be aware that the benefits for you, should I die, are powerful incitements to you to seek my death **pregnant and potential:** obvious and powerful

89. **strange and fastened:** unnatural and confirmed

91. **got:** begot, fathered

91 SD. **Tucket:** trumpet signal

94. **ports:** sea harbors

98. **natural:** i.e., showing natural affection (but the word also had the meaning of "illegitimate," as well as of "legitimate")

99. **capable:** i.e., legally capable of inheriting (in spite of illegitimacy)

101. **Which . . . now:** i.e., which was only just now

111. **tended upon:** i.e., attended

My very character—I'd turn it all
To thy suggestion, plot, and damnèd practice.
And thou must make a dullard of the world   85
If they not thought the profits of my death
Were very pregnant and potential spirits
To make thee seek it."
GLOUCESTER   O strange and fastened villain!
Would he deny his letter, said he?   90
⟨I never got him.⟩   *Tucket within.*
Hark, the Duke's trumpets. I know not ⟨why⟩ he
    comes.
All ports I'll bar. The villain shall not 'scape.
The Duke must grant me that. Besides, his picture   95
I will send far and near, that all the kingdom
May have due note of him. And of my land,
Loyal and natural boy, I'll work the means
To make thee capable.

        Enter Cornwall, Regan, and Attendants.

CORNWALL
How now, my noble friend? Since I came hither,   100
Which I can call but now, I have heard strange
    ⟨news.⟩
REGAN
If it be true, all vengeance comes too short
Which can pursue th' offender. How dost, my
    lord?   105
GLOUCESTER
O madam, my old heart is cracked; it's cracked.
REGAN
What, did my father's godson seek your life?
He whom my father named, your Edgar?
GLOUCESTER
O lady, lady, shame would have it hid!
REGAN
Was he not companion with the riotous knights   110
That tended upon my father?

113. **consort:** company

114. **though:** i.e., if; **ill affected:** evilly inclined

115. **put him on:** i.e., incited him to attempt

116. **expense:** spending; **revenues:** accent on second syllable

123. **childlike office:** service appropriate to a son

125. **He . . . practice:** i.e., Edmund exposed Edgar's plot

130–31. **Make . . . please:** i.e., use my power (against Edgar) however you like

131. **For:** i.e., as for

137. **however else:** i.e., at least

140. **Thus out of season:** i.e., at such an inopportune time

A snail. (1.5.27)
From Thomas Trevelyon's pictorial commonplace book (1608).

GLOUCESTER
I know not, madam. 'Tis too bad, too bad.
EDMUND
Yes, madam, he was of that consort.
REGAN
No marvel, then, though he were ill affected.
'Tis they have put him on the old man's death,   115
To have th' expense and waste of his revenues.
I have this present evening from my sister
Been well informed of them, and with such cautions
That if they come to sojourn at my house
I'll not be there.   120
CORNWALL   Nor I, assure thee, Regan.—
Edmund, I hear that you have shown your father
A childlike office.
EDMUND   It was my duty, sir.
GLOUCESTER
He did bewray his practice, and received   125
This hurt you see striving to apprehend him.
CORNWALL   Is he pursued?
GLOUCESTER   Ay, my good lord.
CORNWALL
If he be taken, he shall never more
Be feared of doing harm. Make your own purpose,   130
How in my strength you please.—For you, Edmund,
Whose virtue and obedience doth this instant
So much commend itself, you shall be ours.
Natures of such deep trust we shall much need.
You we first seize on.   135
EDMUND   I shall serve you, sir,
Truly, however else.
GLOUCESTER   For him I thank your Grace.
CORNWALL
You know not why we came to visit you—
REGAN
Thus out of season, threading dark-eyed night.   140

141. **poise:** weight
144. **which:** i.e., the letters
145. **from:** while away from; **several:** various
146. **attend dispatch:** are waiting to be dismissed
148. **needful:** necessary
149. **instant use:** i.e., immediate action

2.2 Kent meets Oswald at Gloucester's castle (where both await answers to the letters they have brought Regan) and challenges Oswald to fight. The disturbance and Kent's explanations provoke Cornwall into putting Kent into the stocks for punishment.

---

6. **if . . . me:** i.e., please
9. **in Lipsbury pinfold:** A **pinfold** is a pound for animals. Since no such place as **Lipsbury** is known, editors have guessed that Kent means "between my teeth."
14. **broken meats:** i.e., leftover food
15. **base:** low; **three-suited:** Servants were given three suits per year.
15–16. **hundred-pound:** a low yearly income for one who aspires, like Oswald, to the status of gentleman
16. **worsted:** woolen, rather than the preferred silk
16–17. **lily-livered:** cowardly (i.e., with a liver, supposedly the seat of courage, pale from lack of blood)

(continued)

Occasions, noble Gloucester, of some ⟨poise,⟩
Wherein we must have use of your advice.
Our father he hath writ, so hath our sister,
Of differences, which I best ⟨thought⟩ it fit
To answer from our home. The several messengers   145
From hence attend dispatch. Our good old friend,
Lay comforts to your bosom and bestow
Your needful counsel to our businesses,
Which craves the instant use.
GLOUCESTER   I serve you, madam.   150
Your Graces are right welcome.
                                    Flourish. They exit.

                            Scene 2
Enter Kent ⌈in disguise⌉ and ⌈Oswald, the⌉ Steward,
                        severally.

OSWALD Good dawning to thee, friend. Art of this
    house?
KENT Ay.
OSWALD Where may we set our horses?
KENT I' th' mire.   5
OSWALD Prithee, if thou lov'st me, tell me.
KENT I love thee not.
OSWALD Why then, I care not for thee.
KENT If I had thee in Lipsbury pinfold, I would make
    thee care for me.   10
OSWALD Why dost thou use me thus? I know thee not.
KENT Fellow, I know thee.
OSWALD What dost thou know me for?
KENT A knave, a rascal, an eater of broken meats; a
    base, proud, shallow, beggarly, three-suited, hun-   15
    dred-pound, filthy worsted-stocking knave; a lily-
    livered, action-taking, whoreson, glass-gazing, su-
    perserviceable, finical rogue; one-trunk-inheriting

17. **action-taking:** i.e., settling disputes in court, rather than fighting; **glass-gazing:** i.e., fond of admiring himself in a mirror

17-18. **superserviceable:** perhaps, overeager to be of service

18. **one-trunk-inheriting:** i.e., possessing no more than will fit in a single trunk

19-20. **wouldst . . . service:** would, in order to give good service, play pimp or pander

20. **composition:** combination

24. **addition:** title (i.e., the one that I just gave you)

26. **of:** i.e., to

28. **varlet:** rascal

32-33. **make . . . you:** perhaps, fill you so full of holes that you soak up moonlight (A **sop** is a piece of bread soaked in liquid.)

33-34. **cullionly barbermonger:** despicable fop

37. **Vanity the puppet:** probably his name for Goneril (The phrase may mean a figure who personifies the sin of vanity or an actor who plays the allegorical figure Vanity.)

39. **carbonado:** slice up (like meat before it is broiled)

39-40. **Come your ways:** i.e., come on

42-43. **neat slave:** perhaps, elegant rascal

46. **With you:** an offer to fight; **goodman:** a form of address to a man below the rank of gentleman, insulting to Edmund

47. **flesh you:** initiate you into fighting

slave; one that wouldst be a bawd in way of good
service, and art nothing but the composition of a   20
knave, beggar, coward, pander, and the son and heir
of a mongrel bitch; one whom I will beat into
⟨clamorous⟩ whining if thou deny'st the least syllable
of thy addition.

OSWALD Why, what a monstrous fellow art thou thus   25
to rail on one that is neither known of thee nor
knows thee!

KENT What a brazen-faced varlet art thou to deny thou
knowest me! Is it two days ⟨ago⟩ since I tripped up
thy heels and beat thee before the King? ⌜*He draws*   30
his sword.⌝ Draw, you rogue, for though it be night,
yet the moon shines. I'll make a sop o' th' moon-
shine of you, you whoreson, cullionly barbermonger. Draw!

OSWALD Away! I have nothing to do with thee.   35

KENT Draw, you rascal! You come with letters against
the King and take Vanity the puppet's part against
the royalty of her father. Draw, you rogue, or I'll so
carbonado your shanks! Draw, you rascal! Come
your ways.   40

OSWALD Help, ho! Murder! Help!

KENT Strike, you slave! Stand, rogue! Stand, you neat
slave! Strike!   ⌜*He beats Oswald.*⌝

OSWALD Help, ho! Murder, murder!

Enter Bastard ⟨Edmund, with his rapier drawn,⟩
Cornwall, Regan, Gloucester, Servants.

EDMUND How now, what's the matter? Part!   45

KENT With you, goodman boy, if you please. Come, I'll
flesh you. Come on, young master.

GLOUCESTER
Weapons? Arms? What's the matter here?

CORNWALL Keep peace, upon your lives! He dies that
strikes again. What is the matter?   50

52. **your difference:** i.e., the cause of your quarrel
55. **disclaims in:** refuses to acknowledge
59. **stonecutter:** sculptor
60. **ill:** badly
61. **o':** i.e., in
64. **at suit of:** i.e., moved to mercy by
65. **zed:** the letter *z*; **unnecessary:** i.e., not included in the Latin alphabet
67. **unbolted:** unsifted or lumpy; **daub:** plaster
68. **jakes:** outhouse
69. **wagtail:** a bird so-called because of its constantly wagging tail
74–75. **should . . . honesty:** i.e., should wear the symbol of manhood without being honorable
77–78. **oft . . . unloose:** This seems to allude to the Gordian knot, which could not be untied because it was so intricately knotted. (It was cut apart by Alexander the Great.) The **holy cords** may, therefore, refer to marriage bonds, since the Gordian knot often symbolized marriage. **atwain:** in two **intrinse:** intricately tied
78–83. **smooth . . . masters:** i.e., encourage every rebelliously overpowering emotion of their lords by catering to it either through denial or affirmation, changing with every change in their master **smooth:** encourage **Renege:** deny **halcyon:** kingfisher, whose dead body, if hung up, was believed to turn in the direction of the wind **vary:** variation, change

REGAN
 The messengers from our sister and the King.
CORNWALL   What is your difference? Speak.
OSWALD   I am scarce in breath, my lord.
KENT   No marvel, you have so bestirred your valor.
 You cowardly rascal, nature disclaims in thee; a   55
 tailor made thee.
CORNWALL   Thou art a strange fellow. A tailor make a
 man?
KENT   A tailor, sir. A stonecutter or a painter could not
 have made him so ill, though they had been but two   60
 years o' th' trade.
CORNWALL   Speak yet, how grew your quarrel?
OSWALD   This ancient ruffian, sir, whose life I have
 spared at suit of his gray beard—
KENT   Thou whoreson zed, thou unnecessary letter!   65
 —My lord, if you will give me leave, I will tread
 this unbolted villain into mortar and daub the wall
 of a jakes with him.—Spare my gray beard, you
 wagtail?
CORNWALL   Peace, sirrah!   70
 You beastly knave, know you no reverence?
KENT
 Yes, sir, but anger hath a privilege.
CORNWALL   Why art thou angry?
KENT
 That such a slave as this should wear a sword,
 Who wears no honesty. Such smiling rogues as   75
 these,
 Like rats, oft bite the holy cords atwain
 Which are ⟨too⟩ intrinse t' unloose; smooth every
 passion
 That in the natures of their lords rebel,   80
 Being oil to fire, snow to the colder moods,
 ⟨Renege,⟩ affirm, and turn their halcyon beaks
 With every ⟨gale⟩ and vary of their masters,

85. **epileptic:** i.e., distorted

86. **Smile . . . as:** i.e., do you smile . . . as if

87. **Sarum plain:** Salisbury plain (a very large open expanse just north of Salisbury, and, in prehistoric England, the location of the city of Old Sarum)

88. **Camelot:** in the Arthurian legends, the place where King Arthur's court was located (It has been variously placed in Winchester, in Somersetshire, and in Wales.)

94. **likes:** pleases

96. **occupation:** custom, habit; **plain:** i.e., plainspoken, blunt

101-3. **doth . . . nature:** i.e., pretends to be plainspoken, and thus twists plain speech away from its own nature (that is, truth) **saucy:** insolent **garb:** appearance, manner **his:** its

105. **An they:** i.e., if they; **so:** i.e., fine

109. **silly-ducking observants:** ridiculously bowing sycophants

111-14. **Sir . . . front:** Kent here abandons plain speaking and mocks elaborate courtly language. **allowance:** approval **aspect:** (1) look; (2) astrological position (Kent flatteringly associates Cornwall with a heavenly body.) **Phoebus' front:** the sun's forehead

Knowing naught, like dogs, but following.—
A plague upon your epileptic visage!   85
⌈Smile⌉ you my speeches, as I were a fool?
Goose, if I had you upon Sarum plain,
I'd drive you cackling home to Camelot.
CORNWALL   What, art thou mad, old fellow?
GLOUCESTER   How fell you out? Say that.   90
KENT
No contraries hold more antipathy
Than I and such a knave.
CORNWALL
Why dost thou call him "knave"? What is his fault?
KENT   His countenance likes me not.
CORNWALL
No more, perchance, does mine, nor his, nor hers.   95
KENT
Sir, 'tis my occupation to be plain:
I have seen better faces in my time
Than stands on any shoulder that I see
Before me at this instant.
CORNWALL   This is some fellow   100
Who, having been praised for bluntness, doth affect
A saucy roughness and constrains the garb
Quite from his nature. He cannot flatter, he.
An honest mind and plain, he must speak truth!
An they will take it, so; if not, he's plain.   105
These kind of knaves I know, which in this
    plainness
Harbor more craft and more corrupter ends
Than twenty silly-ducking observants
That stretch their duties nicely.   110
KENT
Sir, in good faith, in sincere verity,
Under th' allowance of your great aspect,
Whose influence, like the wreath of radiant fire
On ⌈flick'ring⌉ Phoebus' front—

116. **dialect:** i.e., plainspokenness; **discommend:** disapprove

117–18. **He . . . knave:** i.e., whoever it was who used plain speaking to deceive you was an out-and-out villain

119–20. **though . . . to 't:** perhaps, even though I may displease you (by refusing to be plain) when you ask me to be

124. **late:** recently

125. **upon . . . misconstruction:** i.e., because of the king's misunderstanding me

126. **he, compact:** i.e., Kent, joined in a compact (with the king); **his:** i.e., the king's

127. **being down, insulted:** i.e., I being down, he insulted

128–30. **put . . . self-subdued:** acted like such a courageous man that he made himself appear worthy and won praise from the king by attacking one (namely Oswald) who had already chosen to give up **man:** courage **worthied:** got a reputation for him

131. **fleshment:** excitement arising from a first success

134. **Ajax:** in Greek mythology and in Shakespeare's *Troilus and Cressida,* a dull-witted, blustering Greek warrior in the Trojan War

135. **stocks:** an instrument of punishment that imprisoned the ankles in a wooden frame (See page 92.)

142. **malice:** ill will

143. **grace:** i.e., royal honor

CORNWALL What mean'st by this? 115
KENT   To go out of my dialect, which you discommend
  so much. I know, sir, I am no flatterer. He that
  beguiled you in a plain accent was a plain knave,
  which for my part I will not be, though I should
  win your displeasure to entreat me to 't. 120
CORNWALL, ⌐*to Oswald*¬   What was th' offense you gave
  him?
OSWALD   I never gave him any.
  It pleased the King his master very late
  To strike at me, upon his misconstruction; 125
  When he, compact, and flattering his displeasure,
  Tripped me behind; being down, insulted, railed,
  And put upon him such a deal of man
  That worthied him, got praises of the King
  For him attempting who was self-subdued; 130
  And in the fleshment of this ⟨dread⟩ exploit,
  Drew on me here again.
KENT   None of these rogues and cowards
  But Ajax is their fool.
CORNWALL   Fetch forth the stocks.— 135
  You stubborn ancient knave, you reverent braggart,
  We'll teach you.
KENT   Sir, I am too old to learn.
  Call not your stocks for me. I serve the King,
  On whose employment I was sent to you. 140
  You shall do small ⟨respect,⟩ show too bold
    malice
  Against the grace and person of my master,
  Stocking his messenger.
CORNWALL
  Fetch forth the stocks.—As I have life and honor, 145
  There shall he sit till noon.
REGAN
  Till noon? Till night, my lord, and all night, too.

149. **should:** i.e., would
150. **knave:** (1) servant; (2) villain
151. **color:** nature
152. **away:** i.e., in
155. **check:** rebuke; **purposed . . . correction:** the ignoble punishment you intend
156. **contemned'st:** most despised
161. **answer:** i.e., be accountable for
169. **rubbed:** hindered
170. **watched:** gone without sleep
172. **A . . . heels:** i.e., even good men can have bad luck **grow . . . heels:** decay, like stockings worn through at the heel (perhaps with reference to Kent's position with his heels sticking out of the stocks)
173. **Give:** i.e., God give

A man in the stocks. (2.2.135)
From August Casimir Redel, *Apophtegmata symbolica* . . . (n.d.).

KENT
  Why, madam, if I were your father's dog,
  You should not use me so.
REGAN   Sir, being his knave, I will.   150
CORNWALL
  This is a fellow of the selfsame color
  Our sister speaks of.—Come, bring away the stocks.
                              Stocks brought out.
GLOUCESTER
  Let me beseech your Grace not to do so.
  ⟨His fault is much, and the good king his master
  Will check him for 't. Your purposed low correction   155
  Is such as basest and ⌈contemned'st⌉ wretches
  For pilf'rings and most common trespasses
  Are punished with.⟩ The King must take it ill
  That he, so slightly valued in his messenger,
  Should have him thus restrained.   160
CORNWALL   I'll answer that.
REGAN
  My sister may receive it much more worse
  To have her gentleman abused, assaulted
  ⟨For following her affairs.—Put in his legs.⟩
                    ⌈*Kent is put in the stocks.*⌉
CORNWALL   Come, my ⟨good⟩ lord, away.   165
                  ⌈*All but Gloucester and Kent* exit.⌉
GLOUCESTER
  I am sorry for thee, friend. 'Tis the ⟨Duke's⟩
      pleasure,
  Whose disposition all the world well knows
  Will not be rubbed nor stopped. I'll entreat for thee.
KENT
  Pray, do not, sir. I have watched and traveled hard.   170
  Some time I shall sleep out; the rest I'll whistle.
  A good man's fortune may grow out at heels.
  Give you good morrow.

175. **king:** i.e., Lear; **approve:** prove true; **saw:** proverb

176–77. **out . . . sun:** This proverb ("Out of God's blessing into the warm [i.e., hot] sun") meant "to go from good to bad."

179. **comfortable:** cheering, helpful

183. **obscurèd course:** i.e., actions in disguise

183–85. **shall . . . remedies:** These lines are difficult to interpret, and many editors suspect textual corruption. In stage productions, they are often read as if fragments from Cordelia's letter.

185. **o'erwatched:** tired out from lack of sleep

186. **vantage:** advantage (of your fatigue)

188–89. **turn thy wheel:** i.e., change my luck (Fortune is often depicted turning a wheel on which mortals rise and fall. See page 248.)

2.3 Edgar disguises himself as a madman-beggar to escape his death sentence. (Although Kent remains onstage, a new scene begins because the locale has shifted away from Gloucester's castle, from which Edgar has fled.)

---

1. **proclaimed:** i.e., as an outlaw

2. **happy . . . tree:** i.e., fortunate presence of a hollow tree

5. **attend . . . taking:** i.e., look out for my capture

6. **bethought:** resolved

8. **in contempt of:** i.e., in its contempt for

9. **grime:** begrime, blacken

10. **elf:** twist into elflocks (i.e., mat)

11. **presented:** displayed, offered; **outface:** defy

94

GLOUCESTER
The Duke's to blame in this. 'Twill be ill taken.
He exits.

KENT
Good king, that must approve the common saw, 175
Thou out of heaven's benediction com'st
To the warm sun. ⌐*He takes out a paper.*⌐
Approach, thou beacon to this under globe,
That by thy comfortable beams I may
Peruse this letter. Nothing almost sees miracles 180
But misery. I know 'tis from Cordelia,
Who hath most fortunately been informed
Of my obscurèd course, and shall find time
From this enormous state, seeking to give
Losses their remedies. All weary and o'erwatched, 185
Take vantage, heavy eyes, not to behold
This shameful lodging.
Fortune, good night. Smile once more; turn thy
wheel.
⟨*Sleeps.*⟩

Scene 3
Enter Edgar.

EDGAR I heard myself proclaimed,
And by the happy hollow of a tree
Escaped the hunt. No port is free; no place
That guard and most unusual vigilance
Does not attend my taking. Whiles I may 'scape, 5
I will preserve myself, and am bethought
To take the basest and most poorest shape
That ever penury in contempt of man
Brought near to beast. My face I'll grime with filth,
Blanket my loins, elf all my hairs in knots, 10
And with presented nakedness outface

13. **proof:** example
14. **Bedlam beggars:** See note to 1.2.143.
15. **mortifièd:** deadened
16. **pricks:** skewers
17. **object:** spectacle
17–20. **from . . . charity:** i.e., force country people to give them food   **low:** lowly   **pelting:** paltry   **bans:** curses
20. **Turlygod:** The meaning of this word (unrecorded elsewhere) is unknown.   **Poor Tom:** the name by which the kinds of beggars whom Edgar is imitating called themselves
21. **"Edgar" . . . am:** i.e., as "Edgar," I am nothing

2.4   At Gloucester's castle, Lear is angered that his messenger has been stocked and further angered that Regan and Cornwall refuse to see him. When Goneril arrives, Lear quarrels bitterly with her and with Regan, who claim that he needs no attendants of his own. When each daughter says that he may stay with her only if he dismisses all his knights, he rushes, enraged, out into a storm. Cornwall, Regan, and Goneril shut Gloucester's castle against Lear.

1. **they:** i.e., Regan and Cornwall
5. **remove:** change of residence
10. **cruel:** painful (with a pun on "crewel," thin woolen yarn)
12. **by th' loins:** i.e., around the waist

(continued)

The winds and persecutions of the sky.
The country gives me proof and precedent
Of Bedlam beggars who with roaring voices
Strike in their numbed and mortifièd arms   15
Pins, wooden pricks, nails, sprigs of rosemary,
And, with this horrible object, from low farms,
Poor pelting villages, sheepcotes, and mills,
Sometime with lunatic bans, sometime with prayers,
Enforce their charity. "Poor Turlygod! Poor Tom!"   20
That's something yet. "Edgar" I nothing am.

He exits.

Scene 4
Enter Lear, Fool, and Gentleman.

LEAR
'Tis strange that they should so depart from home
And not send back my ⟨messenger.⟩
GENTLEMAN   As I learned,
The night before there was no purpose in them
Of this remove.   5
KENT, ⌈*waking*⌉   Hail to thee, noble master.
LEAR   Ha?
Mak'st thou this shame thy pastime?
[KENT   No, my lord.]
FOOL   Ha, ha, he wears cruel garters. Horses are tied   10
    by the heads, dogs and bears by th' neck, monkeys
    by th' loins, and men by th' legs. When a ⟨man's⟩
    overlusty at legs, then he wears wooden nether-
    stocks.
LEAR
What's he that hath so much thy place mistook   15
To set thee here?
KENT   It is both he and she,
Your son and daughter.

12–14. **When . . . netherstocks:** Vagabonds were punished by being put in the stocks. **overlusty at legs:** i.e., too eager to wander **netherstocks:** stockings

15–16. **What's . . . To:** i.e., who so mistook your position as to

18. **son:** i.e., son-in-law

23. **Jupiter:** king of the Roman gods

24. **Juno:** queen of the Roman gods, often at odds with Jupiter

28. **upon respect:** i.e., against the king, whose messenger should be respected

29. **Resolve:** inform; **modest:** moderate

30. **usage:** treatment

31. **us:** i.e., me

33. **commend:** deliver

34–35. **Ere . . . kneeling:** i.e., before I could get up from where I knelt to show my duty

35–36. **reeking . . . haste:** i.e., a messenger hot and soaked (with the sweat from his hurried journey)

38. **spite of intermission:** i.e., although he interrupted me

39. **presently:** immediately; **on:** i.e., as a result of

40. **meiny:** train, retinue; **straight:** straightway, immediately

44. **meeting:** i.e., I, meeting

47. **Displayed so saucily:** i.e., put on such an impudent display

48. **more . . . wit:** more courage than intelligence

52–53. **that way:** i.e., south, the direction geese fly as winter approaches (The sense is that things are going to become still worse.)

LEAR No.

KENT Yes.   20

LEAR No, I say.

KENT I say yea.

LEAR By Jupiter, I swear no.

[KENT By Juno, I swear ay.

LEAR]   They durst not do 't.   25
  They could not, would not do 't. 'Tis worse than
    murder
  To do upon respect such violent outrage.
  Resolve me with all modest haste which way
  Thou might'st deserve or they impose this usage,   30
  Coming from us.

KENT   My lord, when at their home
  I did commend your Highness' letters to them,
  Ere I was risen from the place that showed
  My duty kneeling, came there a reeking post,   35
  Stewed in his haste, half breathless, ⟨panting⟩ forth
  From Goneril his mistress salutations;
  Delivered letters, spite of intermission,
  Which presently they read; on ⟨whose⟩ contents
  They summoned up their meiny, straight took   40
    horse,
  Commanded me to follow and attend
  The leisure of their answer, gave me cold looks;
  And meeting here the other messenger,
  Whose welcome, I perceived, had poisoned mine,   45
  Being the very fellow which of late
  Displayed so saucily against your Highness,
  Having more man than wit about me, drew.
  He raised the house with loud and coward cries.
  Your son and daughter found this trespass worth   50
  The shame which here it suffers.

[FOOL Winter's not gone yet if the wild geese fly that
  way.

55. **blind:** i.e., neglectful of their fathers

56. **bags:** i.e., bags of gold

59. **turns the key to:** i.e., opens the door for

60. **dolors for:** sorrows on account of (with a pun on "dollars in exchange for")

61. **tell:** (1) count; (2) relate

62–64. **O, how . . . below:** "The mother" was the name given to hysteria, one symptom of which is the suffocation that Lear is represented as feeling in his rage and grief. (Its medical name is **hysterica passio.**) The disease was thought to be caused by a wandering womb (*hystera*), which belonged **below,** not up near the **heart.**

68. **but:** i.e., other than

70. **chance:** i.e., chances it that

74–81. **We'll . . . after:** The fool explains the desertion of Lear's knights three ways, all of them emphasizing Lear's decline into adversity: Lear is in his **winter** (an unprofitable time for ants, just as following Lear is now unprofitable); Lear stinks with misfortune (so that even a blind man can smell his decay); Lear is like a **great wheel** going downhill, destroying everything attached to it.

84. **sir:** gentleman

86. **follows . . . form:** serves a master only in outward behavior

87. **pack:** hurry off

Fathers that wear rags
   Do make their children blind,   55
But fathers that bear bags
   Shall see their children kind.
Fortune, that arrant whore,
   Ne'er turns the key to th' poor.
But, for all this, thou shalt have as many dolors for   60
thy daughters as thou canst tell in a year.]

LEAR
O, how this mother swells up toward my heart!
Hysterica passio, down, thou climbing sorrow!
Thy element's below.—Where is this daughter?

KENT   With the Earl, sir, here within.   65

LEAR, ⌐*to Fool and Gentleman*⌐ Follow me not. Stay
   here.   *He exits.*

GENTLEMAN
Made you no more offense but what you speak of?

KENT   None.
How chance the King comes with so small a number?   70

FOOL   An thou hadst been set i' th' stocks for that
   question, thou'dst well deserved it.

KENT   Why, Fool?

FOOL   We'll set thee to school to an ant to teach thee
   there's no laboring i' th' winter. All that follow   75
   their noses are led by their eyes but blind men, and
   there's not a nose among twenty but can smell him
   that's stinking. Let go thy hold when a great wheel
   runs down a hill lest it break thy neck with following; but the great one that goes upward, let him   80
   draw thee after. When a wise man gives thee better
   counsel, give me mine again. I would have none but
   knaves follow it, since a Fool gives it.
      That sir which serves
         And seeks for gain,   85
      And follows but for form,
         Will pack when it begins to rain

91. **knave:** servant
92. **knave:** rascal; **perdie:** *par Dieu,* French for "By God"
97. **fetches:** dodges, tricks
98. **images:** signs
102. **unremovable:** immovable
104. **confusion:** ruin
114. **tends:** awaits, expects
115. **service:** homage, fealty, obedience

And leave thee in the storm.
　　But I will tarry; the Fool will stay,
And let the wise man fly.   90
　　The knave turns fool that runs away;
　　The Fool no knave, perdie.
KENT　Where learned you this, Fool?
FOOL　Not i' th' stocks, fool.

Enter Lear and Gloucester.

LEAR
Deny to speak with me? They are sick? They are   95
　weary?
They have traveled all the night? Mere fetches,
The images of revolt and flying off.
Fetch me a better answer.
GLOUCESTER　　　　　　　　My dear lord,   100
You know the fiery quality of the Duke,
How unremovable and fixed he is
In his own course.
LEAR
Vengeance, plague, death, confusion!
"Fiery"? What "quality"? Why Gloucester,   105
　Gloucester,
I'd speak with the Duke of Cornwall and his wife.
[GLOUCESTER
Well, my good lord, I have informed them so.
LEAR
"Informed them"? Dost thou understand me,
　man?]   110
GLOUCESTER　Ay, my good lord.
LEAR
The King would speak with Cornwall. The dear
　father
Would with his daughter speak, commands, tends
　service.   115
[Are they "informed" of this? My breath and
　blood!]

120–121. **still . . . bound:** i.e., always fail in those duties required of us when in good health   **office:** duties

124. **am . . . will:** i.e., am angry with my more impetuous temper

125. **To take:** i.e., in mistaking

126–27. **Death . . . state:** a curse   **my state:** i.e., my royal power

127. **Wherefore:** why

128. **This act:** the stocking of Kent

129. **remotion:** i.e., keeping remote from me

130. **practice:** contrivance, deception;   **Give . . . forth:** release my servant

131. **and 's:** i.e., and his

132. **presently:** immediately

134. **cry . . . death:** i.e., put an end to sleep

137. **cockney:** city dweller

138. **knapped:** knocked

139. **coxcombs:** i.e., heads

140. **wantons:** playful animals (with a secondary sense of "lewd persons")

147. **divorce . . . tomb:** perhaps, divorce your dead mother; or, perhaps, refuse to be buried beside her

"Fiery"? The "fiery" duke? Tell the hot duke that—
No, but not yet. Maybe he is not well.
Infirmity doth still neglect all office   120
Whereto our health is bound. We are not ourselves
When nature, being oppressed, commands the mind
To suffer with the body. I'll forbear,
And am fallen out with my more headier will,
To take the indisposed and sickly fit   125
For the sound man. ⌜*Noticing Kent again.*⌝ Death on
    my state! Wherefore
Should he sit here? This act persuades me
That this remotion of the Duke and her
Is practice only. Give me my servant forth.   130
Go tell the Duke and 's wife I'd speak with them.
Now, presently, bid them come forth and hear me,
Or at their chamber door I'll beat the drum
Till it cry sleep to death.
GLOUCESTER   I would have all well betwixt you.   135
                                       He exits.

LEAR
   O me, my heart, my rising heart! But down!
FOOL   Cry to it, nuncle, as the cockney did to the eels
     when she put 'em i' th' paste alive. She knapped
     'em o' th' coxcombs with a stick and cried "Down,
     wantons, down!" 'Twas her brother that in pure   140
     kindness to his horse buttered his hay.

     Enter Cornwall, Regan, Gloucester, Servants.

LEAR   Good morrow to you both.
CORNWALL   Hail to your Grace.
                        Kent here set at liberty.
REGAN   I am glad to see your Highness.
LEAR
   Regan, I think ⟨you⟩ are. I know what reason   145
   I have to think so: if thou shouldst not be glad,
   I would divorce me from thy ⟨mother's⟩ tomb,

148. **Sepulch'ring:** i.e., since it would be the tomb of   (Lear says that if Regan is not glad to see him, she could not be his daughter. Her mother would therefore be an **adult'ress**.)

151. **naught:** (1) worthless; (2) wicked

154. **quality:** manner

155–57. **I have . . . duty:** i.e., I hope you under-value her merit rather than that she failed in her duty

166. **Nature in you:** i.e., your life

166–67. **verge . . . confine:** i.e., its limit

168. **some . . . that:** i.e., the discretion of someone who; **state:** condition

173. **mark:** see; **house:** i.e., dignity of the royal family

175. **Age . . . unnecessary:** i.e., no one needs old people

Sepulch'ring an adult'ress. ⌜*To Kent.*⌝ O, are you
    free?
Some other time for that.—Belovèd Regan,   150
Thy sister's naught. O Regan, she hath tied
Sharp-toothed unkindness, like a vulture, here.
I can scarce speak to thee. Thou'lt not believe
With how depraved a quality—O Regan!

REGAN
    I pray you, sir, take patience. I have hope   155
    You less know how to value her desert
    Than she to scant her duty.

[LEAR   Say? How is that?

REGAN
    I cannot think my sister in the least
    Would fail her obligation. If, sir, perchance   160
    She have restrained the riots of your followers,
    'Tis on such ground and to such wholesome end
    As clears her from all blame.]

LEAR   My curses on her.

REGAN   O sir, you are old.   165
    Nature in you stands on the very verge
    Of his confine. You should be ruled and led
    By some discretion that discerns your state
    Better than you yourself. Therefore, I pray you
    That to our sister you do make return.   170
    Say you have wronged her.

LEAR   Ask her forgiveness?
    Do you but mark how this becomes the house:
                                ⌜*He kneels.*⌝
    "Dear daughter, I confess that I am old.
    Age is unnecessary. On my knees I beg   175
    That you'll vouchsafe me raiment, bed, and food."

REGAN
    Good sir, no more. These are unsightly tricks.
    Return you to my sister.

180. **abated:** deprived
181. **black:** angrily
184. **top:** i.e., head
185. **taking:** infectious
189–90. **fen-sucked . . . blister:** vapors drawn up from marshes by the sun to fall on and blister her
194. **tender-hefted:** perhaps, moved (i.e., heaved, swayed) by tender emotions
199. **scant my sizes:** diminish my allowance (as if he were a poor university student)
200. **oppose the bolt:** i.e., lock the door
202. **offices of nature:** i.e., natural duties
203. **Effects:** actions

LEAR, ⌐*rising*⌐   Never, Regan.
  She hath abated me of half my train,   180
  Looked black upon me, struck me with her tongue
  Most serpentlike upon the very heart.
  All the stored vengeances of heaven fall
  On her ingrateful top! Strike her young bones,
  You taking airs, with lameness!   185
CORNWALL   Fie, sir, fie!
LEAR
  You nimble lightnings, dart your blinding flames
  Into her scornful eyes! Infect her beauty,
  You fen-sucked fogs drawn by the powerful sun
  To fall and blister!   190
REGAN
  O, the blest gods! So will you wish on me
  When the rash mood is on.
LEAR
  No, Regan, thou shalt never have my curse.
  Thy tender-hefted nature shall not give
  Thee o'er to harshness. Her eyes are fierce, but   195
    thine
  Do comfort and not burn. 'Tis not in thee
  To grudge my pleasures, to cut off my train,
  To bandy hasty words, to scant my sizes,
  And, in conclusion, to oppose the bolt   200
  Against my coming in. Thou better know'st
  The offices of nature, bond of childhood,
  Effects of courtesy, dues of gratitude.
  Thy half o' th' kingdom hast thou not forgot,
  Wherein I thee endowed.   205
REGAN   Good sir, to' th' purpose.
                    Tucket within.
LEAR
  Who put my man i' th' stocks?
CORNWALL   What trumpet's that?

209. **approves:** confirms

213. **grace:** favor

214. **varlet:** rascal

217. **on 't:** i.e., of it

219–20. **sway / Allow:** government approves

226–27. **that . . . so:** i.e., that is thought so by those who lack judgment and that is named so by the senile

228. **sides:** i.e., sides of his body

232. **advancement:** preferment, promotion

REGAN
  I know 't—my sister's. This approves her letter,
  That she would soon be here.   210

                Enter ⌐Oswald, the⌐ Steward.

                              Is your lady come?
LEAR
  This is a slave whose easy-borrowed pride
  Dwells in the ⟨fickle⟩ grace of her he follows.—
  Out, varlet, from my sight!
CORNWALL   What means your Grace?   215
LEAR
  Who stocked my servant? Regan, I have good hope
  Thou didst not know on 't.

                Enter Goneril.

                              Who comes here? O heavens,
  If you do love old men, if your sweet sway
  Allow obedience, if you yourselves are old,   220
  Make it your cause. Send down and take my part.
  ⌐To Goneril.⌐ Art not ashamed to look upon this
      beard?   ⌐Regan takes Goneril's hand.⌐
  O Regan, will you take her by the hand?
GONERIL
  Why not by th' hand, sir? How have I offended?   225
  All's not offense that indiscretion finds
  And dotage terms so.
LEAR   O sides, you are too tough!
  Will you yet hold?—How came my man i' th'
      stocks?   230
CORNWALL
  I set him there, sir, but his own disorders
  Deserved much less advancement.
LEAR   You? Did you?
REGAN
  I pray you, father, being weak, seem so.
  If till the expiration of your month   235

238. **from home:** i.e., away from my home

239. **entertainment:** proper care

242. **wage:** contend, struggle

244. **Necessity's . . . pinch:** i.e., I choose the pains of poverty and distress

247. **knee:** i.e., kneel before

249. **sumpter:** packhorse

252. **mad:** insane

258. **embossèd carbuncle:** swollen, inflamed tumor

260. **call:** invoke

261. **thunder-bearer:** i.e., the king of Roman gods (called both **Jove** and Jupiter)

268. **fit:** appropriate

269. **mingle . . . passion:** i.e., rationally assess your intemperate behavior

Jove, "the thunder-bearer." (2.4.261–62)
From Vincenzo Cartari, *Le vere e noue Imagini* . . . (1615).

You will return and sojourn with my sister,
Dismissing half your train, come then to me.
I am now from home and out of that provision
Which shall be needful for your entertainment.

LEAR
 Return to her? And fifty men dismissed?   240
 No! Rather I abjure all roofs, and choose
 To wage against the enmity o' th' air,
 To be a comrade with the wolf and owl,
 Necessity's sharp pinch. Return with her?
 Why the hot-blooded France, that dowerless took 245
 Our youngest born—I could as well be brought
 To knee his throne and, squire-like, pension beg
 To keep base life afoot. Return with her?
 Persuade me rather to be slave and sumpter
 To this detested groom.   ⌐*He indicates Oswald.*⌐ 250

GONERIL   At your choice, sir.

LEAR
 I prithee, daughter, do not make me mad.
 I will not trouble thee, my child. Farewell.
 We'll no more meet, no more see one another.
 But yet thou art my flesh, my blood, my daughter, 255
 Or, rather, a disease that's in my flesh,
 Which I must needs call mine. Thou art a boil,
 A plague-sore or embossèd carbuncle
 In my corrupted blood. But I'll not chide thee.
 Let shame come when it will; I do not call it. 260
 I do not bid the thunder-bearer shoot,
 Nor tell tales of thee to high-judging Jove.
 Mend when thou canst. Be better at thy leisure.
 I can be patient. I can stay with Regan,
 I and my hundred knights.   265

REGAN Not altogether so.
 I looked not for you yet, nor am provided
 For your fit welcome. Give ear, sir, to my sister,
 For those that mingle reason with your passion

275. **sith that:** since; **charge:** expense
278. **Hold amity:** i.e., remain peaceful
281. **slack:** neglect (their duty to)
286. **notice:** acknowledgment
289. **depositaries:** trustees (of my power)
290. **kept a reservation:** i.e., reserved for myself the right
291–92. **to . . . With:** i.e., to have as my own attendants
294. **well-favored:** attractive
296. **Stands . . . praise:** i.e., deserves a measure of praise

Must be content to think you old, and so— 270
But she knows what she does.
LEAR Is this well spoken?
REGAN
    I dare avouch it, sir. What, fifty followers?
    Is it not well? What should you need of more?
    Yea, or so many, sith that both charge and danger 275
    Speak 'gainst so great a number? How in one house
    Should many people under two commands
    Hold amity? 'Tis hard, almost impossible.
GONERIL
    Why might not you, my lord, receive attendance
    From those that she calls servants, or from mine? 280
REGAN
    Why not, my lord? If then they chanced to slack
      you,
    We could control them. If you will come to me
    (For now I spy a danger), I entreat you
    To bring but five-and-twenty. To no more 285
    Will I give place or notice.
LEAR   I gave you all—
REGAN   And in good time you gave it.
LEAR
    Made you my guardians, my depositaries,
    But kept a reservation to be followed 290
    With such a number. What, must I come to you
    With five-and-twenty? Regan, said you so?
REGAN
    And speak 't again, my lord. No more with me.
LEAR
    Those wicked creatures yet do look well-favored
    When others are more wicked. Not being the worst 295
    Stands in some rank of praise. ⌜*To Goneril.*⌝ I'll go
      with thee.
    Thy fifty yet doth double five-and-twenty,
    And thou art twice her love.
GONERIL Hear me, my lord. 300

302. **follow:** attend on you

305. **reason not:** i.e., do not argue in terms of

306. **Are . . . superfluous:** i.e., own something that exceeds what they actually need

307. **nature . . . nature:** i.e., humans . . . animals

309–11. **If . . . warm:** i.e., if dressing warmly were the only beauty a lady needed, then you would not need your gorgeous clothes, which hardly keep you warm anyway

317–18. **fool . . . To:** do not make me such a fool as to

327. **flaws:** fragments

328. **Or ere:** before

331. **bestowed:** accommodated

What need you five-and-twenty, ten, or five,
To follow in a house where twice so many
Have a command to tend you?
REGAN   What need one?
LEAR
  O, reason not the need! Our basest beggars   305
  Are in the poorest thing superfluous.
  Allow not nature more than nature needs,
  Man's life is cheap as beast's. Thou art a lady;
  If only to go warm were gorgeous,
  Why, nature needs not what thou gorgeous wear'st,   310
  Which scarcely keeps thee warm. But, for true
      need—
  You heavens, give me that patience, patience I need!
  You see me here, you gods, a poor old man
  As full of grief as age, wretched in both.   315
  If it be you that stirs these daughters' hearts
  Against their father, fool me not so much
  To bear it tamely. Touch me with noble anger,
  And let not women's weapons, water drops,
  Stain my man's cheeks.—No, you unnatural hags,   320
  I will have such revenges on you both
  That all the world shall—I will do such things—
  What they are yet I know not, but they shall be
  The terrors of the earth! You think I'll weep.
  No, I'll not weep.   325
  I have full cause of weeping, but this heart
                          Storm and tempest.
  Shall break into a hundred thousand flaws
  Or ere I'll weep.—O Fool, I shall go mad!
                          ⟨*Lear, Kent, and Fool*⟩ *exit*
                    ⌐*with Gloucester and the Gentleman.*⌐
CORNWALL   Let us withdraw. 'Twill be a storm.
REGAN
  This house is little. The old man and 's people   330
  Cannot be well bestowed.

332. **his . . . himself:** i.e., his fault that has put him

333. **taste:** experience

334. **For . . . particular:** i.e., as for him in particular

341. **will:** i.e., will go

342. **give him way:** i.e., let him have his own way; **He . . . himself:** i.e., he will take no one's advice

345. **sorely ruffle:** fiercely blow

350. **a desperate train:** i.e., a troop of violent supporters

351–52. **being . . . abused:** i.e., being easily misled or deceived

GONERIL
  'Tis his own blame hath put himself from rest,
  And must needs taste his folly.
REGAN
  For his particular, I'll receive him gladly,
  But not one follower.   335
GONERIL
  So am I purposed. Where is my lord of Gloucester?
CORNWALL
  Followed the old man forth.

                    Enter Gloucester.

                              He is returned.
GLOUCESTER   The King is in high rage.
[CORNWALL   Whither is he going?   340
GLOUCESTER
  He calls to horse,] but will I know not whither.
CORNWALL
  'Tis best to give him way. He leads himself.
GONERIL, ⌜*to Gloucester*⌝
  My lord, entreat him by no means to stay.
GLOUCESTER
  Alack, the night comes on, and the high winds
  Do sorely ruffle. For many miles about   345
  There's scarce a bush.
REGAN   O sir, to willful men
  The injuries that they themselves procure
  Must be their schoolmasters. Shut up your doors.
  He is attended with a desperate train,   350
  And what they may incense him to, being apt
  To have his ear abused, wisdom bids fear.
CORNWALL
  Shut up your doors, my lord. 'Tis a wild night.
  My Regan counsels well. Come out o' th' storm.
                                        They exit.

The Tragedy of

KING LEAR

ACT 3

3.1 Kent, searching for Lear, meets a Gentleman and learns that Lear and the Fool are alone in the storm. Kent tells the Gentleman that French forces are on their way to England.

---

0 SD. **Storm still:** i.e., the storm continues

5. **Bids:** i.e., he bids

6. **main:** mainland

10. **make nothing of:** i.e., treat irreverently; or, scatter and reduce to nothing as he tears it out

13. **cub-drawn:** i.e., ravenous, with her dugs sucked dry by her cubs

14. **couch:** i.e., stay in her den

17. **bids . . . take all:** The desperate gambler betting the last of his money cries "Take all!"

19–20. **outjest . . . injuries:** i.e., use jokes to relieve the injuries that have struck the king to the heart

Wind swelling "the curlèd waters." (3.1.6)
From Lodovico Dolce, *Imprese nobili* . . . (1583).

ACT 3

Scene 1
Storm still. Enter Kent ⌈in disguise,⌉ and a Gentleman, severally.

KENT Who's there, besides foul weather?

GENTLEMAN
One minded like the weather, most unquietly.

KENT I know you. Where's the King?

GENTLEMAN
Contending with the fretful elements;
Bids the wind blow the earth into the sea   5
Or swell the curlèd waters 'bove the main,
That things might change or cease; ⟨tears his white
    hair,
Which the impetuous blasts with eyeless rage
Catch in their fury and make nothing of;   10
Strives in his little world of man to outscorn
The to-and-fro conflicting wind and rain.
This night, wherein the cub-drawn bear would
    couch,
The lion and the belly-pinchèd wolf   15
Keep their fur dry, unbonneted he runs
And bids what will take all.⟩

KENT   But who is with him?

GENTLEMAN
None but the Fool, who labors to outjest
His heart-struck injuries.   20

123

22. **upon . . . note:** i.e., justified by what I have observed in you

23. **Commend:** entrust, commit; **a dear:** an important, precious

26. **that . . . stars:** i.e., whom the fates or destinies

27. **seem no less:** i.e., appear to be real servants

28. **spies, speculations:** Both words mean **spies.**

29. **Intelligent of:** giving information about

30. **snuffs:** rages (against each other); **packings:** plots

33. **furnishings:** outer trappings

34. **a power:** an armed force

35. **scattered:** divided

36. **Wise in:** knowledgeable about; **feet:** i.e. footholds

37. **at point:** in readiness

38. **their open banner:** i.e., their banner openly

39. **credit:** credibility

41. **making just:** i.e., for making a true

42. **bemadding:** maddening

43. **plain:** complain about

44. **blood:** noble birth

46. **office:** duty (i.e., to go to Dover)

50. **outwall:** outward appearance

54. **that fellow is:** i.e., who I am

KENT   Sir, I do know you
And dare upon the warrant of my note
Commend a dear thing to you. There is division,
Although as yet the face of it is covered
With mutual cunning, 'twixt Albany and Cornwall,   25
[Who have—as who have not, that their great stars
Throned and set high?—servants, who seem no less,
Which are to France the spies and speculations
Intelligent of our state. What hath been seen,
Either in snuffs and packings of the dukes,   30
Or the hard rein which both of them hath borne
Against the old kind king, or something deeper,
Whereof perchance these are but furnishings—]
⟨But true it is, from France there comes a power
Into this scattered kingdom, who already,   35
Wise in our negligence, have secret feet
In some of our best ports and are at point
To show their open banner. Now to you:
If on my credit you dare build so far
To make your speed to Dover, you shall find   40
Some that will thank you, making just report
Of how unnatural and bemadding sorrow
The King hath cause to plain.
I am a gentleman of blood and breeding,
And from some knowledge and assurance offer   45
This office to you.⟩
GENTLEMAN
I will talk further with you.
KENT   No, do not.
For confirmation that I am much more
Than my outwall, open this purse and take   50
What it contains.
                ⌜*Kent hands him a purse and a ring.*⌝
                If you shall see Cordelia
(As fear not but you shall), show her this ring,
And she will tell you who that fellow is

58. **to effect:** i.e., in their significance

59–61. **in . . . this:** i.e., in which effort, you seek him that way while I go this way

3.2 Lear rages against the elements while the Fool begs him to return to his daughters for shelter; when Kent finds them, he leads them toward a hovel.

---

1. **crack your cheeks:** On maps of the time, the winds are pictured as puffing out their cheeks as they blow.

2. **cataracts and hurricanoes:** waterspouts, tornadoes occurring over water

4. **cocks:** i.e., weathercocks, weathervanes (on the top of **steeples**)

5. **thought-executing:** acting as quickly as thought; or, destroying thought; **fires:** i.e., lightning

6. **Vaunt-couriers:** forerunners

10. **Crack . . . molds:** destroy the molds in which nature fashions life; **germens:** seeds; **spill:** destroy

12. **court holy water:** flattering speeches

18. **tax:** accuse

That yet you do not know. Fie on this storm! 55
I will go seek the King.

GENTLEMAN
Give me your hand. Have you no more to say?

KENT
Few words, but, to effect, more than all yet:
That when we have found the King—in which your
  pain 60
That way, I'll this—he that first lights on him
Holla the other.

                    They exit ⌜separately.⌝

Scene 2
Storm still. Enter Lear and Fool.

LEAR
Blow winds, and crack your cheeks! Rage, blow!
You cataracts and hurricanoes, spout
Till you have drenched our steeples, ⟨drowned⟩ the
  cocks.
You sulph'rous and thought-executing fires, 5
Vaunt-couriers of oak-cleaving thunderbolts,
Singe my white head. And thou, all-shaking
  thunder,
Strike flat the thick rotundity o' th' world.
Crack nature's molds, all germens spill at once 10
That makes ingrateful man.

FOOL   O nuncle, court holy water in a dry house is
      better than this rainwater out o' door. Good nun-
      cle, in. Ask thy daughters' blessing. Here's a night
      pities neither wise men nor fools. 15

LEAR
Rumble thy bellyful! Spit, fire! Spout, rain!
Nor rain, wind, thunder, fire are my daughters.
I tax not you, you elements, with unkindness.

20. **subscription:** submission, allegiance

23. **ministers:** underlings, agents

25. **high-engendered battles:** heavenly battalions

28. **headpiece:** helmet; brain

29. **codpiece:** a showy appendage to the front of a man's breeches; here meaning the genitals themselves; **house:** lodge, take shelter (in sexual activity)

30. **any:** i.e., a house in which to live

31. **louse:** become infested with lice

37–38. **made mouths . . . glass:** i.e., made faces in a mirror

42. **Marry:** a mild oath (originally on the name of the Virgin Mary)

46. **Gallow:** frighten, terrify

47. **keep:** stay within

50. **carry:** endure

I never gave you kingdom, called you children;
You owe me no subscription. Then let fall   20
Your horrible pleasure. Here I stand your slave,
A poor, infirm, weak, and despised old man.
But yet I call you servile ministers,
That will with two pernicious daughters join
Your high-engendered battles 'gainst a head   25
So old and white as this. O, ho, 'tis foul!
FOOL   He that has a house to put 's head in has a good
    headpiece.
            The codpiece that will house
                Before the head has any,   30
            The head and he shall louse;
                So beggars marry many.
            The man that makes his toe
                What he his heart should make,
            Shall of a corn cry woe,   35
                And turn his sleep to wake.
    For there was never yet fair woman but she made
    mouths in a glass.
LEAR
    No, I will be the pattern of all patience.
    I will say nothing.   40

            Enter Kent ⌈in disguise.⌉

KENT   Who's there?
FOOL   Marry, here's grace and a codpiece; that's a
    wise man and a fool.
KENT
    Alas, sir, are you here? Things that love night
    Love not such nights as these. The wrathful skies   45
    Gallow the very wanderers of the dark
    And make them keep their caves. Since I was man,
    Such sheets of fire, such bursts of horrid thunder,
    Such groans of roaring wind and rain I never
    Remember to have heard. Man's nature cannot carry   50
    Th' affliction nor the fear.

53. **pudder:** pother, confusion

54. **Find out:** discover, expose

56. **of:** i.e., by

57. **perjured:** i.e., perjurer; **simular:** simulator, imitator

58. **Caitiff:** wretch, villain

59. **seeming:** deception

60. **practiced on:** plotted against; **Close pent-up:** hidden, confined

61. **Rive . . . concealing continents:** tear open that which contains and conceals you

61–62. **cry . . . grace:** i.e., cry for mercy from the elements—i.e., **These dreadful summoners** (**Summoners** were officers of church courts.)

66. **hard:** near

70–71. **Which . . . come in:** i.e., the residents of which forbade my entrance   **demanding:** i.e., I asking

72. **scanted:** withheld; deficient

LEAR   Let the great gods
  That keep this dreadful pudder o'er our heads
  Find out their enemies now. Tremble, thou wretch,
  That hast within thee undivulgèd crimes   55
  Unwhipped of justice. Hide thee, thou bloody hand,
  Thou perjured, and thou simular of virtue
  That art incestuous. Caitiff, to pieces shake,
  That under covert and convenient seeming
  Has practiced on man's life. Close pent-up guilts,   60
  Rive your concealing continents and cry
  These dreadful summoners grace. I am a man
  More sinned against than sinning.
KENT   Alack,
    bareheaded?   65
  Gracious my lord, hard by here is a hovel.
  Some friendship will it lend you 'gainst the tempest.
  Repose you there while I to this hard house—
  More harder than the stones whereof 'tis raised,
  Which even but now, demanding after you,   70
  Denied me to come in—return and force
  Their scanted courtesy.
LEAR   My wits begin to turn.—
  Come on, my boy. How dost, my boy? Art cold?
  I am cold myself.—Where is this straw, my fellow?   75
  The art of our necessities is strange
  And can make vile things precious. Come, your
    hovel.—
  Poor Fool and knave, I have one part in my heart
  That's sorry yet for thee.   80
FOOL ⌜*sings*⌝
      He that has and a little tiny wit,
          With heigh-ho, the wind and the rain,
      Must make content with his fortunes fit,
          Though the rain it raineth every day.
LEAR
  True, ⟨my good⟩ boy.—Come, bring us to this hovel.   85
                          ⌜*Lear and Kent*⌝ *exit.*

86. **brave:** fine

88–101. **When . . . used with feet:** This speech is a parody of a well-known prophecy known as "Merlin's Prophecy." The first few lines seem to present, as a vision of the future, the actual state of affairs in an imperfect world.

88. **more . . . matter:** i.e., preach virtue better than they practice it

89. **mar:** i.e., dilute

90. **nobles . . . tutors:** i.e., noblemen teach their tailors (perhaps, about what is fashionable)

91. **heretics burned:** The traditional punishment for religious heretics was being burned at the stake.

92–97. **When . . . build:** These lines represent a utopia or perfect world. **right:** just **cutpurses . . . throngs:** purse-stealers do not haunt crowds **usurers . . . field:** moneylenders count their money in public **bawds:** procurers of women as prostitutes

98. **Albion:** England

99. **confusion:** ruin

101. **going . . . feet:** i.e., walking will be done on foot

3.3 Gloucester tells Edmund that he has decided to go to Lear's aid; he also tells him about an incriminating letter he has received about the French invasion. After Gloucester leaves to find Lear, Edmund announces his plan to betray his father to Cornwall.

3. **pity:** have pity on
8. **Go to:** an expression of impatience
11. **closet:** private chamber

[FOOL This is a brave night to cool a courtesan. I'll
speak a prophecy ere I go:
  When priests are more in word than matter,
  When brewers mar their malt with water,
  When nobles are their tailors' tutors,   90
  No heretics burned but wenches' suitors,
  When every case in law is right,
  No squire in debt, nor no poor knight;
  When slanders do not live in tongues,
  Nor cutpurses come not to throngs,   95
  When usurers tell their gold i' th' field,
  And bawds and whores do churches build,
  Then shall the realm of Albion
  Come to great confusion;
  Then comes the time, who lives to see 't,   100
  That going shall be used with feet.
This prophecy Merlin shall make, for I live before
his time.
He exits.]

Scene 3
Enter Gloucester and Edmund.

GLOUCESTER Alack, alack, Edmund, I like not this
unnatural dealing. When I desired their leave that I
might pity him, they took from me the use of mine
own house, charged me on pain of perpetual
displeasure neither to speak of him, entreat for   5
him, or any way sustain him.

EDMUND Most savage and unnatural.

GLOUCESTER Go to; say you nothing. There is division
between the dukes, and a worse matter than that. I
have received a letter this night; 'tis dangerous to   10
be spoken; I have locked the letter in my closet.
These injuries the King now bears will be revenged

13. **home:** i.e., completely; **power:** armed force; **footed:** i.e., landed

14. **incline to:** i.e., take the side of; **look:** i.e., look for; **privily:** secretly

16. **of:** i.e., by

19. **toward:** about to happen

21. **This . . . thee:** i.e., the forbidden kindness to the king that you are about to show

23. **This . . . deserving:** i.e., this (treachery to my father) will seem (to Cornwall) to deserve a reward

3.4 Lear, Kent, and the Fool reach the hovel, where they find Edgar disguised as Poor Tom, a madman-beggar. When Gloucester finds them, he leads them to the shelter of a house.

---

2. **open night:** i.e., night in the open air

3. **nature:** i.e., human nature

10. **fixed:** lodged, rooted

home; there is part of a power already footed. We
must incline to the King. I will look him and privily
relieve him. Go you and maintain talk with the   15
Duke, that my charity be not of him perceived. If he
ask for me, I am ill and gone to bed. If I die for it, as
no less is threatened me, the King my old master
must be relieved. There is strange things toward,
Edmund. Pray you, be careful.   *He exits.*   20

EDMUND
This courtesy forbid thee shall the Duke
Instantly know, and of that letter too.
This seems a fair deserving, and must draw me
That which my father loses—no less than all.
The younger rises when the old doth fall.   25
          He exits.

Scene 4
Enter Lear, Kent ⌐in disguise,⌐ and Fool.

KENT
Here is the place, my lord. Good my lord, enter.
The tyranny of the open night's too rough
For nature to endure.   *Storm still.*
LEAR   Let me alone.
KENT
Good my lord, enter here.   5
LEAR   Wilt break my heart?
KENT
I had rather break mine own. Good my lord, enter.
LEAR
Thou think'st 'tis much that this contentious storm
Invades us to the skin. So 'tis to thee.
But where the greater malady is fixed,   10
The lesser is scarce felt. Thou'dst shun a bear,
But if ⟨thy⟩ flight lay toward the roaring sea,

13. **i' th' mouth:** i.e., head-on
14. **free:** i.e., at peace
18. **as:** i.e., as if
23. **frank:** generous
29. **would:** i.e., that would
33. **bide:** suffer, endure
35. **looped and windowed:** i.e., holey (as if filled with loopholes and windows)
38. **Take physic:** i.e., cure yourself; **pomp:** i.e., you who are powerful
40. **superflux:** excess, surplus (that you have)
42. **Fathom and half:** cry of a sailor taking soundings

Thou'dst meet the bear i' th' mouth. When the
   mind's free,
The body's delicate. ⟨This⟩ tempest in my mind   15
Doth from my senses take all feeling else
Save what beats there. Filial ingratitude!
Is it not as this mouth should tear this hand
For lifting food to 't? But I will punish home.
No, I will weep no more. [In such a night   20
To shut me out? Pour on. I will endure.]
In such a night as this? O Regan, Goneril,
Your old kind father whose frank heart gave all!
O, that way madness lies. Let me shun that;
No more of that.   25
KENT   Good my lord, enter here.
LEAR
Prithee, go in thyself. Seek thine own ease.
This tempest will not give me leave to ponder
On things would hurt me more. But I'll go in.—
[In, boy; go first.—You houseless poverty—   30
Nay, get thee in. I'll pray, and then I'll sleep.]
                     ⌜*Fool*⌝ *exits.*
Poor naked wretches, wheresoe'er you are,
That bide the pelting of this pitiless storm,
How shall your houseless heads and unfed sides,
Your looped and windowed raggedness defend   35
   you
From seasons such as these? O, I have ta'en
Too little care of this. Take physic, pomp.
Expose thyself to feel what wretches feel,
That thou may'st shake the superflux to them   40
And show the heavens more just.
[EDGAR ⌜*within*⌝ Fathom and half, fathom and half!
Poor Tom!

                Enter Fool.]

FOOL   Come not in here, nuncle; here's a spirit. Help
   me, help me!   45

48. **grumble:** i.e., mumble, mutter

50. **Away:** go away; **foul fiend:** devil (Edgar, in disguise as Poor Tom, pretends to be possessed.)

50–51. **Through . . . wind:** a line from a ballad

58. **that:** i.e., the fiend; **his:** i.e., Poor Tom's

59. **halters:** hangman's ropes (Like **knives** and **ratsbane,** the ropes were temptations to suicide.); **porridge:** thick soup

61. **four-inched bridges:** i.e., very narrow bridges; **course:** hunt

62. **for:** as; **five wits:** five senses (According to Stephen Hawes in *The Pastime of Pleasure,* the five wits are common wit, imagination, fantasy, estimation, and memory.)

64. **star-blasting:** i.e., the evil influence of stars; **taking:** being put under a magic spell; being attacked by disease

68. **pass:** predicament

71. **else:** otherwise

73. **pendulous:** pendent, overhanging

74. **fated:** fatefully, ominously

KENT   Give me thy hand. Who's there?

FOOL   A spirit, a spirit! He says his name's Poor Tom.

KENT   What art thou that dost grumble there i' th' straw? Come forth.

Enter Edgar ⌜in disguise.⌝

EDGAR   Away. The foul fiend follows me. Through the   50
sharp hawthorn ⟨blows the cold wind.⟩ Hum! Go to
thy ⟨cold⟩ bed and warm thee.

LEAR   Didst thou give all to thy daughters? And art thou
come to this?

EDGAR   Who gives anything to Poor Tom, whom the   55
foul fiend hath led ⟨through⟩ fire and through flame,
through ⟨ford⟩ and whirlpool, o'er bog and quag-
mire; that hath laid knives under his pillow and
halters in his pew, set ratsbane by his porridge,
made him proud of heart to ride on a bay trotting   60
horse over four-inched bridges to course his own
shadow for a traitor? Bless thy five wits! Tom's
a-cold. O, do de, do de, do de. Bless thee from
whirlwinds, star-blasting, and taking! Do Poor Tom
some charity, whom the foul fiend vexes. There   65
could I have him now, and there—and there again
—and there.   *Storm still.*

LEAR
Has his daughters brought him to this pass?—
Couldst thou save nothing? Wouldst thou give 'em
all?   70

FOOL   Nay, he reserved a blanket, else we had been all
shamed.

LEAR
Now all the plagues that in the pendulous air
Hang fated o'er men's faults light on thy daughters!

KENT   He hath no daughters, sir.   75

LEAR
Death, traitor! Nothing could have subdued nature
To such a lowness but his unkind daughters.

79. **flesh:** i.e., bodies (See Edgar's description at 2.3.6–12 of how he will turn his body into a "horrible object.")

81. **pelican:** Young pelicans were thought to feed on their parents' blood. (See page 144.)

82. **Pillicock:** a term of endearment and a name for the phallus

87. **keep . . . justice:** i.e., keep your word

87–88. **commit . . . spouse:** i.e., do not commit adultery

89. **array:** dress, clothing

91. **servingman:** literally, servant; figuratively, a lover (in service to his beloved)

92. **gloves:** A lover honored his mistress by wearing her glove in his hat.

98. **out-paramoured the Turk:** i.e., had sex with more women than the Turkish sultan with his harem

99. **light of ear:** i.e., ready to listen to malicious talk

101. **prey:** i.e., preying

103. **plackets:** openings in petticoats or in skirts

104. **lenders:** moneylenders

106. **Dolphin . . . sessa:** perhaps a fragment of a song

108. **answer:** stand up to

111. **worm:** i.e., silkworm

112. **cat:** civet cat, from whose secretions perfume is made (See page 160.); **on 's:** i.e., of us

113. **sophisticated:** not pure or genuine

113–14. **unaccommodated:** unfurnished (with items taken from other animals)

Is it the fashion that discarded fathers
Should have thus little mercy on their flesh?
Judicious punishment! 'Twas this flesh begot   80
Those pelican daughters.
EDGAR   Pillicock sat on Pillicock Hill. Alow, alow, loo,
    loo.
FOOL   This cold night will turn us all to fools and
    madmen.   85
EDGAR   Take heed o' th' foul fiend. Obey thy parents,
    keep thy word's justice, swear not, commit not with
    man's sworn spouse, set not thy sweet heart on
    proud array. Tom's a-cold.
LEAR   What hast thou been?   90
EDGAR   A servingman, proud in heart and mind, that
    curled my hair, wore gloves in my cap, served the
    lust of my mistress' heart and did the act of
    darkness with her, swore as many oaths as I spake
    words and broke them in the sweet face of heaven;   95
    one that slept in the contriving of lust and waked to
    do it. Wine loved I ⟨deeply,⟩ dice dearly, and in
    woman out-paramoured the Turk. False of heart,
    light of ear, bloody of hand; hog in sloth, fox in
    stealth, wolf in greediness, dog in madness, lion in   100
    prey. Let not the creaking of shoes nor the rustling
    of silks betray thy poor heart to woman. Keep thy
    foot out of brothels, thy hand out of plackets, thy
    pen from lenders' books, and defy the foul fiend.
    Still through the hawthorn blows the cold wind;   105
    says suum, mun, nonny. Dolphin my boy, boy, sessa!
    Let him trot by.   *Storm still.*
LEAR   Thou wert better in a grave than to answer with
    thy uncovered body this extremity of the skies.—Is
    man no more than this? Consider him well.—Thou   110
    ow'st the worm no silk, the beast no hide, the sheep
    no wool, the cat no perfume. Ha, here's three on 's
    are sophisticated. Thou art the thing itself; unac-
    commodated man is no more but such a poor, bare,

115. **lendings:** i.e., clothes

117. **naughty:** wicked

118. **wild:** uncultivated

120. **on 's:** i.e., of his

122. **Flibbertigibbet:** a name for the devil borrowed from Samuel Harsnett's *Declaration of Egregious Popish Impostures* (1603), an attack on Catholics for exploiting popular belief in demonic possession

123. **curfew:** i.e., 9 p.m., when the curfew bell was rung; **first cock:** the first crowing of the cock (midnight)

124. **web . . . pin:** cataract of the eye; **squints:** i.e., makes squint

125. **white:** ripening

127. **Swithold:** Saint Withold, who appears in this charm against the devil in the role of an exorcist; **footed:** crossed on foot; **'old:** wold, open country

128. **nightmare:** incubus; **nine fold:** nine offspring

130. **plight:** i.e., pledge (to do no more harm)

131. **aroint:** begone, get away

137. **water:** i.e., water newt

139. **sallets:** tasty things

140. **ditch-dog:** dead dog thrown in a ditch; **green mantle:** scum

141–42. **tithing to tithing:** i.e., place to place (Beggars were ordered whipped from one place to the next until they returned to their own district.) **tithing:** originally the name of a community of ten families

143. **three suits:** See note to 2.2.15.

146. **deer:** animals

forked animal as thou art. Off, off, you lendings!   115
Come, unbutton here.   ⌜*Tearing off his clothes.*⌝
FOOL   Prithee, nuncle, be contented. 'Tis a naughty
night to swim in. Now, a little fire in a wild field
were like an old lecher's heart—a small spark, all
the rest on 's body cold.   120

Enter Gloucester, with a torch.

Look, here comes a walking fire.
EDGAR   This is the foul ⟨fiend⟩ Flibbertigibbet. He be-
gins at curfew and walks ⟨till the⟩ first cock. He
gives the web and the pin, squints the eye, and
makes the harelip, mildews the white wheat, and   125
hurts the poor creature of earth.
    Swithold footed thrice the 'old,
    He met the nightmare and her ninefold,
      Bid her alight,
      And her troth plight,   130
    And aroint thee, witch, aroint thee.
KENT   How fares your Grace?
LEAR   What's he?
KENT   Who's there? What is 't you seek?
GLOUCESTER   What are you there? Your names?   135
EDGAR   Poor Tom, that eats the swimming frog, the
toad, the tadpole, the wall newt, and the water;
that, in the fury of his heart, when the foul fiend
rages, eats cow dung for sallets, swallows the old
rat and the ditch-dog, drinks the green mantle of   140
the standing pool; who is whipped from tithing to
tithing, and stocked, punished, and imprisoned;
who hath ⟨had⟩ three suits to his back, six shirts to
his body,
    Horse to ride, and weapon to wear;   145
    But mice and rats and such small deer
    Have been Tom's food for seven long year.

148. **my follower:** i.e., the fiend that attends me

148, 151, 152. **Smulkin, Modo, Mahu:** names of devils in Harsnett's *Declaration*

153. **flesh and blood:** i.e., children

154. **what gets it:** i.e., parents **gets:** i.e., begets

156–57. **suffer / T' obey:** i.e., tolerate obeying

165. **Theban:** citizen of Thebes, capital of ancient Boetiae in Greece

166. **your study:** the specialty that you study

167. **prevent:** forestall

169. **Importune:** implore, beg (accent on second syllable)

A pelican and its young. (3.4.81)
From Conrad Lycosthenes, *Prodigiorum* . . . (1557).

Beware my follower. Peace, Smulkin! Peace, thou
fiend!
GLOUCESTER
What, hath your Grace no better company?   150
EDGAR The Prince of Darkness is a gentleman. Modo
he's called, and Mahu.
GLOUCESTER
Our flesh and blood, my lord, is grown so vile
That it doth hate what gets it.
EDGAR Poor Tom's a-cold.   155
GLOUCESTER
Go in with me. My duty cannot suffer
T' obey in all your daughters' hard commands.
Though their injunction be to bar my doors
And let this tyrannous night take hold upon you,
Yet have I ventured to come seek you out   160
And bring you where both fire and food is ready.
LEAR
First let me talk with this philosopher.
⌜To Edgar.⌝ What is the cause of thunder?
KENT
Good my lord, take his offer; go into th' house.
LEAR
I'll talk a word with this same learnèd Theban.— 165
What is your study?
EDGAR How to prevent the fiend and to kill vermin.
LEAR Let me ask you one word in private.
                              ⌜They talk aside.⌝
KENT, ⌜to Gloucester⌝
Importune him once more to go, my lord.
His wits begin t' unsettle.   170
GLOUCESTER   Canst thou blame him?
                                        Storm still.
His daughters seek his death. Ah, that good Kent!
He said it would be thus, poor banished man.
Thou sayest the King grows mad; I'll tell thee,
    friend,   175

177. **outlawed from my blood:** i.e., (1) disinherited; (2) condemned as an outlaw
182. **cry you mercy:** i.e., excuse me
189. **keep still:** i.e., continue to stay
190. **soothe:** indulge
191. **Take . . . on:** i.e., bring him along
193. **Athenian:** i.e., philosopher
195–97. **Child . . . man:** Edgar gives to the hero of Charlemagne legends, Rowland or Roland (whose title **Child** shows that he was a candidate for knighthood), the words of the giant in "Jack and the Beanstalk." **word:** motto **still:** always

3.5 Edmund tells Cornwall about Gloucester's decision to help Lear and about the incriminating letter from France; in return, Cornwall makes Edmund earl of Gloucester.

———

3. **censured:** judged; **that:** i.e., because; **nature:** i.e., natural affection for my father
4. **something fears:** somewhat frightens

I am almost mad myself. I had a son,
Now outlawed from my blood. He sought my life
But lately, very late. I loved him, friend,
No father his son dearer. True to tell thee,
The grief hath crazed my wits. What a night's this!   180
—I do beseech your Grace—
LEAR   O, cry you mercy, sir.
⌐*To Edgar.*¬ Noble philosopher, your company.
EDGAR   Tom's a-cold.
GLOUCESTER, ⌐*to Edgar*¬
In fellow, there, into th' hovel. Keep thee warm.   185
LEAR   Come, let's in all.
KENT   This way, my lord.
LEAR, ⌐*indicating Edgar*¬   With him.
I will keep still with my philosopher.
KENT, ⌐*to Gloucester*¬
Good my lord, soothe him. Let him take the fellow.   190
GLOUCESTER, ⌐*to Kent*¬   Take him you on.
KENT, ⌐*to Edgar*¬
Sirrah, come on: go along with us.
LEAR   Come, good Athenian.
GLOUCESTER   No words, no words. Hush.
EDGAR
          Child Rowland to the dark tower came.   195
          His word was still "Fie, foh, and fum,
          I smell the blood of a British man."
                              They exit.

                    Scene 5
Enter Cornwall, and Edmund ⌐*with a paper.*¬

CORNWALL   I will have my revenge ere I depart his
          house.
EDMUND   How, my lord, I may be censured, that nature
          thus gives way to loyalty, something fears me to
          think of.   5

7. **his:** i.e., Gloucester's

8. **provoking merit:** perhaps, Edgar's virtue incited or provoked; or, perhaps, Gloucester's deserving (of death) provoked

8–9. **reprovable . . . himself:** blameworthy evil in Gloucester

12. **approves him:** i.e., proves him to be

12–13. **intelligent . . . France:** one giving information that aids the king of France

20. **apprehension:** arrest

21. **comforting:** i.e., relieving the misery of

22. **his suspicion:** perhaps, Cornwall's suspicion of Gloucester

24. **my blood:** i.e., attachment to my blood relations

3.6 Lear, in his madness, imagines that Goneril and Regan are on trial before a tribunal made up of Edgar, the Fool, Kent, and himself. Gloucester returns to announce that Lear's death is being plotted and to urge Kent to rush Lear to Cordelia at Dover.

---

2. **piece out:** i.e., increase

5. **impatience:** incapacity to endure more suffering

6. **Frateretto:** another devil found in Harsnett's *Declaration*; **Nero:** brutal and self-indulgent emperor of Rome in first century A.D. (here doomed to fish in hell)

CORNWALL I now perceive it was not altogether your
  brother's evil disposition made him seek his death,
  but a provoking merit set awork by a reprovable
  badness in himself.

EDMUND How malicious is my fortune that I must   10
  repent to be just! This is the letter he spoke of,
  which approves him an intelligent party to the
  advantages of France. O heavens, that this treason
  were not, or not I the detector.

CORNWALL Go with me to the Duchess.   15

EDMUND If the matter of this paper be certain, you
  have mighty business in hand.

CORNWALL True or false, it hath made thee Earl of
  Gloucester. Seek out where thy father is, that he
  may be ready for our apprehension.   20

EDMUND, ⌜*aside*⌝ If I find him comforting the King, it
  will stuff his suspicion more fully.—I will persevere
  in my course of loyalty, though the conflict be sore
  between that and my blood.

CORNWALL I will lay trust upon thee, and thou shalt   25
  find a ⟨dearer⟩ father in my love.

                                        They exit.

                         Scene 6
        Enter Kent ⌜*in disguise,*⌝ *and Gloucester.*

GLOUCESTER Here is better than the open air. Take it
  thankfully. I will piece out the comfort with what
  addition I can. I will not be long from you.

KENT All the power of his wits have given way to his
  impatience. The gods reward your kindness!   5
                              ⌜*Gloucester*⌝ *exits.*

  Enter Lear, Edgar ⌜*in disguise,*⌝ *and Fool.*

EDGAR Frateretto calls me and tells me Nero is an

10. **yeoman:** rank below gentleman

12–13. **to his son:** i.e., as a son

14. **before him:** i.e., before he has achieved the rank himself

20–59. **I will arraign . . . 'scape:** In this passage Lear stages an arraignment and trial of the absent Goneril and Regan.

20. **straight:** straightway, immediately

25. **he:** perhaps one of Poor Tom's fiends, or perhaps Lear

25–26. **Want'st . . . trial:** perhaps, "Do you lack onlookers at your trial?" or, perhaps, "Can't you see who is judging you?"

27. **Come . . . me:** the first line of a ballad first printed in 1558 (The Fool's continuation of it does not follow the original.) **burn:** stream, brook

32. **Hoppedance:** One of Harsnett's devils is called "Hobberdidance."

33. **white:** unsmoked; **Croak not:** Edgar may be alluding to the rumbling of an empty stomach.

35. **amazed:** confused (as if lost in a maze)

37. **their evidence:** the witnesses against them

angler in the lake of darkness. Pray, innocent, and
beware the foul fiend.

FOOL Prithee, nuncle, tell me whether a madman be a
gentleman or a yeoman. 10

LEAR A king, a king!

[FOOL No, he's a yeoman that has a gentleman to his
son, for he's a mad yeoman that sees his son a
gentleman before him.

LEAR]
To have a thousand with red burning spits 15
Come hissing in upon 'em!

⟨EDGAR The foul fiend bites my back.

FOOL He's mad that trusts in the tameness of a wolf, a
horse's health, a boy's love, or a whore's oath.

LEAR
It shall be done. I will arraign them straight. 20
⌐*To Edgar.*¬ Come, sit thou here, most learnèd
justice.
⌐*To Fool.*¬ Thou sapient sir, sit here. ⌐Now,¬ you
she-foxes—

EDGAR Look where he stands and glares!—Want'st 25
thou eyes at trial, madam?
⌐*Sings.*¬ Come o'er the ⌐burn,¬ Bessy, to me—

FOOL ⌐*sings*¬
Her boat hath a leak,
And she must not speak
Why she dares not come over to thee. 30

EDGAR The foul fiend haunts Poor Tom in the voice of
a nightingale. Hoppedance cries in Tom's belly for
two white herring.—Croak not, black angel. I have
no food for thee.

KENT, ⌐*to Lear*¬
How do you, sir? Stand you not so amazed. 35
Will you lie down and rest upon the cushions?

LEAR
I'll see their trial first. Bring in their evidence.

40. **yokefellow of equity:** fellow justice in a court of equity

41. **Bench:** i.e., sit on the bench

41–42. **o' th' commission:** authorized to be a judge

45–48. **Sleepest . . . harm:** These lines echo songs, ballads, and catches from the period, including the nursery song "Little Boy Blue."

46. **corn:** i.e., wheat

47. **minikin:** pretty, dainty

49. **Purr the cat: Purr** is a devil named by Harsnett, although here the word may refer instead to the sound made by the cat.

51. **kicked:** i.e., she kicked

55. **I . . . joint stool:** a stock joke meaning "I did not notice you" (Here the fresh point may be that while Goneril is not onstage, a stool may be.) **joint stool:** a stool made of parts joined or fitted together

56. **warped:** (1) twisted, bent; (2) perverse

57. **store:** stock, material; **on:** i.e., of

58. **Corruption in the place:** i.e., even the law court is corrupt

60. **five wits:** See note to 3.4.62.

61. **patience:** self-control

64. **counterfeiting:** i.e., disguise

67. **Avaunt:** i.e., get away

69. **or . . . or:** i.e., either . . . or

⌜*To Edgar.*⌝ Thou robèd man of justice, take thy
  place,
⌜*To Fool.*⌝ And thou, his yokefellow of equity,   40
Bench by his side. ⌜*To Kent.*⌝ You are o' th'
  commission;
Sit you, too.
EDGAR Let us deal justly.
  ⌜*Sings.*⌝ Sleepest or wakest, thou jolly shepherd?   45
        Thy sheep be in the corn.
      And for one blast of thy minikin mouth,
        Thy sheep shall take no harm.
  Purr the cat is gray.
LEAR Arraign her first; 'tis Goneril. I here take my oath   50
  before this honorable assembly, kicked the poor
  king her father.
FOOL Come hither, mistress. Is your name Goneril?
LEAR She cannot deny it.
FOOL Cry you mercy, I took you for a joint stool.   55
LEAR
  And here's another whose warped looks proclaim
  What store her heart is made on. Stop her there!
  Arms, arms, sword, fire! Corruption in the place!
  False justicer, why hast thou let her 'scape?⟩
EDGAR Bless thy five wits!   60
KENT, ⌜*to Lear*⌝
  O pity! Sir, where is the patience now
  That you so oft have boasted to retain?
EDGAR, ⌜*aside*⌝
  My tears begin to take his part so much
  They mar my counterfeiting.
LEAR The little dogs and all,   65
  Tray, Blanch, and Sweetheart, see, they bark at me.
EDGAR Tom will throw his head at them. —Avaunt, you
  curs!
      Be thy mouth or black or white,
      Tooth that poisons if it bite,   70

72. **brach:** bitch-hound; **lym:** bloodhound
73. **Bobtail tike:** dog with its tail cut short; **trundle-tail:** long-tailed dog
76. **hatch:** bottom half of a divided door
77. **wakes:** festivals
78. **horn:** large ox horns worn by beggars from which to drink (The phrase "my horn is dry" was a plea for more drink.)
80. **anatomize:** dissect
82. **make:** i.e., makes
83. **entertain for:** take into service as
85. **Persian:** i.e., gorgeous and exotic
88. **curtains:** i.e., imaginary bed curtains
94. **upon:** i.e., against
101. **Stand in . . . loss:** i.e., will certainly be lost

"Poor Tom, thy horn is dry." (3.6.78–79)
From *Bagford Ballads*, printed in 1878.

Mastiff, greyhound, mongrel grim,
Hound or spaniel, brach, or ⌜lym,⌝
Bobtail ⟨tike,⟩ or ⟨trundle-tail,⟩
Tom will make him weep and wail;
For, with throwing thus my head,   75
Dogs leapt the hatch, and all are fled.
Do de, de, de. Sessa! Come, march to wakes
and fairs and market towns. Poor Tom, thy horn
is dry.
LEAR   Then let them anatomize Regan; see what breeds   80
about her heart. Is there any cause in nature that
make these hard hearts? ⌜*To Edgar.*⌝ You, sir, I
entertain for one of my hundred; only I do not like
the fashion of your garments. You will say they are
Persian, but let them be changed.   85
KENT
Now, good my lord, lie here and rest awhile.
LEAR, ⌜*lying down*⌝ Make no noise, make no noise.
Draw the curtains. So, so, we'll go to supper i' th'
morning.
[FOOL   And I'll go to bed at noon.]   90

Enter Gloucester.

GLOUCESTER, ⌜*to Kent*⌝
Come hither, friend. Where is the King my master?
KENT
Here, sir, but trouble him not; his wits are gone.
GLOUCESTER
Good friend, I prithee, take him in thy arms.
I have o'erheard a plot of death upon him.
There is a litter ready; lay him in 't,   95
And drive toward Dover, friend, where thou shalt
   meet
Both welcome and protection. Take up thy master.
If thou shouldst dally half an hour, his life,
With thine and all that offer to defend him,   100
Stand in assurèd loss. Take up, take up,

102–3. **to some . . . conduct:** i.e., quickly take you to where you can find supplies

105. **balmed:** soothed; **sinews:** nerves

107. **Stand . . . cure:** i.e., are not likely to be cured

111. **bearing . . . woes:** suffering woes like ours

112. **We . . . foes:** perhaps, we almost forget our own suffering

114. **free:** carefree; **shows:** scenes

115. **sufferance:** i.e., suffering

116. **bearing:** enduring; **fellowship:** company

117. **portable:** endurable

120. **He childed . . . fathered:** i.e., his children are like my father (in driving him away; or, in seeking his life)

121. **Mark . . . noises:** pay attention to news of those in high places, i.e., those in power; **bewray:** reveal

124. **In thy just proof:** upon your being proved right; **repeals:** recalls; **reconciles:** i.e., reconciles you with your accusers

125. **What . . . King:** i.e., whatever more happens tonight, may the king escape safely

3.7 Cornwall dispatches men to capture Gloucester, whom he calls a traitor. Sending Edmund and Goneril to tell Albany about the landing of the French army, Cornwall puts out Gloucester's eyes. Cornwall is himself seriously wounded by one of his own servants, who tries to stop the torture of Gloucester.

———————

1. **Post speedily:** hasten

And follow me, that will to some provision
Give thee quick conduct.
⟨KENT   Oppressèd nature sleeps.
This rest might yet have balmed thy broken sinews,   105
Which, if convenience will not allow,
Stand in hard cure. ⌜*To the Fool.*⌝ Come, help to
   bear thy master.
Thou must not stay behind.
GLOUCESTER⟩   Come, come away.   110
           ⌜*All but Edgar*⌝ *exit,* ⌜*carrying Lear.*⌝
⟨EDGAR
When we our betters see bearing our woes,
We scarcely think our miseries our foes.
Who alone suffers suffers most i' th' mind,
Leaving free things and happy shows behind.
But then the mind much sufferance doth o'erskip   115
When grief hath mates and bearing fellowship.
How light and portable my pain seems now
When that which makes me bend makes the King
   bow!
He childed as I fathered. Tom, away.   120
Mark the high noises, and thyself bewray
When false opinion, whose wrong thoughts defile
   thee,
In thy just proof repeals and reconciles thee.
What will hap more tonight, safe 'scape the King!   125
Lurk, lurk.⟩
                              ⌜*He exits.*⌝

Scene 7
Enter Cornwall, Regan, Goneril, ⌜*Edmund, the*⌝ *Bastard,*
and Servants.

CORNWALL, ⌜*to Goneril*⌝ Post speedily to my lord your
   husband. Show him this letter. ⌜*He gives her a*
   paper.⌝ The army of France is landed.—Seek out
   the traitor Gloucester.   ⌜*Some Servants exit.*⌝

8. **our sister:** i.e., Goneril

8–9. **are bound:** (1) are obligated; (2) cannot fail

10–11. **Advise . . . preparation:** i.e., advise Albany, to whom you are going, to make speedy preparation (for war)   **festinate:** speedy, hasty

12. **to the like:** i.e., to do the same thing; **posts:** messengers

13. **intelligent:** i.e., will carry intelligence (information)

14. **lord of Gloucester:** i.e., Edmund (Oswald will immediately use the same title to refer to Edmund's father.)

18. **Hot questrists:** keen seekers

19. **the lord's:** i.e., Gloucester's

26. **Pinion:** bind

27. **pass . . . life:** i.e., condemn him to death

29. **do a court'sy:** i.e., yield, bow down, defer

REGAN Hang him instantly.   5
GONERIL Pluck out his eyes.
CORNWALL Leave him to my displeasure.—Edmund,
   keep you our sister company. The revenges we are
   bound to take upon your traitorous father are not
   fit for your beholding. Advise the Duke, where you   10
   are going, to a most festinate preparation; we are
   bound to the like. Our posts shall be swift and
   intelligent betwixt us.—Farewell, dear sister.—
   Farewell, my lord of Gloucester.

           Enter ⌜*Oswald, the*⌝ *Steward.*

   How now? Where's the King?   15
OSWALD
   My lord of Gloucester hath conveyed him hence.
   Some five- or six-and-thirty of his knights,
   Hot questrists after him, met him at gate,
   Who, with some other of the lord's dependents,
   Are gone with him toward Dover, where they boast   20
   To have well-armèd friends.
CORNWALL Get horses for your mistress.
                                    ⌜*Oswald exits.*⌝
GONERIL Farewell, sweet lord, and sister.
CORNWALL
   Edmund, farewell.   ⌜*Goneril and Edmund*⌝ *exit.*
                   Go seek the traitor Gloucester.   25
   Pinion him like a thief; bring him before us.
                                ⌜*Some Servants exit.*⌝
   Though well we may not pass upon his life
   Without the form of justice, yet our power
   Shall do a court'sy to our wrath, which men
   May blame but not control.   30

           Enter Gloucester and Servants.

                        Who's there? The
   traitor?

34. **corky:** dry and withered
40. **none:** i.e., not a traitor
46. **Naughty:** wicked
48. **quicken:** come to life
49. **my . . . favors:** perhaps, the features (face) of your host; or, perhaps, my hospitable kindnesses to you
50. **ruffle:** bully, treat roughly
51. **late:** recently
52. **simple-answered:** i.e., direct in answering
54. **footed:** landed
57. **guessingly set down:** i.e., written without certainty; containing only speculations

A civet cat. (3.4.112)
From Edward Topsell, *The historie of foure-footed beastes* . . . (1607).

REGAN   Ingrateful fox! 'Tis he.
CORNWALL   Bind fast his corky arms.
GLOUCESTER
  What means your Graces? Good my friends, consider   35
  You are my guests; do me no foul play, friends.
CORNWALL
  Bind him, I say.
REGAN   Hard, hard. O filthy traitor!
GLOUCESTER
  Unmerciful lady as you are, I'm none.   40
CORNWALL
  To this chair bind him.   ⌜*Servants bind Gloucester.*⌝
                       Villain, thou shalt find—
               ⌜*Regan plucks Gloucester's beard.*⌝
GLOUCESTER
  By the kind gods, 'tis most ignobly done
  To pluck me by the beard.
REGAN
  So white, and such a traitor?   45
GLOUCESTER   Naughty lady,
  These hairs which thou dost ravish from my chin
  Will quicken and accuse thee. I am your host;
  With robber's hands my hospitable favors
  You should not ruffle thus. What will you do?   50
CORNWALL
  Come, sir, what letters had you late from France?
REGAN
  Be simple-answered, for we know the truth.
CORNWALL
  And what confederacy have you with the traitors
  Late footed in the kingdom?
REGAN   To whose hands   55
  You have sent the lunatic king. Speak.
GLOUCESTER
  I have a letter guessingly set down

64. **Wherefore:** why

67. **I . . . course:** i.e., I am like a bear in a bearbaiting, tied to a stake, facing the attack of the dogs, i.e., the **course** (See page 164.)

71. **anointed:** i.e., with holy oil at his coronation

73–74. **buoyed up . . . fires:** i.e., risen up and extinguished the stars **stellèd fires:** (1) starry fires; (2) fixed stars

75. **holp:** helped

77–78. **turn the key:** i.e., let them in

79. **All . . . subscribe:** perhaps, all cruel creatures, except for you, give in to feelings of compassion **subscribe:** submit, yield

80. **wingèd vengeance:** probably, divine vengeance

83. **will think:** i.e., hopes, expects

Which came from one that's of a neutral heart,
And not from one opposed.

CORNWALL Cunning. 60

REGAN And false.

CORNWALL Where hast thou sent the King?

GLOUCESTER To Dover.

REGAN

Wherefore to Dover? Wast thou not charged at
    peril— 65

CORNWALL

Wherefore to Dover? Let him answer that.

GLOUCESTER

I am tied to th' stake, and I must stand the course.

REGAN Wherefore to Dover?

GLOUCESTER

Because I would not see thy cruel nails
Pluck out his poor old eyes, nor thy fierce sister 70
In his anointed flesh stick boarish fangs.
The sea, with such a storm as his bare head
In hell-black night endured, would have buoyed up
And quenched the stellèd fires;
Yet, poor old heart, he holp the heavens to rain. 75
If wolves had at thy gate howled that stern time,
Thou shouldst have said "Good porter, turn the
    key."
All cruels else subscribe. But I shall see
The wingèd vengeance overtake such children. 80

CORNWALL

See 't shalt thou never.—Fellows, hold the chair.—
Upon these eyes of thine I'll set my foot.

GLOUCESTER

He that will think to live till he be old,
Give me some help!

⌜*As Servants hold the chair, Cornwall forces out*
one of Gloucester's eyes.⌝

O cruel! O you gods! 85

88. **Hold . . . hand:** stop, refrain

95. **I'd . . . quarrel:** i.e., I'd defy you openly in this cause; **What . . . mean?:** an expression of astonishment and disbelief

96. **villain:** servant

97. **chance of anger:** i.e., risks of an angry fight

100. **mischief:** harm, injury

105. **sparks of nature:** i.e., natural feelings (as a son)

106. **quit:** requite, avenge

107. **Out:** an exclamation (here expressing disagreement or denial)

109. **overture:** revelation, disclosure

A bear "tied to th' stake." (3.7.67)
From Franco Giacomo, *Habiti d'huomeni de donne Venetiane* . . . (1609?).

REGAN
  One side will mock another. Th' other too.
CORNWALL   If you see vengeance—
⌜FIRST⌝ SERVANT   Hold your hand,
    my lord.
  I have served you ever since I was a child,   90
  But better service have I never done you
  Than now to bid you hold.
REGAN   How now, you dog?
⌜FIRST⌝ SERVANT
  If you did wear a beard upon your chin,
  I'd shake it on this quarrel. What do you mean?   95
CORNWALL   My villain?   ⟨*Draw and fight.*⟩
⌜FIRST⌝ SERVANT
  Nay, then, come on, and take the chance of anger.
REGAN, ⌜*to an Attendant*⌝
  Give me thy sword. A peasant stand up thus?
                    ⟨*She takes a sword and runs*
                      at him behind;⟩ *kills him.*
⌜FIRST⌝ SERVANT
  O, I am slain! My lord, you have one eye left
  To see some mischief on him. O!   ⌜*He dies.*⌝   100
CORNWALL
  Lest it see more, prevent it. Out, vile jelly!
            ⌜*Forcing out Gloucester's other eye.*⌝
  Where is thy luster now?
GLOUCESTER
  All dark and comfortless! Where's my son
    Edmund?—
  Edmund, enkindle all the sparks of nature   105
  To quit this horrid act.
REGAN   Out, treacherous villain!
  Thou call'st on him that hates thee. It was he
  That made the overture of thy treasons to us,
  Who is too good to pity thee.   110

111. **abused:** wronged
112. **prosper him:** cause him to flourish
115. **How look you:** i.e., how are you
117. **this slave:** i.e., the dead servant
123. **old:** usual, customary
125. **Bedlam:** i.e., Bedlam beggar, Tom o' Bedlam (Edgar in disguise)
126–27. **His ... anything:** i.e., as a madman-vagabond, he can do anything
128. **flax and whites of eggs:** prescribed (in the Renaissance) for wounded eyes

GLOUCESTER
  O my follies! Then Edgar was abused.
  Kind gods, forgive me that, and prosper him.
REGAN
  Go thrust him out at gates, and let him smell
  His way to Dover.
                    ⌜*Some Servants*⌝ *exit with Gloucester.*
                    How is 't, my lord? How look you?   115
CORNWALL
  I have received a hurt. Follow me, lady.—
  Turn out that eyeless villain. Throw this slave
  Upon the dunghill.—Regan, I bleed apace.
  Untimely comes this hurt. Give me your arm.
                    ⌜*Cornwall and Regan*⌝ *exit.*
⟨⌜SECOND⌝ SERVANT
  I'll never care what wickedness I do   120
  If this man come to good.
⌜THIRD⌝ SERVANT   If she live long
  And in the end meet the old course of death,
  Women will all turn monsters.
⌜SECOND⌝ SERVANT
  Let's follow the old earl and get the Bedlam   125
  To lead him where he would. His roguish madness
  Allows itself to anything.
⌜THIRD⌝ SERVANT
  Go thou. I'll fetch some flax and whites of eggs
  To apply to his bleeding face. Now heaven help him!
                    ⌜*They*⌝ *exit.*⟩

The Tragedy of

KING LEAR

ACT 4

4.1   Edgar, still in disguise as Poor Tom, meets the blinded Gloucester and agrees to lead him to Dover.

––––––––––

   1. **Yet . . . contemned:** i.e., it is better to be a beggar and openly despised
   2. **Than . . . flattered:** i.e., than to be despised but flattered
   3. **most dejected thing of:** i.e., the thing most cast down by
   4. **still:** always; **esperance:** hope
   6. **The . . . laughter:** i.e., any change from the worst is necessarily for the better
   9. **Owes nothing to:** i.e., and therefore has nothing to fear from
   10. **poorly led:** i.e., led by a poor peasant
   11. **But that:** i.e., except that
   12. **yield to age:** perhaps, accept old age and death
   16. **Thy comforts:** i.e., the relief that you can offer

ACT 4

Scene 1
Enter Edgar ⌈in disguise.⌉

EDGAR
  Yet better thus, and known to be contemned,
  Than still contemned and flattered. To be worst,
  The lowest and most dejected thing of fortune,
  Stands still in esperance, lives not in fear.
  The lamentable change is from the best;   5
  The worst returns to laughter. [Welcome, then,
  Thou unsubstantial air that I embrace.
  The wretch that thou hast blown unto the worst
  Owes nothing to thy blasts.] But who comes here?

Enter Gloucester and an old man.

  My father, poorly led? World, world, O world,   10
  But that thy strange mutations make us hate thee,
  Life would not yield to age.
OLD MAN
  O my good lord, I have been your tenant
  And your father's tenant these fourscore years.
GLOUCESTER
  Away, get thee away. Good friend, begone.   15
  Thy comforts can do me no good at all;
  Thee they may hurt.
OLD MAN   You cannot see your way.

171

19. **want:** need

21. **Our . . . us:** i.e., our resources (while in prosperity) make us careless; **mere defects:** utter deficiencies

22. **commodities:** advantages

23. **abusèd:** deceived

35. **He . . . reason:** i.e., he is not completely mad

41. **wanton:** undisciplined

42. **sport:** amusement, fun

44. **trade:** i.e., occupation; **play . . . sorrow:** i.e., play the role of a fool to my grieving father

45. **Ang'ring:** irritating, vexing

GLOUCESTER
　I have no way and therefore want no eyes.
　I stumbled when I saw. Full oft 'tis seen　　　　　20
　Our means secure us, and our mere defects
　Prove our commodities. O dear son Edgar,
　The food of thy abusèd father's wrath,
　Might I but live to see thee in my touch,
　I'd say I had eyes again.　　　　　　　　　　25
OLD MAN　　　　　　　　　How now? Who's there?
EDGAR, ⌈*aside*⌉
　O gods, who is 't can say "I am at the worst"?
　I am worse than e'er I was.
OLD MAN　　　　　　　　　'Tis poor mad Tom.
EDGAR, ⌈*aside*⌉
　And worse I may be yet. The worst is not　　　30
　So long as we can say "This is the worst."
OLD MAN
　Fellow, where goest?
GLOUCESTER　　　　　Is it a beggar-man?
OLD MAN　Madman and beggar too.
GLOUCESTER
　He has some reason, else he could not beg.　　35
　I' th' last night's storm, I such a fellow saw,
　Which made me think a man a worm. My son
　Came then into my mind, and yet my mind
　Was then scarce friends with him. I have heard
　　more since.　　　　　　　　　　　　　40
　As flies to wanton boys are we to th' gods;
　They kill us for their sport.
EDGAR, ⌈*aside*⌉　　　　　　How should this be?
　Bad is the trade that must play fool to sorrow,
　Ang'ring itself and others.—Bless thee, master.　45
GLOUCESTER
　Is that the naked fellow?
OLD MAN　　　　　　　　Ay, my lord.
GLOUCESTER
　⟨Then, prithee,⟩ get thee away. If for my sake

49. **o'ertake us:** i.e., catch up to us; **twain:** two

50. **ancient:** long-established

52. **Which:** i.e., whom

54. **time's plague:** i.e., a sign of the sickness of our time

56. **Above the rest:** i.e., above all

57. **'parel:** apparel, clothes

58. **on 't:** of it

60. **daub it further:** i.e., act my part of Poor Tom anymore **daub:** literally, cover over with mortar

68–70. **Obidicut, Hobbididance, Mahu, Modo, Flibbertigibbet:** all names for devils based on Harsnett's *Declaration*

70. **mopping and mowing:** grimacing and making faces; **since:** i.e., since then

75. **humbled . . . strokes:** i.e., reduced to a humble acceptance of all miseries

77. **superfluous . . . man:** he who has more than he needs and who feeds his desires

78. **slaves your ordinance:** enslaves (to his own interest) the divine decree (to share)

Thou wilt o'ertake us hence a mile or twain
I' th' way toward Dover, do it for ancient love,   50
And bring some covering for this naked soul,
Which I'll entreat to lead me.
OLD MAN Alack, sir, he is mad.
GLOUCESTER
'Tis the time's plague when madmen lead the blind.
Do as I bid thee, or rather do thy pleasure.   55
Above the rest, begone.
OLD MAN
I'll bring him the best 'parel that I have,
Come on 't what will.   *He exits.*
GLOUCESTER   Sirrah, naked fellow—
EDGAR
Poor Tom's a-cold. ⌜*Aside.*⌝ I cannot daub it further.   60
GLOUCESTER Come hither, fellow.
EDGAR, ⌜*aside*⌝
And yet I must.—Bless thy sweet eyes, they bleed.
GLOUCESTER Know'st thou the way to Dover?
EDGAR Both stile and gate, horseway and footpath.
Poor Tom hath been ⟨scared⟩ out of his good wits.   65
Bless thee, good man's son, from the foul fiend.
⟨Five fiends have been in Poor Tom at once: of lust,
as Obidicut; Hobbididance, prince of dumbness;
Mahu, of stealing; Modo, of murder; ⌜Flibbertigib-
bet,⌝ of ⌜mopping⌝ and ⌜mowing,⌝ who since pos-   70
sesses chambermaids and waiting women. So, bless
thee, master.⟩
GLOUCESTER, ⌜*giving him money*⌝
Here, take this purse, thou whom the heavens'
   plagues
Have humbled to all strokes. That I am wretched   75
Makes thee the happier. Heavens, deal so still:
Let the superfluous and lust-dieted man,
That slaves your ordinance, that will not see
Because he does not feel, feel your power quickly.

83. **bending:** overhanging
84. **fearfully:** frighteningly; **in . . . deep:** i.e., into
the waters of the English Channel, **confinèd,** in the
Straits of Dover, between England's cliffs and
France's shore
87. **rich:** i.e., valuable; **about me:** i.e., that I have
with me

4.2 Goneril and Edmund arrive at Albany and
Goneril's castle. After Goneril has sent Edmund back
to Cornwall, Albany enters and fiercely rebukes
Goneril for her treatment of Lear. A messenger
reports Gloucester's blinding and the death of the
duke of Cornwall.

---

2. **Not met:** i.e., did not meet
10. **sot:** dolt, fool
12. **pleasant:** pleasing
13. **What like:** i.e., what he should like

So distribution should undo excess   80
And each man have enough. Dost thou know Dover?
EDGAR   Ay, master.
GLOUCESTER
There is a cliff, whose high and bending head
Looks fearfully in the confinèd deep.
Bring me but to the very brim of it,   85
And I'll repair the misery thou dost bear
With something rich about me. From that place
I shall no leading need.
EDGAR   Give me thy arm.
Poor Tom shall lead thee.   90

                                              They exit.

                        Scene 2
        Enter Goneril and ⌐Edmund, the⌐ Bastard.

GONERIL
Welcome, my lord. I marvel our mild husband
Not met us on the way.

              ⟨*Enter ⌐Oswald, the⌐ Steward.*⟩

                      Now, where's your master?
OSWALD
Madam, within, but never man so changed.
I told him of the army that was landed;   5
He smiled at it. I told him you were coming;
His answer was "The worse." Of Gloucester's
    treachery
And of the loyal service of his son
When I informed him, then he called me "sot"   10
And told me I had turned the wrong side out.
What most he should dislike seems pleasant to him;
What like, offensive.
GONERIL, ⌐*to Edmund*⌐ Then shall you go no further.

15. **cowish:** cowardly

16. **undertake:** commit himself to an enterprise; **feel wrongs:** i.e., acknowledge offenses

17. **tie . . . answer:** i.e., would require him to retaliate; **wishes . . . way:** hopes expressed during our journey

18. **prove effects:** i.e., be fulfilled; **brother:** i.e., brother-in-law, Cornwall

19. **musters:** gathering of soldiers; **powers:** troops

20. **change names:** i.e., exchange roles with Albany; **distaff:** spinning staff (See page 184.)

22. **like:** i.e., likely

29. **Conceive:** i.e., understand (my unspoken meaning)

35. **My fool:** i.e., my husband, who is a fool; **usurps:** possesses forcibly and without right

37. **worth the whistle:** Proverbial: "It is a poor dog that is not worth the whistling."

40. **fear your disposition:** am fearful about your nature

41. **contemns:** despises

42. **Cannot . . . itself:** cannot be securely contained within itself; or, can have no reliable boundaries

43–44. **herself will sliver . . . sap:** i.e., tear herself away (from Lear) as if she were a branch tearing itself away from the tree that sustains it (See page 192.)

45. **deadly use:** i.e., destruction (of herself and others)

46. **text:** i.e., theme of your sermon

It is the cowish terror of his spirit, 15
That dares not undertake. He'll not feel wrongs
Which tie him to an answer. Our wishes on the way
May prove effects. Back, Edmund, to my brother.
Hasten his musters and conduct his powers.
I must change names at home and give the distaff 20
Into my husband's hands. This trusty servant
Shall pass between us. Ere long you are like to
    hear—
If you dare venture in your own behalf—
A mistress's command. Wear this; spare speech. 25
⌜*She gives him a favor.*⌝
Decline your head. ⌜*She kisses him.*⌝ This kiss, if it
    durst speak,
Would stretch thy spirits up into the air.
Conceive, and fare thee well.

EDMUND
Yours in the ranks of death.   *He exits.* 30

GONERIL   My most dear
    Gloucester!
[O, the difference of man and man!]
To thee a woman's services are due;
My fool usurps my body. 35

OSWALD   Madam, here comes my lord.   ⟨*He exits.*⟩

Enter Albany.

GONERIL   I have been worth the whistle.

ALBANY   O Goneril,
    You are not worth the dust which the rude wind
    Blows in your face. ⟨I fear your disposition. 40
    That nature which contemns its origin
    Cannot be bordered certain in itself.
    She that herself will sliver and disbranch
    From her material sap perforce must wither
    And come to deadly use. 45

GONERIL   No more. The text is foolish.

51. **head-lugged:** tugged by the head (hence, bad-tempered)

53. **barbarous, degenerate:** i.e., barbarously, degenerately

54. **madded:** driven mad

55. **brother:** i.e., brother-in-law; **suffer:** allow

62. **Milk-livered:** i.e., white-livered, cowardly

63. **bear'st . . . blows:** i.e., when you are struck, you turn the other cheek

64–65. **hast . . . suffering:** i.e., cannot tell the difference between what must be resisted in the defense of your honor and what may be permitted (i.e., suffered)

66–67. **Fools . . . mischief:** i.e., only fools have pity on villains who are punished before they can do harm

69. **France:** i.e., the king of France; **noiseless:** quiet, peaceful

70. **helm:** helmet; **thy . . . threat:** i.e., begins to threaten your power

71. **moral:** i.e., moralizing

74–75. **Proper . . . woman:** i.e., the ugliness that is **proper** (appropriate) for the devil **shows** (appears) more horrible in a woman

76. **vain:** idle, useless

77. **changèd:** transformed; **self-covered:** i.e., your true nature as a fiend concealed by your womanly appearance; or, perhaps, your true nature as a woman now covered up by your fiendishness

78. **Bemonster . . . feature:** i.e., do not deform yourself into a monster **feature:** shape; **my fitness:** appropriate for me

79. **blood:** feelings

ALBANY
Wisdom and goodness to the vile seem vile.
Filths savor but themselves. What have you done?
Tigers, not daughters, what have you performed?
A father, and a gracious agèd man,   50
Whose reverence even the head-lugged bear would
    lick,
Most barbarous, most degenerate, have you
    madded.
Could my good brother suffer you to do it?   55
A man, a prince, by him so benefited!
If that the heavens do not their visible spirits
Send quickly down to tame ⌜these⌝ vile offenses,
It will come:
Humanity must perforce prey on itself,   60
Like monsters of the deep.⟩
GONERIL   Milk-livered man,
That bear'st a cheek for blows, a head for wrongs;
Who hast not in thy brows an eye discerning
Thine honor from thy suffering; ⟨that not know'st   65
Fools do those villains pity who are punished
Ere they have done their mischief. Where's thy
    drum?
France spreads his banners in our noiseless land.
With plumèd helm thy state begins ⌜to threat⌝   70
Whilst thou, a moral fool, sits still and cries
"Alack, why does he so?"⟩
ALBANY   See thyself, devil!
Proper deformity ⟨shows⟩ not in the fiend
So horrid as in woman.   75
GONERIL   O vain fool!
⟨ALBANY
Thou changèd and self-covered thing, for shame
Bemonster not thy feature. Were 't my fitness
To let these hands obey my blood,
They are apt enough to dislocate and tear   80

81. **Howe'er:** i.e., however much

82. **shield:** i.e., protect you (from violence at my hands)

83. **Marry:** i.e., indeed; **mew:** a sound of derision

86. **going to:** i.e., as Cornwall was going to

89. **he bred:** i.e., Cornwall raised; **thrilled with remorse:** pierced with compassion

90. **Opposed against:** i.e., stood in opposition to

90–91. **bending . . . To:** i.e., turning his sword against

92. **amongst them:** i.e., in a melee; or, between them (Cornwall and Regan)

93–94. **But . . . after:** i.e., but not before Cornwall suffered the wound that has since killed him

96. **justicers:** i.e., heavenly justices

96–97. **our . . . venge:** i.e., can so quickly avenge the crimes committed in our world beneath the heavens

102. **One way . . . well:** i.e., in one way I am glad to hear that Cornwall is dead

103. **But . . . widow:** i.e., but Regan now being a widow

104. **all . . . pluck:** i.e., pull down the dreams I have constructed

106. **tart:** sour

Thy flesh and bones. Howe'er thou art a fiend,
A woman's shape doth shield thee.
GONERIL
Marry, your manhood, mew—⟩

Enter a Messenger.

⟨ALBANY   What news?⟩
MESSENGER
O, my good lord, the Duke of Cornwall's dead,   85
Slain by his servant, going to put out
The other eye of Gloucester.
ALBANY   Gloucester's eyes?
MESSENGER
A servant that he bred, thrilled with remorse,
Opposed against the act, bending his sword   90
To his great master, who, ⟨thereat⟩ enraged,
Flew on him and amongst them felled him dead,
But not without that harmful stroke which since
Hath plucked him after.
ALBANY   This shows you are above,   95
You ⟨justicers,⟩ that these our nether crimes
So speedily can venge. But, O poor Gloucester,
Lost he his other eye?
MESSENGER   Both, both, my lord.—
This letter, madam, craves a speedy answer.   100
                        ⌜*Giving her a paper.*⌝
'Tis from your sister.
GONERIL, ⌜*aside*⌝   One way I like this well.
But being widow and my Gloucester with her
May all the building in my fancy pluck
Upon my hateful life. Another way   105
The news is not so tart.—I'll read, and answer.
                        ⟨*She exits.*⟩
ALBANY
Where was his son when they did take his eyes?
MESSENGER
Come with my lady hither.

110. **back:** i.e., going back

4.3 In the French camp Kent and a Gentleman discuss Cordelia's love of Lear, which has brought her back to Britain at the head of the French army; they say that Lear is in the town of Dover, and that, though he is sometimes sane, his shame at his earlier action makes him refuse to see Cordelia.

———————

5. **imports:** i.e., would cause
8. **general:** i.e., as general
14. **trilled:** rolled
16. **passion, who:** i.e., emotion, which

Woman with a distaff. (4.2.20)
From Johann Engel, *Astrolabium* (1488).

ALBANY   He is not here.

MESSENGER

No, my good lord. I met him back again.   110

ALBANY   Knows he the wickedness?

MESSENGER

Ay, my good lord. 'Twas he informed against him
And quit the house on purpose, that their punishment
Might have the freer course.

ALBANY   Gloucester, I live   115
To thank thee for the love thou show'd'st the King,
And to revenge thine eyes.—Come hither, friend.
Tell me what more thou know'st.

They exit.

⌜Scene 3⌝
⟨*Enter Kent* ⌜*in disguise*⌝ *and a Gentleman.*

KENT   Why the King of France is so suddenly gone
    back know you no reason?

GENTLEMAN   Something he left imperfect in the state,
    which since his coming forth is thought of, which
    imports to the kingdom so much fear and danger   5
    that his personal return was most required and
    necessary.

KENT   Who hath he left behind him general?

GENTLEMAN   The Marshal of France, Monsieur La Far.

KENT   Did your letters pierce the Queen to any demon-   10
    stration of grief?

GENTLEMAN

Ay, ⌜sir,⌝ she took them, read them in my
    presence,
And now and then an ample tear trilled down
Her delicate cheek. It seemed she was a queen   15
Over her passion, who, most rebel-like,
Fought to be king o'er her.

KENT   O, then it moved her.

19. **Patience:** self-control
20. **Who . . . goodliest:** i.e., about which would make her appear most beautiful
22. **like:** i.e., like sunshine and rain; **a better way:** i.e., but more lovely
24. **which:** i.e., the tears
26. **rarity most beloved:** i.e., something precious and sought after
27. **If . . . it:** i.e., if sorrow could be so becoming to others
28. **Made . . . question?:** i.e., did she say anything?
34. **believed:** i.e., believed to exist
36. **clamor moistened:** i.e., moistened her outburst of grief with tears
39. **conditions:** mental dispositions
40–41. **Else . . . issues:** i.e., otherwise the same couple could not conceive such different offspring **self:** same **make:** mate, partner **issues:** offspring
44. **King:** i.e., of France; **returned:** i.e., to France
47. **better tune:** i.e., less jangled, more rational, state

GENTLEMAN
  Not to a rage. Patience and sorrow ⌜strove⌝
  Who should express her goodliest. You have seen   20
  Sunshine and rain at once; her smiles and tears
  Were like a better way. Those happy smilets
  That played on her ripe lip ⌜seemed⌝ not to know
  What guests were in her eyes, which parted thence
  As pearls from diamonds dropped. In brief,   25
  Sorrow would be a rarity most beloved
  If all could so become it.
KENT   Made she no verbal question?
GENTLEMAN
  Faith, once or twice she heaved the name of
      "father"   30
  Pantingly forth, as if it pressed her heart;
  Cried "Sisters, sisters, shame of ladies, sisters!
  Kent, father, sisters! What, i' th' storm, i' th' night?
  Let pity not be believed!" There she shook
  The holy water from her heavenly eyes,   35
  And clamor moistened. Then away she started,
  To deal with grief alone.
KENT   It is the stars.
  The stars above us govern our conditions,
  Else one self mate and make could not beget   40
  Such different issues. You spoke not with her
      since?
GENTLEMAN   No.
KENT
  Was this before the King returned?
GENTLEMAN   No, since.   45
KENT
  Well, sir, the poor distressèd Lear's i' th' town,
  Who sometime in his better tune remembers
  What we are come about, and by no means
  Will yield to see his daughter.
GENTLEMAN   Why, good sir?   50

51. **sovereign:** overpowering; **elbows him:** i.e., jostles (his mind)

53. **from . . . benediction:** i.e., of his blessing

53–54. **turned . . . casualties:** i.e., sent her away to take her chances in a foreign land

59. **powers:** armed forces

60. **afoot:** i.e., on the march

62. **attend:** wait upon; **dear:** important

64. **aright:** i.e., as Kent

64–65. **grieve . . . me:** i.e., regret having extended this acquaintanceship to me

4.4 In the French camp Cordelia orders out a search party for Lear.

---

0 SD. **Drum and Colors:** i.e., drummers and soldiers carrying banners

3–5. **fumiter, furrow-weeds, hardocks, hemlock, nettles, cuckooflowers, Darnel:** Most of these weeds and plants may be called **idle** (i.e., worthless), but some (e.g., **fumiter**) were used as medicines for diseases of the brain.

6. **our sustaining corn:** wheat, which gives us sustenance; **A century:** a troop of one hundred soldiers

9. **What . . . wisdom:** i.e., what can human knowledge do

KENT
A sovereign shame so elbows him—his own
  unkindness,
That stripped her from his benediction, turned her
To foreign casualties, gave her dear rights
To his dog-hearted daughters—these things sting   55
His mind so venomously that burning shame
Detains him from Cordelia.
GENTLEMAN   Alack, poor gentleman!
KENT
Of Albany's and Cornwall's powers you heard not?
GENTLEMAN   'Tis so. They are afoot.   60
KENT
Well, sir, I'll bring you to our master Lear
And leave you to attend him. Some dear cause
Will in concealment wrap me up awhile.
When I am known aright, you shall not grieve
Lending me this acquaintance. I pray you, go   65
Along with me.
                         ⌜*They*⌝ *exit.*⟩

Scene ⌜4⌝
Enter with Drum and Colors, Cordelia, ⟨Doctor,⟩
Gentlemen, and Soldiers.

CORDELIA
Alack, 'tis he! Why, he was met even now
As mad as the vexed sea, singing aloud,
Crowned with rank fumiter and furrow-weeds,
With hardocks, hemlock, nettles, cuckooflowers,
Darnel, and all the idle weeds that grow   5
In our sustaining corn. A century send forth.
Search every acre in the high-grown field
And bring him to our eye.   ⌜*Soldiers exit.*⌝
                  What can man's wisdom

10. **his bereavèd sense:** i.e., his mind, of which he is bereaved

11. **outward worth:** i.e., wealth

14–15. **That . . . operative:** i.e., there are many medicinal plants or herbs (**simples**) that will be effective (**operative**) in inducing sleep in him

18. **unpublished:** perhaps, hidden; or, unknown; **virtues:** healing powers

19. **Spring:** grow; **Be . . . remediate:** i.e., be aids and remedies

21. **rage:** madness

22. **wants . . . means:** i.e., lacks the resources

29. **importuned:** importuning, pleading

30. **blown:** puffed-up, swollen

4.5 Regan questions Oswald about Goneril and Edmund, states her intention to marry Edmund, and asks Oswald to dissuade Goneril from pursuing Edmund.

---

1. **my brother's powers:** i.e., Albany's armies

In the restoring his bereavèd sense? 10
He that helps him take all my outward worth.
⟨DOCTOR⟩   There is means, madam.
Our foster nurse of nature is repose,
The which he lacks. That to provoke in him
Are many simples operative, whose power 15
Will close the eye of anguish.
CORDELIA   All blest secrets,
All you unpublished virtues of the earth,
Spring with my tears. Be aidant and remediate
In the good man's ⟨distress.⟩ Seek, seek for him, 20
Lest his ungoverned rage dissolve the life
That wants the means to lead it.

Enter Messenger.

MESSENGER   News, madam.
The British powers are marching hitherward.
CORDELIA
'Tis known before. Our preparation stands 25
In expectation of them.—O dear father,
It is thy business that I go about.
Therefore great France
My mourning and importuned tears hath pitied.
No blown ambition doth our arms incite, 30
But love, dear love, and our aged father's right.
Soon may I hear and see him.
                                             They exit.

Scene ⌜5⌝
Enter Regan and ⌜Oswald, the⌝ Steward.

REGAN
But are my brother's powers set forth?
OSWALD   Ay, madam.
REGAN   Himself in person there?

4. **ado:** fuss and trouble

8. **What . . . letter:** i.e., what could my sister's letter say?

10. **is . . . hence:** has hurried away

15. **nighted:** i.e., made as dark as night; **descry:** discover by observation

21. **charged my duty:** i.e., exhorted me to be dutiful

23. **Belike:** probably; or, possibly

28. **at . . . here:** when she was here recently

29. **eliads:** oeillades, loving looks

30. **of her bosom:** in her confidence

32. **Y' are:** i.e., you are

"She that herself will . . . disbranch. . . ." (4.2.43)
From Henry Peacham, *Minerua Britanna* . . . (1612).

OSWALD   Madam, with much ado.
 Your sister is the better soldier.   5
REGAN
 Lord Edmund spake not with your lord at home?
OSWALD   No, madam.
REGAN
 What might import my sister's letter to him?
OSWALD   I know not, lady.
REGAN
 Faith, he is posted hence on serious matter.   10
 It was great ignorance, Gloucester's eyes being out,
 To let him live. Where he arrives he moves
 All hearts against us. Edmund, I think, is gone,
 In pity of his misery, to dispatch
 His nighted life; moreover to descry   15
 The strength o' th' enemy.
OSWALD
 I must needs after him, madam, with my letter.
REGAN
 Our troops set forth tomorrow. Stay with us.
 The ways are dangerous.
OSWALD   I may not, madam.   20
 My lady charged my duty in this business.
REGAN
 Why should she write to Edmund? Might not you
 Transport her purposes by word? Belike,
 Some things—I know not what. I'll love thee much—
 Let me unseal the letter.   25
OSWALD   Madam, I had rather—
REGAN
 I know your lady does not love her husband;
 I am sure of that; and at her late being here,
 She gave strange eliads and most speaking looks
 To noble Edmund. I know you are of her bosom.   30
OSWALD   I, madam?
REGAN
 I speak in understanding. Y' are; I know 't.

33. **take this note:** i.e., take note of the following

35–36. **more . . . lady's:** i.e., it is more appropriate that he marry me than Goneril

36. **gather:** infer, guess

37. **this:** Editors and readers can only guess what Regan is sending to Edmund.

38. **thus much:** i.e., what I am telling you

39. **call . . . her:** i.e., call back her good sense

4.6 To cure Gloucester of despair, Edgar pretends to aid him in a suicide attempt, a fall from Dover Cliff to the beach far below. When Gloucester wakes from his faint, Edgar (now in the disguise of a peasant) tells him that the gods intervened to save his life. The two meet the mad Lear, who talks with Gloucester about lechery, abuses of power, and other human follies. Lear runs off when some of Cordelia's search party come upon him. When Oswald appears and tries to kill Gloucester, Edgar kills Oswald and finds on his body a letter from Goneril to Edmund plotting Albany's death.

---

1. **that . . . hill:** i.e., above the cliffs of Dover, to which Gloucester asked to be led

8. **By:** i.e., because of

Therefore I do advise you take this note:
My lord is dead; Edmund and I have talked,
And more convenient is he for my hand   35
Than for your lady's. You may gather more.
If you do find him, pray you, give him this,
And when your mistress hears thus much from you,
I pray, desire her call her wisdom to her.
So, fare you well.   40
If you do chance to hear of that blind traitor,
Preferment falls on him that cuts him off.

OSWALD
Would I could meet ⟨him,⟩ madam. I should show
What party I do follow.

REGAN   Fare thee well.   45

They exit.

Scene ⌜6⌝
Enter Gloucester and Edgar ⌜dressed as a peasant.⌝

GLOUCESTER
When shall I come to th' top of that same hill?

EDGAR
You do climb up it now. Look how we labor.

GLOUCESTER
Methinks the ground is even.

EDGAR   Horrible steep.
Hark, do you hear the sea?   5

GLOUCESTER   No, truly.

EDGAR
Why then, your other senses grow imperfect
By your eyes' anguish.

GLOUCESTER   So may it be indeed.
Methinks thy voice is altered and thou speak'st   10
In better phrase and matter than thou didst.

17. **so low:** i.e., so far down

18. **wing . . . air:** i.e., are flying halfway down

19. **gross:** large

20. **samphire:** an aromatic herb; **dreadful:** terrifying

23–24. **bark . . . buoy:** i.e., ship appears no larger than its cockboat (a small ship's boat), and her cockboat appears the size of a buoy

25. **for sight:** i.e., to be seen

26. **unnumbered:** innumerable; **pebble:** pebbles (of the beach)

28–29. **the . . . Topple:** i.e., the unsteadiness of my perception causes me to topple

33. **upright:** i.e., up into the air

35. **'s:** i.e., is

37. **Prosper . . . thee:** i.e., make it increase and make you prosper

EDGAR
  You're much deceived; in nothing am I changed
  But in my garments.
GLOUCESTER   Methinks you're better spoken.
EDGAR
  Come on, sir. Here's the place. Stand still. How   15
    fearful
  And dizzy 'tis to cast one's eyes so low!
  The crows and choughs that wing the midway air
  Show scarce so gross as beetles. Halfway down
  Hangs one that gathers samphire—dreadful trade;   20
  Methinks he seems no bigger than his head.
  The fishermen that ⟨walk⟩ upon the beach
  Appear like mice, and yond tall anchoring bark
  Diminished to her cock, her cock a buoy
  Almost too small for sight. The murmuring surge   25
  That on th' unnumbered idle pebble chafes
  Cannot be heard so high. I'll look no more
  Lest my brain turn and the deficient sight
  Topple down headlong.
GLOUCESTER   Set me where you stand.   30
EDGAR
  Give me your hand. You are now within a foot
  Of th' extreme verge. For all beneath the moon
  Would I not leap upright.
GLOUCESTER   Let go my hand.
  Here, friend, 's another purse; in it a jewel   35
  Well worth a poor man's taking. Fairies and gods
  Prosper it with thee.   ⌜*He gives Edgar a purse.*⌝
              Go thou further off.
  Bid me farewell, and let me hear thee going.
EDGAR, ⌜*walking away*⌝
  Now fare you well, good sir.   40
GLOUCESTER   With all my heart.
EDGAR, ⌜*aside*⌝
  Why I do trifle thus with his despair
  Is done to cure it.

48. **To quarrel with:** i.e., into rebellion against; **opposeless:** irresistible

49–50. **My snuff . . . out:** i.e., my useless and despised life could end itself naturally   **snuff:** partially burnt candle wick   **part:** remainder

53. **conceit:** imagination, thought

55. **Yields to:** i.e., cooperates in

58. **pass:** die

59. **What:** i.e., who

61. **aught:** anything

63. **Thou'dst shivered:** i.e., you would have broken to pieces

65. **heavy:** i.e., solid

67. **at each:** end to end

71. **chalky bourn:** i.e., chalk cliff (of Dover)

72. **a-height:** high; **shrill-gorged:** shrill-throated, shrill-voiced

77. **beguile:** foil, cheat

GLOUCESTER   O you mighty gods!   (*He kneels.*)
  This world I do renounce, and in your sights   45
  Shake patiently my great affliction off.
  If I could bear it longer, and not fall
  To quarrel with your great opposeless wills,
  My snuff and loathèd part of nature should
  Burn itself out. If Edgar live, O, bless him!—   50
  Now, fellow, fare thee well.   (*He falls.*)
EDGAR   Gone, sir. Farewell.—
  And yet I know not how conceit may rob
  The treasury of life, when life itself
  Yields to the theft. Had he been where he thought,   55
  By this had thought been past. Alive or dead?—
  Ho you, sir! Friend, hear you. Sir, speak.—
  Thus might he pass indeed. Yet he revives.—
  What are you, sir?
GLOUCESTER   Away, and let me die.   60
EDGAR
  Hadst thou been aught but gossamer, feathers, air,
  So many fathom down precipitating,
  Thou'dst shivered like an egg; but thou dost
    breathe,
  Hast heavy substance, bleed'st not, speak'st, art   65
    sound.
  Ten masts at each make not the altitude
  Which thou hast perpendicularly fell.
  Thy life's a miracle. Speak yet again.
GLOUCESTER   But have I fall'n or no?   70
EDGAR
  From the dread summit of this chalky bourn.
  Look up a-height. The shrill-gorged lark so far
  Cannot be seen or heard. Do but look up.
GLOUCESTER   Alack, I have no eyes.
  Is wretchedness deprived that benefit   75
  To end itself by death? 'Twas yet some comfort
  When misery could beguile the tyrant's rage
  And frustrate his proud will.

88. **whelked:** twisted

89. **happy father:** fortunate old man

90–92. **clearest . . . impossibilities:** i.e., most serene gods, who win veneration by doing what humans cannot do

94–95. **till . . . die:** i.e., until it ends; or, until I die

98. **free:** innocent (i.e., guilt-free); carefree

100–1. **safer sense . . . thus:** i.e., a sane mind will never allow its possessor to dress in this way

102. **touch:** censure; **coining:** counterfeiting

104. **side-piercing:** heart-rending

106. **press-money:** money paid a new recruit upon enlistment (Lear speaks as if he were a recruiting officer.)

106–7. **like a crowkeeper:** i.e., inexpertly, like someone guarding a cornfield from crows

107. **Draw . . . yard:** i.e., draw your bow to a full arrow's length (the length of a **clothier's yard**)

EDGAR   Give me your arm.
                      ⌜*He raises Gloucester.*⌝
  Up. So, how is 't? Feel you your legs? You stand.   80
GLOUCESTER
  Too well, too well.
EDGAR   This is above all strangeness.
  Upon the crown o' th' cliff, what thing was that
  Which parted from you?
GLOUCESTER   A poor unfortunate beggar.   85
EDGAR
  As I stood here below, methought his eyes
  Were two full moons; he had a thousand noses,
  Horns whelked and waved like the enragèd sea.
  It was some fiend. Therefore, thou happy father,
  Think that the clearest gods, who make them   90
    honors
  Of men's impossibilities, have preserved thee.
GLOUCESTER
  I do remember now. Henceforth I'll bear
  Affliction till it do cry out itself
  "Enough, enough!" and die. That thing you speak of,   95
  I took it for a man. Often 'twould say
  "The fiend, the fiend!" He led me to that place.
EDGAR
  Bear free and patient thoughts.

                      Enter Lear.

                      But who comes here?
  The safer sense will ne'er accommodate   100
  His master thus.
LEAR No, they cannot touch me for ⟨coining.⟩ I am the
    King himself.
EDGAR O, thou side-piercing sight!
LEAR Nature's above art in that respect. There's your   105
    press-money. That fellow handles his bow like a
    crowkeeper. Draw me a clothier's yard. Look, look,

109. **prove it on:** uphold my quarrel in a fight

110. **brown bills:** i.e., soldiers carrying brown bills (weapons painted brown to prevent rust); **O, well flown, bird:** perhaps referring to the flight of an (imaginary) arrow

111. **clout:** bull's-eye; **Hewgh:** possibly, the sound of an arrow in flight; **word:** password

116. **like a dog:** i.e., as if they were dogs fawning on me; **white hairs:** representing wisdom

119. **divinity:** theology (Compare James 5.12: "Let your yea be yea and your nay, nay.")

122. **found:** exposed; **Go to:** an expression of impatience

124. **ague-proof:** immune to chills and fevers (**Ague** is pronounced ay-gue.)

125. **trick:** peculiarity

129. **thy cause:** the accusation against you

132. **lecher:** play the lecher (i.e., copulate)

134. **got:** begotten, conceived

135. **luxury:** lechery

136–37. **whose . . . snow:** i.e., whose looks predict a cold (i.e., icily chaste) response   **forks:** perhaps, instruments for propping up a woman's hair; or, perhaps, legs

137. **minces virtue:** enacts virtue mincingly (i.e., in an affected way)

138. **The fitchew:** i.e., neither the polecat

139. **soiled:** perhaps, put out to stud; or, perhaps, lively because fed with green fodder

140. **centaurs:** mythological monsters that were bestial below the waist (See page 206.)

141. **girdle:** i.e., waist

142. **inherit:** possess

a mouse! Peace, peace! This piece of toasted cheese
will do 't. There's my gauntlet; I'll prove it on a
giant. Bring up the brown bills. O, well flown, bird!   110
I' th' clout, i' th' clout! Hewgh! Give the word.
EDGAR   Sweet marjoram.
LEAR   Pass.
GLOUCESTER   I know that voice.
LEAR   Ha! Goneril with a white beard? They flattered   115
me like a dog and told me I had the white hairs in
my beard ere the black ones were there. To say "ay"
and "no" to everything that I said "ay" and "no" to
was no good divinity. When the rain came to wet me
once and the wind to make me chatter, when the   120
thunder would not peace at my bidding, there I
found 'em, there I smelt 'em out. Go to. They are
not men o' their words; they told me I was everything. 'Tis a lie. I am not ague-proof.
GLOUCESTER
The trick of that voice I do well remember.   125
Is 't not the King?
LEAR   Ay, every inch a king.
When I do stare, see how the subject quakes.
I pardon that man's life. What was thy cause?
Adultery? Thou shalt not die. Die for adultery? No.   130
The wren goes to 't, and the small gilded fly does
lecher in my sight. Let copulation thrive, for
Gloucester's bastard son was kinder to his father
than my daughters got 'tween the lawful sheets. To
't, luxury, pell-mell, for I lack soldiers. Behold yond   135
simp'ring dame, whose face between her forks
presages snow, that minces virtue and does shake
the head to hear of pleasure's name. The fitchew
nor the soiled horse goes to 't with a more riotous
appetite. Down from the waist they are centaurs,   140
though women all above. But to the girdle do the
gods inherit; beneath is all the fiend's. There's hell,

145. **civet:** musky perfume; **apothecary:** pharmacist

150. **so:** in the same way

152. **squinny:** squint; **Cupid:** the Roman god of love, often depicted as blindfolded

156. **take:** believe, credit; **It is:** i.e., it is actually taking place

159. **case:** i.e., sockets

160. **are . . . me:** i.e., is this what you mean?

162. **heavy case:** sad condition; **light:** i.e., empty

164. **feelingly:** (1) by the sense of touch; (2) by feeling pain

167. **simple:** humble, ordinary

168. **handy-dandy:** a trick in which one asks a child to choose which of one's hands holds a treat

173. **image:** likeness, model

173–74. **a dog's . . . office:** i.e., even a dog is obeyed when it's in a position of power

"Blind Cupid." (4.6.152)
Anonymous engraving inserted in Jacques Callot, *Le petit passion* . . . (n.d.).

there's darkness, there is the sulphurous pit; burn-
ing, scalding, stench, consumption! Fie, fie, fie, pah,
pah! Give me an ounce of civet, good apothecary;   145
sweeten my imagination. There's money for thee.
GLOUCESTER   O, let me kiss that hand!
LEAR   Let me wipe it first; it smells of mortality.
GLOUCESTER
O ruined piece of nature! This great world
Shall so wear out to naught. Dost thou know me?   150
LEAR   I remember thine eyes well enough. Dost thou
squinny at me? No, do thy worst, blind Cupid, I'll
not love. Read thou this challenge. Mark but the
penning of it.
GLOUCESTER
Were all thy letters suns, I could not see.   155
EDGAR, ⌈*aside*⌉
I would not take this from report. It is,
And my heart breaks at it.
LEAR   Read.
GLOUCESTER   What, with the case of eyes?
LEAR   Oho, are you there with me? No eyes in your   160
head, nor no money in your purse? Your eyes are in
a heavy case, your purse in a light, yet you see how
this world goes.
GLOUCESTER   I see it feelingly.
LEAR   What, art mad? A man may see how this world   165
goes with no eyes. Look with thine ears. See how
yond justice rails upon yond simple thief. Hark in
thine ear. Change places and, handy-dandy, which
is the justice, which is the thief? Thou hast seen a
farmer's dog bark at a beggar?   170
GLOUCESTER   Ay, sir.
LEAR   And the creature run from the cur? There thou
might'st behold the great image of authority: a
dog's obeyed in office.

175. **beadle:** inferior parish officer responsible for punishing petty offenders

177. **kind:** way

178. **usurer:** moneylender

179. **cozener:** cheat, fraud, impostor

181. **Plate:** i.e., arm in plate armor

183. **hurtless:** i.e., harmlessly

185. **able:** authorize; vouch for

192. **matter and impertinency:** sense and absurdity

198. **Mark:** pay attention

201. **This':** i.e., this is; **block:** style of hat

202. **delicate:** wonderfully ingenious

203. **put 't in proof:** i.e., put it to the test

A centaur. (4.6.140)
From Gabriel Rollenhagen, *Nucleus emblematum selectissimorum* . . . (1611).

Thou rascal beadle, hold thy bloody hand!   175
Why dost thou lash that whore? Strip thy own back.
Thou hotly lusts to use her in that kind
For which thou whipp'st her. The usurer hangs the
  cozener.
Through tattered clothes ⟨small⟩ vices do appear.   180
Robes and furred gowns hide all. [⌜Plate sin⌝ with
  gold,
And the strong lance of justice hurtless breaks.
Arm it in rags, a pygmy's straw does pierce it.
None does offend, none, I say, none; I'll able 'em.   185
Take that of me, my friend, who have the power
To seal th' accuser's lips.] Get thee glass eyes,
And like a scurvy politician
Seem to see the things thou dost not. Now, now,
  now, now.   190
Pull off my boots. Harder, harder. So.
EDGAR, ⌜*aside*⌝
  O, matter and impertinency mixed,
  Reason in madness!
LEAR
  If thou wilt weep my fortunes, take my eyes.
  I know thee well enough; thy name is Gloucester.   195
  Thou must be patient. We came crying hither;
  Thou know'st the first time that we smell the air
  We wawl and cry. I will preach to thee. Mark.
GLOUCESTER   Alack, alack the day!
LEAR
  When we are born, we cry that we are come   200
  To this great stage of fools.—This' a good block.
  It were a delicate stratagem to shoe
  A troop of horse with felt. I'll put 't in proof,
  And when I have stol'n upon these son-in-laws,
  Then kill, kill, kill, kill, kill, kill!   205

    Enter a Gentleman ⌜*and Attendants.*⌝

210. **natural fool of fortune:** one born to be the plaything of fortune

214. **seconds:** attendants, supporters

215. **of salt:** i.e., of tears

218. **bravely:** (1) courageously; (2) gorgeously dressed; **smug:** neat, trim in appearance

222. **an:** if

223. **Sa . . . sa:** a cry to hunting dogs to chase their prey

224. **meanest:** of lowest degree, poorest

226. **general:** universal

227. **her:** i.e., nature

228. **gentle:** noble

229. **speed:** i.e., God speed (May God make you prosper!)

230. **toward:** about to happen

231. **vulgar:** of common knowledge

231–32. **Everyone . . . sound:** i.e., everyone who can hear hears of the battle

GENTLEMAN, ⌜*noticing Lear*⌝
  O, here he is. ⌜*To an Attendant.*⌝ Lay hand upon
    him.—Sir,
  Your most dear daughter—
LEAR
  No rescue? What, a prisoner? I am even
  The natural fool of fortune. Use me well.   210
  You shall have ransom. Let me have surgeons;
  I am cut to' th' brains.
GENTLEMAN You shall have anything.
LEAR No seconds? All myself?
  Why, this would make a man a man of salt,   215
  To use his eyes for garden waterpots,
  ⟨Ay, and laying autumn's dust.⟩
  I will die bravely like a smug bridegroom. What?
  I will be jovial. Come, come, I am a king,
  Masters, know you that?   220
GENTLEMAN
  You are a royal one, and we obey you.
LEAR Then there's life in 't. Come, an you get it, you
    shall get it by running. Sa, sa, sa, sa.
      ⟨*The King exits running* ⌜*pursued by Attendants.*⌝⟩
GENTLEMAN
  A sight most pitiful in the meanest wretch,
  Past speaking of in a king. Thou hast a daughter   225
  Who redeems nature from the general curse
  Which twain have brought her to.
EDGAR Hail, gentle sir.
GENTLEMAN Sir, speed you. What's your will?
EDGAR
  Do you hear aught, sir, of a battle toward?   230
GENTLEMAN
  Most sure and vulgar. Everyone hears that,
  Which can distinguish sound.
EDGAR   But, by your favor,
  How near 's the other army?

235–36. **The . . . thought:** i.e., the main part of the army is expected every hour to be in sight

238. **Though that:** i.e., although; **on:** because of

244. **father:** common term of address to an old man

245. **what:** i.e., who

246. **tame:** servile, meek

247. **known:** experienced; **feeling:** deeply felt, acute

248. **pregnant:** inclined

249. **biding:** dwelling

251–52. **The bounty . . . boot:** i.e., and, besides my thanks, I pray that you receive the gifts and blessing of heaven as your reward **To boot:** into the bargain

253. **happy:** fortunate, lucky

256. **thyself remember:** i.e., recall and repent your sins

GENTLEMAN
Near and on speedy foot. The main descry 235
Stands on the hourly thought.

EDGAR   I thank you, sir. That's all.

GENTLEMAN
Though that the Queen on special cause is here,
Her army is moved on.

EDGAR   I thank you, sir. 240

⌜Gentleman⌝ exits.

GLOUCESTER
You ever-gentle gods, take my breath from me;
Let not my worser spirit tempt me again
To die before you please.

EDGAR   Well pray you, father.

GLOUCESTER   Now, good sir, what are you? 245

EDGAR
A most poor man, made tame to fortune's blows,
Who, by the art of known and feeling sorrows,
Am pregnant to good pity. Give me your hand;
I'll lead you to some biding.

⌜He takes Gloucester's hand.⌝

GLOUCESTER   Hearty thanks. 250
The bounty and the benison of heaven
To boot, and boot.

Enter ⌜Oswald, the⌝ Steward.

OSWALD, *⌜drawing his sword⌝*
                    A proclaimed prize! Most happy!
That eyeless head of thine was first framed flesh
To raise my fortunes. Thou old unhappy traitor, 255
Briefly thyself remember; the sword is out
That must destroy thee.

GLOUCESTER   Now let thy friendly hand
Put strength enough to 't.

⌜Edgar steps between Gloucester and Oswald.⌝

OSWALD   Wherefore, bold peasant, 260

261. **published:** proclaimed

262. **Lest:** i.e., to prevent the possibility

263. **Like:** similar

264. **Chill:** i.e., I will; **vurther 'casion:** further occasion or cause (Here Edgar assumes a dialect that signaled that the speaker was from the country.)

266. **gait:** way

267–68. **An . . . life:** if I could have been killed by mere swaggering or blustering

268–69. **'twould . . . vortnight:** it (my life) would not have been so long as it is by a fortnight

270. **che vor' ye:** I warn you; **Ise:** I will; **costard:** head (slang)

271. **ballow:** perhaps, walking stick (This word is not recorded elsewhere.)

273–74. **no matter . . . foins:** i.e., I do not care about your (sword) thrusts

275. **Villain:** i.e., villein, peasant

277. **about:** upon

279. **Upon:** on; **party:** side

280. **serviceable:** active and diligent in service

287. **deathsman:** executioner

288. **Leave:** i.e., give me leave; permit me; **wax:** i.e., the seal on the letter

292–93. **your will want not:** i.e., you do not lack the will

293. **fruitfully:** (1) fully, completely; (2) so as to produce good results

Dar'st thou support a published traitor? Hence,
Lest that th' infection of his fortune take
Like hold on thee. Let go his arm.

EDGAR   Chill not let go, zir, without vurther 'casion.

OSWALD   Let go, slave, or thou diest!   265

EDGAR   Good gentleman, go your gait, and let poor
volk pass. An 'chud ha' bin zwaggered out of my
life, 'twould not ha' bin zo long as 'tis by a vortnight. Nay, come not near th' old man. Keep out,
che vor' ye, or Ise try whether your costard or my   270
ballow be the harder. Chill be plain with you.

OSWALD   Out, dunghill.

EDGAR   Chill pick your teeth, zir. Come, no matter vor
your foins.   ⟨*They fight.*⟩

OSWALD, ⌜*falling*⌝
Slave, thou hast slain me. Villain, take my purse.   275
If ever thou wilt thrive, bury my body,
And give the letters which thou find'st about me
To Edmund, Earl of Gloucester. Seek him out
Upon the English party. O, untimely death! Death!
                              ⟨*He dies.*⟩

EDGAR
I know thee well, a serviceable villain,   280
As duteous to the vices of thy mistress
As badness would desire.

GLOUCESTER   What, is he dead?

EDGAR   Sit you down, father; rest you.
Let's see these pockets. The letters that he speaks of   285
May be my friends. He's dead; I am only sorry
He had no other deathsman. Let us see.
                    ⌜*He opens a letter.*⌝
Leave, gentle wax, and, manners, blame us not.
To know our enemies' minds, we rip their hearts.
Their papers is more lawful.   *Reads the letter.*   290
Let our reciprocal vows be remembered. You have
many opportunities to cut him off. If your will want
not, time and place will be fruitfully offered. There is

296–97. **supply . . . labor:** i.e., take his place as a reward for the labor (of killing him)

299. **for . . . venture:** i.e., empowered to put herself at risk for you   **venture:** an enterprise involving risk

300. **indistinguished . . . will:** boundlessness of woman's desire

303. **rake up:** i.e., bury in a shallow grave; **post:** messenger

304. **in the mature time:** in due time

305. **ungracious:** wicked

306. **death-practiced duke:** i.e., duke whose death has been plotted

308–10. **How stiff . . . sorrows:** i.e., how stubborn is my disgusting sanity that it keeps me standing and makes me aware of my great sorrows

310. **distract:** distracted, insane

312. **wrong imaginations:** false beliefs, delusions

316. **bestow:** house, lodge

4.7   In the French camp, Lear is waked by the doctor treating him and is reunited with Cordelia.

———————

4. **o'erpaid:** i.e., to be paid too much

nothing done if he return the conqueror. Then am I
the prisoner, and his bed my jail, from the loathed   295
warmth whereof deliver me and supply the place for
your labor.
　　　Your (wife, so I would say) affectionate servant,
　　　⟨*and, for you, her own for venture,*⟩　　*Goneril.*
O indistinguished space of woman's will!   300
A plot upon her virtuous husband's life,
And the exchange my brother.—Here, in the sands
Thee I'll rake up, the post unsanctified
Of murderous lechers; and in the mature time
With this ungracious paper strike the sight   305
Of the death-practiced duke. For him 'tis well
That of thy death and business I can tell.

GLOUCESTER
The King is mad. How stiff is my vile sense
That I stand up and have ingenious feeling
Of my huge sorrows! Better I were distract.   310
So should my thoughts be severed from my griefs,
And woes, by wrong imaginations, lose
The knowledge of themselves.　　*Drum afar off.*

EDGAR　　　　　　　　　　Give me your hand.
Far off methinks I hear the beaten drum.   315
Come, father, I'll bestow you with a friend.
　　　　　　　　　　　　　　They exit.

Scene 7
Enter Cordelia, Kent ⌐*in disguise,*⌐ ⟨*Doctor,*⟩ *and*
Gentleman.

CORDELIA
O, thou good Kent, how shall I live and work
To match thy goodness? My life will be too short,
And every measure fail me.

KENT
To be acknowledged, madam, is o'erpaid.

5. **All . . . go:** perhaps, may all reports about me conform; or, perhaps, all my reports to you have conformed

6. **Nor . . . clipped:** i.e., neither more nor less

7. **suited:** dressed

8. **weeds:** clothes; **memories:** reminders

11. **to . . . intent:** i.e., to be recognized would make the plan I have formed fall short

12. **My . . . not:** i.e., I ask you, as a favor, not to acknowledge me

13. **meet:** fitting

15. **sleeps:** i.e., he sleeps

18. **wind up:** put in tune

19. **child-changèd:** (1) changed (driven mad) by his children; (2) changed to a child

24. **I' th' sway:** i.e., according to the authority

28. **I . . . temperance:** i.e., I do not fear he will lose self-control

All my reports go with the modest truth,   5
Nor more, nor clipped, but so.
CORDELIA   Be better suited.
These weeds are memories of those worser hours.
I prithee put them off.
KENT   Pardon, dear madam.   10
Yet to be known shortens my made intent.
My boon I make it that you know me not
Till time and I think meet.
CORDELIA
Then be 't so, my good lord.—How does the King?
⟨DOCTOR⟩   Madam, sleeps still.   15
CORDELIA   O, you kind gods,
Cure this great breach in his abusèd nature!
Th' untuned and jarring senses, O, wind up,
Of this child-changèd father!
⟨DOCTOR⟩   So please your Majesty   20
That we may wake the King? He hath slept
    long.
CORDELIA
Be governed by your knowledge, and proceed
I' th' sway of your own will. Is he arrayed?

    Enter Lear in a chair carried by Servants.

GENTLEMAN
Ay, madam. In the heaviness of sleep,   25
We put fresh garments on him.
⌜DOCTOR⌝
Be by, good madam, when we do awake him.
I doubt ⟨not⟩ of his temperance.
⟨CORDELIA   Very well.
                                   ⌜*Music.*⌝
DOCTOR
Please you, draw near.—Louder the music there.⟩   30
CORDELIA, ⌜*kissing Lear*⌝
O, my dear father, restoration hang

32. **Thy medicine:** i.e., medicine for you

34. **thy reverence:** i.e., you, whom they should hold in reverence

36. **Had you:** i.e., even if you had; **flakes:** i.e., hairs

37. **challenge:** require, demand

39. **deep:** i.e., deep-voiced; **dread-bolted thunder:** i.e., dreadful bolts of thunder

41. **cross-lightning:** zigzag lightning; **perdu:** i.e., a *sentinel perdu,* or solitary sentinel standing watch in a very dangerous place

42. **helm:** helmet (i.e., his thin hair)

44. **Against:** i.e., by; **fain:** glad

45. **rogues forlorn:** wretched vagabonds

46. **short:** i.e., broken

48. **concluded all:** all come to an end

53. **wheel of fire:** Those condemned to death were sometimes bound to a wheel and tortured. Here, the reference to fire seems to suggest torture in hell. (See page 220.)

57. **wide:** i.e., wide of the mark (in a deluded state)

60. **abused:** (1) wronged; (2) deceived; (3) worn out

Thy medicine on my lips, and let this kiss
Repair those violent harms that my two sisters
Have in thy reverence made.
KENT   Kind and dear princess.   35
CORDELIA
Had you not been their father, these white flakes
Did challenge pity of them. Was this a face
To be opposed against the jarring winds?
⟨To stand against the deep dread-bolted thunder,
In the most terrible and nimble stroke   40
Of quick cross-lightning? To watch, poor *perdu*,
With this thin helm?⟩ Mine enemy's dog,
Though he had bit me, should have stood that night
Against my fire. And wast thou fain, poor father,
To hovel thee with swine and rogues forlorn   45
In short and musty straw? Alack, alack,
'Tis wonder that thy life and wits at once
Had not concluded all.—He wakes. Speak to him.
⟨DOCTOR⟩   Madam, do you; 'tis fittest.
CORDELIA
How does my royal lord? How fares your Majesty?   50
LEAR
You do me wrong to take me out o' th' grave.
Thou art a soul in bliss, but I am bound
Upon a wheel of fire, that mine own tears
Do scald like molten lead.
CORDELIA   Sir, do you know me?   55
LEAR
You are a spirit, I know. Where did you die?
CORDELIA   Still, still, far wide.
⟨DOCTOR⟩
He's scarce awake. Let him alone awhile.
LEAR
Where have I been? Where am I? Fair daylight?
I am mightily abused; I should e'en die with pity   60

61. **thus:** i.e., in my condition
69. **fond:** silly; dazed
74. **mainly:** entirely
90. **abuse:** deceive; or, mistreat
91. **rage:** madness, insanity
92. **danger:** i.e., dangerous
93. **even o'er:** i.e., fill in; **lost:** forgotten

"Bound upon a wheel of fire." (4.7.52–53)
From Giovanni Ferro, *Teatro d'imprese* . . . (1623).

To see another thus. I know not what to say.
I will not swear these are my hands. Let's see.
I feel this pinprick. Would I were assured
Of my condition!
CORDELIA   O, look upon me, sir,   65
And hold your hand in benediction o'er me.
⟨No, sir,⟩ you must not kneel.
LEAR   Pray do not mock:
I am a very foolish fond old man,
Fourscore and upward, not an hour more nor less,   70
And to deal plainly,
I fear I am not in my perfect mind.
Methinks I should know you and know this man,
Yet I am doubtful, for I am mainly ignorant
What place this is, and all the skill I have   75
Remembers not these garments; nor I know not
Where I did lodge last night. Do not laugh at me,
For, as I am a man, I think this lady
To be my child Cordelia.
CORDELIA, ⌈*weeping*⌉ And so I am; I am.   80
LEAR
Be your tears wet? Yes, faith. I pray, weep not.
If you have poison for me, I will drink it.
I know you do not love me, for your sisters
Have, as I do remember, done me wrong.
You have some cause; they have not.   85
CORDELIA   No cause, no
    cause.
LEAR   Am I in France?
KENT   In your own kingdom, sir.
LEAR   Do not abuse me.   90
⟨DOCTOR⟩
Be comforted, good madam. The great rage,
You see, is killed in him, ⟨and yet it is danger
To make him even o'er the time he has lost.⟩

95. **settling:** calming (of his mind)

100. **Holds it true:** i.e., is it a fact

103. **conductor:** leader

108. **powers . . . kingdom:** i.e., armies of Britain

109. **arbitrament:** settlement of the dispute; **like:** i.e., likely

111. **My . . . period:** i.e., the conclusion (of my life; or, perhaps, of my plans); **throughly wrought:** worked out completely

112. **Or . . . or:** either . . . or; **as . . . fought:** according to the outcome of today's battle

Desire him to go in. Trouble him no more
Till further settling. 95
CORDELIA Will 't please your Highness walk?
LEAR You must bear with me.
Pray you now, forget, and forgive. I am old and
    foolish. ⟨*They exit. Kent and Gentleman remain.*⟩
⟨GENTLEMAN Holds it true, sir, that the Duke of Corn- 100
wall was so slain?
KENT Most certain, sir.
GENTLEMAN Who is conductor of his people?
KENT As 'tis said, the bastard son of Gloucester.
GENTLEMAN They say Edgar, his banished son, is with 105
the Earl of Kent in Germany.
KENT Report is changeable. 'Tis time to look about.
The powers of the kingdom approach apace.
GENTLEMAN The arbitrament is like to be bloody. Fare
you well, sir.   ⌈*He exits.*⌉ 110
KENT
My point and period will be throughly wrought,
Or well, or ill, as this day's battle's fought.
He exits.⟩

The Tragedy of

KING LEAR

ACT 5

5.1 Albany joins his forces with Regan's (led by Edmund) to oppose the French invasion. Edgar, still in disguise, approaches Albany with the letter plotting Albany's death, and promises to produce a champion to maintain the authenticity of the letter in a trial by combat. Edmund then enters and, when alone, reflects upon his possible marriage to either Goneril or Regan and upon his intention to have Cordelia and Lear killed if the British forces are victorious.

---

1. **Know . . . hold:** i.e., learn from Albany if he is firm in his latest decision
2. **since:** i.e., since then
3. **alteration:** changes (of mind)
4. **constant pleasure:** settled intention
5. **man:** i.e., Oswald; **miscarried:** come to harm, perished
6. **doubted:** feared
11. **honored:** i.e., honorable
13. **forfended:** forbidden
14. **That . . . you:** i.e., you wrong yourself in having such a thought
15. **doubtful:** fearful
15–16. **conjunct . . . bosomed:** united and intimate

ACT 5

Scene 1

Enter, with Drum and Colors, Edmund, Regan,
Gentlemen, and Soldiers.

EDMUND, ⌜*to a Gentleman*⌝
Know of the Duke if his last purpose hold,
Or whether since he is advised by aught
To change the course. He's full of alteration
And self-reproving. Bring his constant pleasure.
                                        ⌜*A Gentleman exits.*⌝
REGAN
Our sister's man is certainly miscarried.   5
EDMUND
'Tis to be doubted, madam.
REGAN   Now, sweet lord,
You know the goodness I intend upon you;
Tell me but truly, but then speak the truth,
Do you not love my sister?   10
EDMUND   In honored love.
REGAN
But have you never found my brother's way
To the forfended place?
⟨EDMUND   That thought abuses you.
REGAN
I am doubtful that you have been conjunct   15
And bosomed with her as far as we call hers.⟩
EDMUND   No, by mine honor, madam.

227

20. **Fear me not:** do not doubt me

23. **bemet:** met

25. **rigor . . . state:** harshness of our government

26. **Where:** i.e., in situations where; **honest:** honorable

27. **For:** i.e., as for

28. **touches us:** concerns or moves me; **as . . . land:** i.e., in that it is a French invasion

29–30. **Not . . . oppose:** i.e., not insofar as France emboldens Lear and others who oppose us for just and serious reasons

32. **reasoned:** i.e., being discussed

34. **particular broils:** personal quarrels

36. **determine:** decide

37. **th' ancient of war:** i.e., our officers with the most military experience

38. **presently:** at once

39. **us:** i.e., me

41. **convenient:** (1) suitable; (2) morally proper

REGAN
  I never shall endure her. Dear my lord,
  Be not familiar with her.

EDMUND
  Fear ⟨me⟩ not. She and the Duke, her husband.   20

Enter, with Drum and Colors, Albany, Goneril, Soldiers.

⟨GONERIL, ⌐*aside*⌐
  I had rather lose the battle than that sister
  Should loosen him and me.⟩

ALBANY
  Our very loving sister, well bemet.—
  Sir, this I heard: the King is come to his daughter,
  With others whom the rigor of our state   25
  Forced to cry out. ⟨Where I could not be honest,
  I never yet was valiant. For this business,
  It touches us as France invades our land,
  Not bolds the King, with others whom, I fear,
  Most just and heavy causes make oppose.   30

EDMUND
  Sir, you speak nobly.⟩

REGAN   Why is this reasoned?

GONERIL
  Combine together 'gainst the enemy,
  For these domestic and particular broils
  Are not the question here.   35

ALBANY   Let's then determine
  With th' ancient of war on our proceeding.

⟨EDMUND
  I shall attend you presently at your tent.⟩

REGAN   Sister, you'll go with us?

GONERIL   No.   40

REGAN
  'Tis most convenient. Pray, go with us.

GONERIL, ⌐*aside*⌐
  Oho, I know the riddle.—I will go.
                    ⌐*They begin to exit.*⌐

47–48. **sound / For:** i.e., summon

49. **prove:** i.e., establish as true in a trial by combat

50. **avouchèd:** asserted; **miscarry:** lose; are killed

57. **o'erlook:** read

58. **powers:** armed forces

60. **discovery:** reconnaissance

62. **greet the time:** i.e., be ready when the time comes

64. **jealous:** suspicious

Enter Edgar ⌜dressed as a peasant.⌝

EDGAR, ⌜*to Albany*⌝
If e'er your Grace had speech with man so poor,
Hear me one word.
ALBANY, ⌜*to those exiting*⌝
⠀⠀⠀⠀⠀⠀⠀⠀I'll overtake you.—Speak.⠀⠀⠀⠀⠀45
⠀⠀⠀⠀⠀⠀⠀⠀⠀⠀*Both the armies exit.*
EDGAR, ⌜*giving him a paper*⌝
Before you fight the battle, ope this letter.
If you have victory, let the trumpet sound
For him that brought it. Wretched though I seem,
I can produce a champion that will prove
What is avouchèd there. If you miscarry,⠀⠀⠀50
Your business of the world hath so an end,
And machination ceases. Fortune ⟨love⟩ you.
ALBANY⠀⠀Stay till I have read the letter.
EDGAR⠀⠀I was forbid it.
When time shall serve, let but the herald cry⠀⠀55
And I'll appear again.⠀⠀⠀⠀⠀*He exits.*
ALBANY
Why, fare thee well. I will o'erlook thy paper.

Enter Edmund.

EDMUND
The enemy's in view. Draw up your powers.
⠀⠀⠀⠀⠀⠀⌜*Giving him a paper.*⌝
Here is the guess of their true strength and forces
By diligent discovery. But your haste⠀⠀⠀60
Is now urged on you.
ALBANY⠀⠀⠀⠀⠀⠀We will greet the time.
⠀⠀⠀⠀⠀⠀⠀⠀⠀⠀⠀*He exits.*
EDMUND
To both these sisters have I sworn my love,
Each jealous of the other as the stung
Are of the adder. Which of them shall I take?⠀⠀65

69. **hardly:** with difficulty
70. **Her:** i.e., Goneril's
71. **countenance:** rank and position; repute in the world
73. **taking off:** murder
76. **Shall:** i.e., they shall
76–77. **my state / Stands on me:** my position depends on me

5.2   Cordelia's French army is defeated.

———————

0 SD. **Alarum:** call to arms ("All arm")
1. **father:** a polite address to an old man
5 SD. **Retreat:** trumpet call for a retreat
7. **ta'en:** i.e., have been taken

Both? One? Or neither? Neither can be enjoyed
If both remain alive. To take the widow
Exasperates, makes mad her sister Goneril,
And hardly shall I carry out my side,
Her husband being alive. Now, then, we'll use   70
His countenance for the battle, which, being done,
Let her who would be rid of him devise
His speedy taking off. As for the mercy
Which he intends to Lear and to Cordelia,
The battle done and they within our power,   75
Shall never see his pardon, for my state
Stands on me to defend, not to debate.
                                        He exits.

Scene 2
Alarum within. Enter, with Drum and Colors, Lear,
Cordelia, and Soldiers, over the stage, and exit.
Enter Edgar and Gloucester.

EDGAR
Here, father, take the shadow of this tree
For your good host. Pray that the right may thrive.
If ever I return to you again,
I'll bring you comfort.
GLOUCESTER   Grace go with you, sir.   5
                        ⌜*Edgar*⌝ *exits.*
                        Alarum and Retreat within.

                        Enter Edgar.

EDGAR
Away, old man. Give me thy hand. Away.
King Lear hath lost, he and his daughter ta'en.
Give me thy hand. Come on.
GLOUCESTER
No further, sir. A man may rot even here.

5.3 Edmund sends Lear and Cordelia to prison and secretly commissions their assassination. Albany confronts Edmund and Goneril with their intended treachery against him and calls for the champion that Edgar said he would produce. Edgar himself, in full armor, appears to accuse Edmund of treachery. In the ensuing trial by combat, Edgar mortally wounds Edmund. Edgar reveals his identity, tells about his life as Poor Tom, and describes Gloucester's death. A messenger announces the deaths of Regan (who has been poisoned by Goneril) and Goneril (who has committed suicide). Kent, no longer in disguise, arrives in search of Lear. Edmund confesses that he has ordered the deaths of Lear and of Cordelia. While a messenger rushes to the prison to save them, Lear enters bearing the dead Cordelia. As Albany makes plans to restore Lear to the throne, Lear himself dies.

----

1. **Good guard:** i.e., guard them well
3. **censure:** pronounce judicial sentence on
5. **meaning:** purposes
7. **else:** otherwise
8. **daughters . . . sisters:** i.e., Goneril and Regan
18. **wear out:** outlast
20. **That . . . moon:** i.e., whose fortunes change with the tides

EDGAR
What, in ill thoughts again? Men must endure   10
Their going hence even as their coming hither.
Ripeness is all. Come on.
[GLOUCESTER   And that's true too.]
                                        They exit.

                              Scene 3
Enter in conquest, with Drum and Colors, Edmund;
Lear and Cordelia as prisoners; Soldiers, Captain.

EDMUND
Some officers take them away. Good guard
Until their greater pleasures first be known
That are to censure them.
CORDELIA, ⌜*to Lear*⌝   We are not the first
Who with best meaning have incurred the worst.   5
For thee, oppressèd king, I am cast down.
Myself could else outfrown false Fortune's frown.
Shall we not see these daughters and these sisters?
LEAR
No, no, no, no. Come, let's away to prison.
We two alone will sing like birds i' th' cage.   10
When thou dost ask me blessing, I'll kneel down
And ask of thee forgiveness. So we'll live,
And pray, and sing, and tell old tales, and laugh
At gilded butterflies, and hear poor rogues
Talk of court news, and we'll talk with them too—   15
Who loses and who wins; who's in, who's out—
And take upon 's the mystery of things,
As if we were God's spies. And we'll wear out,
In a walled prison, packs and sects of great ones
That ebb and flow by th' moon.   20
EDMUND   Take them away.
LEAR
Upon such sacrifices, my Cordelia,

23. **throw incense:** The image is of a rite of sacrifice in which those celebrating the ritual throw incense on the burnt offering. Here, it is the gods themselves who celebrate the sacrifice.

25. **shall:** i.e., will have to; **brand:** i.e., piece of burning wood

26. **fire us . . . foxes:** i.e., drive us apart with fire as foxes are driven out of their dens

27. **good years:** It has been suggested that this should be printed as "goodyears," and that it is a rare plural form of a term used to denote an unnamed evil power. It seems just as likely that the Folio's **good years** is the correct reading and that Lear is simply referring to the passage of time. **fell:** skin

37. **Does . . . sword:** i.e., is not fitting for a soldier

38. **bear:** allow for

41. **write "happy":** i.e., regard yourself as fortunate; **th':** thou

42. **carry it so:** i.e., carry it out exactly

46. **strain:** (1) disposition; (2) lineage

48. **opposites of:** opponents in

The gods themselves throw incense. Have I caught
    thee?
He that parts us shall bring a brand from heaven   25
And fire us hence like foxes. Wipe thine eyes.
The good years shall devour them, flesh and fell,
Ere they shall make us weep. We'll see 'em starved
    first.
Come.   30

⌐*Lear and Cordelia*⌐ exit, ⌐*with Soldiers.*⌐

EDMUND Come hither, captain. Hark.
                    ⌐*Handing him a paper.*⌐
Take thou this note. Go follow them to prison.
One step I have advanced thee. If thou dost
As this instructs thee, thou dost make thy way
To noble fortunes. Know thou this: that men   35
Are as the time is; to be tender-minded
Does not become a sword. Thy great employment
Will not bear question. Either say thou'lt do 't,
Or thrive by other means.
CAPTAIN   I'll do 't, my lord.   40
EDMUND
About it, and write "happy" when th' hast done.
Mark, I say, instantly, and carry it so
As I have set it down.
⟨CAPTAIN
I cannot draw a cart, nor eat dried oats.
If it be man's work, I'll do 't.⟩   *Captain exits.* 45

Flourish. Enter Albany, Goneril, Regan, Soldiers ⌐*and a
                    Captain.*⌐

ALBANY, ⌐*to Edmund*⌐
Sir, you have showed today your valiant strain,
And Fortune led you well. You have the captives
Who were the opposites of this day's strife.
I do require them of you, so to use them
As we shall find their merits and our safety   50
May equally determine.

54. **retention . . . guard:** confinement under a specially appointed guard

55–57. **Whose . . . eyes:** i.e., Lear's old age and title will persuade the populace to take his side, and our own lancers (drafted from the populace) will turn against us

58. **Which:** i.e., who

61. **further space:** i.e., a later date

64–65. **And . . . sharpness:** i.e., before the heat of battle has cooled, the best of causes are cursed by those who have had to endure the pain of the battle

68. **by . . . patience:** a polite phrase, like "by your leave"

69. **hold:** regard; **but a subject of:** i.e., only as a subordinate in

71. **we list:** I choose; **grace:** confer dignity (or a title) on

72. **pleasure:** wishes; **demanded:** consulted

74. **place:** position

75. **immediacy:** i.e., direct connection to me

79. **your addition:** the title you give him

80–81. **In . . . invested:** i.e., endowed with my power and authority

81. **compeers:** is equal to

82. **That were the most:** i.e., that would be the most (that you could invest him with)

83. **Jesters . . . prophets:** Here Regan combines two proverbs: "There is many a true word spoken in jest" and "Fools [**jesters**] and children do often prophesy."

85. **That . . . asquint:** Goneril replies by alluding to another proverb: "Love, being jealous, makes a good eye look asquint."

EDMUND Sir, I thought it fit
To send the old and miserable king
To some retention ⟨and appointed guard,⟩
Whose age had charms in it, whose title more,   55
To pluck the common bosom on his side
And turn our impressed lances in our eyes,
Which do command them. With him I sent the
   Queen,
My reason all the same, and they are ready   60
Tomorrow, or at further space, t' appear
Where you shall hold your session. ⟨At this time
We sweat and bleed. The friend hath lost his friend,
And the best quarrels in the heat are cursed
By those that feel their sharpness.   65
The question of Cordelia and her father
Requires a fitter place.⟩
ALBANY   Sir, by your patience,
I hold you but a subject of this war,
Not as a brother.   70
REGAN   That's as we list to grace him.
Methinks our pleasure might have been demanded
Ere you had spoke so far. He led our powers,
Bore the commission of my place and person,
The which immediacy may well stand up   75
And call itself your brother.
GONERIL   Not so hot.
In his own grace he doth exalt himself
More than in your addition.
REGAN   In my rights,   80
By me invested, he compeers the best.
⟨GONERIL⟩
That were the most if he should husband you.
REGAN
Jesters do oft prove prophets.
GONERIL   Holla, holla!
That eye that told you so looked but asquint.   85

87. **full-flowing stomach:** i.e., with a great flow of angry words (**Stomach** often meant "anger.")

90. **the . . . thine:** Regan surrenders herself like a walled town or fortress.

91. **Witness the world:** i.e., let the world witness

94. **let-alone:** i.e., granting or withholding of permission

96. **Half-blooded:** illegitimate

97. **strike:** as a signal for battle

99. **On . . . treason:** for high treason; **in thine attaint:** (1) as another tainted by your crime; (2) as your accuser (as Goneril has become through Albany's possession of her letter to Edmund)

103. **subcontracted:** i.e., contracted, engaged

104. **your banns:** i.e., the proclamation of your marriage to Edmund

106. **bespoke:** already spoken for

107. **an interlude:** i.e., a play

112. **make it:** i.e., prove it true

113. **in nothing less:** i.e., in no respect less criminal

REGAN
　　Lady, I am not well, else I should answer
　　From a full-flowing stomach. ⌜*To Edmund.*⌝
　　　General,
　　Take thou my soldiers, prisoners, patrimony.
　　[Dispose of them, of me; the walls is thine.]   90
　　Witness the world that I create thee here
　　My lord and master.
GONERIL　　　　　　　　Mean you to enjoy him?
ALBANY
　　The let-alone lies not in your goodwill.
EDMUND
　　Nor in thine, lord.   95
ALBANY　　　　　　　Half-blooded fellow, yes.
REGAN, ⌜*to Edmund*⌝
　　Let the drum strike, and prove my title thine.
ALBANY
　　Stay yet, hear reason.—Edmund, I arrest thee
　　On capital treason; and, in ⟨thine attaint,⟩
　　This gilded serpent.—For your claim, fair   100
　　　⟨sister,⟩
　　I bar it in the interest of my wife.
　　'Tis she is subcontracted to this lord,
　　And I, her husband, contradict your banns.
　　If you will marry, make your loves to me.   105
　　My lady is bespoke.
[GONERIL　　　　　　An interlude!]
ALBANY
　　Thou art armed, Gloucester. Let the trumpet sound.
　　If none appear to prove upon thy person
　　Thy heinous, manifest, and many treasons,   110
　　There is my pledge.　　⌜*He throws down a glove.*⌝
　　　　　　　　I'll make it on thy heart,
　　Ere I taste bread, thou art in nothing less
　　Than I have here proclaimed thee.

116. **medicine:** i.e., poison
118. **What:** i.e., whoever
121. **who not:** i.e., whoever
125. **thy single virtue:** i.e., your own strength alone
133. **quality or degree:** rank
136. **He:** i.e., Edmund
139 SD. **armed:** dressed in full armor

An armed knight.
From Henry Peacham, *Minerua Britanna* . . . (1612).

REGAN Sick, O, sick!   115
GONERIL, ⌈*aside*⌉ If not, I'll ne'er trust medicine.
EDMUND
  There's my exchange.   ⌈*He throws down a glove.*⌉
                              What in the world ⟨he is⟩
  That names me traitor, villain-like he lies.
  Call by the trumpet. He that dares approach,   120
  On him, on you, who not, I will maintain
  My truth and honor firmly.
ALBANY A herald, ho!
⟨EDMUND   A herald, ho, a herald!⟩
⟨ALBANY⟩
  Trust to thy single virtue, for thy soldiers,   125
  All levied in my name, have in my name
  Took their discharge.
REGAN   My sickness grows upon me.
ALBANY
  She is not well. Convey her to my tent.
                              ⌈*Regan is helped to exit.*⌉

              Enter a Herald.

  Come hither, herald. Let the trumpet sound,   130
  And read out this.   ⌈*He hands the Herald a paper.*⌉
⟨CAPTAIN Sound, trumpet!⟩
                              A trumpet sounds.
HERALD *reads.*
  If any man of quality or degree, within the lists of the
  army, will maintain upon Edmund, supposed Earl of
  Gloucester, that he is a manifold traitor, let him   135
  appear by the third sound of the trumpet. He is bold in
  his defense.   [*First trumpet* ⌈*sounds.*⌉
HERALD Again!   *Second trumpet* ⌈*sounds.*⌉
HERALD Again!   *Third trumpet* ⌈*sounds.*⌉
                              Trumpet answers within.]

          Enter Edgar armed.

142. **What:** who

146. **canker-bit:** destroyed like a rosebud by the caterpillar

148. **cope:** encounter

156–58. **mine   honors . . . oath . . . profession:** All these refer to Edgar's status as a knight.

159. **Maugre:** in spite of

160. **fire-new:** brand new

163. **Conspirant:** conspiring; or, conspirator

164. **upward:** top

165. **descent:** lowest part

166. **toad-spotted:** loathsomely tainted; **Say thou:** i.e., if you say

167. **bent:** directed

170. **wisdom:** prudence

ALBANY, ⌜*to Herald*⌝
　Ask him his purposes, why he appears   140
　Upon this call o' th' trumpet.
HERALD   What are you?
　Your name, your quality, and why you answer
　This present summons?
EDGAR   Know my name is lost,   145
　By treason's tooth bare-gnawn and canker-bit.
　Yet am I noble as the adversary
　I come to cope.
ALBANY   Which is that adversary?
EDGAR
　What's he that speaks for Edmund, Earl of   150
　　Gloucester?
EDMUND
　Himself. What sayest thou to him?
EDGAR   Draw thy sword,
　That if my speech offend a noble heart,
　Thy arm may do thee justice. Here is mine.   155
　　　　　　　　　　　⌜*He draws his sword.*⌝
　Behold, it is my privilege, the privilege of mine
　　honors,
　My oath, and my profession. I protest,
　Maugre thy strength, place, youth, and eminence,
　⟨Despite⟩ thy victor-sword and fire-new fortune,   160
　Thy valor, and thy heart, thou art a traitor,
　False to thy gods, thy brother, and thy father,
　Conspirant 'gainst this high illustrious prince,
　And from th' extremest upward of thy head
　To the descent and dust below thy foot,   165
　A most toad-spotted traitor. Say thou "no,"
　This sword, this arm, and my best spirits are bent
　To prove upon thy heart, whereto I speak,
　Thou liest.
EDMUND   In wisdom I should ask thy name,   170
　But since thy outside looks so fair and warlike,

172. **that:** i.e., since; **say:** assay, sign; **breeding:** i.e., noble birth

173–74. **What . . . disdain:** i.e., I disdain the cautious course of claiming my right, under the rules of knighthood, to refuse combat with a challenger whose name and rank I do not know

175. **treasons to:** i.e., accusations of treason at

176. **the . . . lie:** i.e., the lie that charges me with treason, which I hate as I hate hell

177–79. **for . . . forever:** i.e., because my countercharges glance off your armor without even bruising you, I will now use my sword to open a passage to your heart, where they will forever lodge

180. **Save him:** i.e., spare his life

181. **This is practice:** i.e., you were tricked into fighting

184. **cozened and beguiled:** duped and deceived

186. **stopple:** close with a stopple or plug; **Hold, sir:** Perhaps this repeats Albany's earlier command to Edgar to spare Edmund's life.

194. **Govern:** (1) restrain; (2) look after

198. **fortune on:** success over

And that thy tongue some say of breeding breathes,
[What safe and nicely I might well delay]
By rule of knighthood, I disdain and spurn.
Back do I toss these treasons to thy head,   175
With the hell-hated lie o'erwhelm thy heart,
Which, for they yet glance by and scarcely bruise,
This sword of mine shall give them instant way,
Where they shall rest forever. Trumpets, speak!
⌜*He draws his sword.*⌝ *Alarums. Fights.*
⌜*Edmund falls, wounded.*⌝

ALBANY, ⌜*to Edgar*⌝
Save him, save him!   180
GONERIL   This is practice, Gloucester.
By th' law of war, thou wast not bound to answer
An unknown opposite. Thou art not vanquished,
But cozened and beguiled.
ALBANY   Shut your mouth, dame,   185
Or with this paper shall I ⟨stopple⟩ it.—Hold, sir.—
Thou worse than any name, read thine own evil.
No tearing, lady. I perceive you know it.
GONERIL
Say if I do; the laws are mine, not thine.
Who can arraign me for 't?   190
ALBANY   Most monstrous! O!
Know'st thou this paper?
⟨GONERIL⟩   Ask me not what I know.
She exits.

ALBANY
Go after her, she's desperate. Govern her.
⌜*A Soldier exits.*⌝
EDMUND, ⌜*to Edgar*⌝
What you have charged me with, that have I done,   195
And more, much more. The time will bring it out.
'Tis past, and so am I. But what art thou
That hast this fortune on me? If thou 'rt noble,
I do forgive thee.

201. **no . . . blood:** i.e., am of no less honorable birth or descent

202. **If more:** i.e., because I am legitimate and the firstborn; **th':** thou

204. **pleasant:** pleasure-giving

206. **thee he got:** he begot you

209. **wheel:** i.e., Fortune's wheel, which draws up one to a position of power and then casts one down as it continues to turn; **here:** i.e., at the bottom of the wheel, where I began

217. **List:** listen to

219. **The . . . escape:** i.e., in order to escape from the proclamation condemning me to death

224. **this habit:** these garments

225. **rings:** i.e., eye sockets

229. **past:** ago

230. **success:** result

232. **flawed:** damaged

Fortune's wheel. (5.3.209)
From John Lydgate, *The hystorye, sege and dystruccyon of Troye* (1513).

EDGAR　　　　　　　Let's exchange charity.　　　　　200
　I am no less in blood than thou art, Edmund;
　If more, the more th' hast wronged me.
　My name is Edgar and thy father's son.
　The gods are just, and of our pleasant vices
　Make instruments to plague us.　　　　　205
　The dark and vicious place where thee he got
　Cost him his eyes.
EDMUND　　　　　　Th' hast spoken right. 'Tis true.
　The wheel is come full circle; I am here.
ALBANY, ⌈to Edgar⌉
　Methought thy very gait did prophesy　　　210
　A royal nobleness. I must embrace thee.
　Let sorrow split my heart if ever I
　Did hate thee or thy father!
EDGAR　Worthy prince, I know 't.
ALBANY　Where have you hid yourself?　　　215
　How have you known the miseries of your father?
EDGAR
　By nursing them, my lord. List a brief tale,
　And when 'tis told, O, that my heart would burst!
　The bloody proclamation to escape
　That followed me so near—O, our lives' sweetness,　220
　That we the pain of death would hourly die
　Rather than die at once!—taught me to shift
　Into a madman's rags, t' assume a semblance
　That very dogs disdained, and in this habit
　Met I my father with his bleeding rings,　　　225
　Their precious stones new lost; became his guide,
　Led him, begged for him, saved him from despair.
　Never—O fault!—revealed myself unto him
　Until some half hour past, when I was armed.
　Not sure, though hoping of this good success,　230
　I asked his blessing, and from first to last
　Told him our pilgrimage. But his flawed heart
　(Alack, too weak the conflict to support)

242. **period:** highest point (of woe)

243. **another:** i.e., another sorrowful event

244. **To amplify too much:** i.e., to increase what was already too sorrowful

245. **top extremity:** i.e., overtop the utmost point

246. **big in clamor:** i.e., loudly lamenting Gloucester's death

251. **As:** i.e., as if; **threw . . . father:** i.e., grief-stricken, threw himself on Gloucester's body

254. **puissant:** powerful

256. **tranced:** in a trance

259. **enemy king:** Lear, who could be called Kent's enemy for having banished him

'Twixt two extremes of passion, joy and grief,
Burst smilingly. 235
EDMUND   This speech of yours hath moved me,
And shall perchance do good. But speak you on.
You look as you had something more to say.
ALBANY
If there be more, more woeful, hold it in,
For I am almost ready to dissolve, 240
Hearing of this.
⟨EDGAR   This would have seemed a period
To such as love not sorrow; but another,
To amplify too much, would make much more
And top extremity. Whilst I 245
Was big in clamor, came there in a man
Who, having seen me in my worst estate,
Shunned my abhorred society; but then, finding
Who 'twas that so endured, with his strong arms
He fastened on my neck and bellowed out 250
As he'd burst heaven, threw ⌐him⌐ on my father,
Told the most piteous tale of Lear and him
That ever ear received, which, in recounting,
His grief grew puissant, and the strings of life
Began to crack. Twice then the trumpets sounded, 255
And there I left him tranced.
ALBANY   But who was this?
EDGAR
Kent, sir, the banished Kent, who in disguise
Followed his enemy king and did him service
Improper for a slave.⟩ 260

Enter a Gentleman ⟨with a bloody knife.⟩

GENTLEMAN Help, help, O, help!
EDGAR What kind of help?
[ALBANY, ⌐*to Gentleman*⌐ Speak, man!]
EDGAR What means this bloody knife?

265. **smokes:** steams
277. **compliment:** formal greeting
278. **very:** mere
280. **aye:** forever
285. **object:** spectacle

GENTLEMAN
  'Tis hot, it smokes! It came even from the heart   265
  Of—O, she's dead!
ALBANY Who dead? Speak, man.
GENTLEMAN
  Your lady, sir, your lady. And her sister
  By her is poisoned. She confesses it.
EDMUND
  I was contracted to them both. All three   270
  Now marry in an instant.
[EDGAR   Here comes Kent.

                Enter Kent.]

ALBANY, ⌜*to the Gentleman*⌝
  Produce the bodies, be they alive or dead.
                        ⌜*Gentleman exits.*⌝
  This judgment of the heavens, that makes us
    tremble,   275
  Touches us not with pity. O, is this he?
  ⌜*To Kent.*⌝ The time will not allow the compliment
  Which very manners urges.
KENT   I am come
  To bid my king and master aye goodnight.   280
  Is he not here?
ALBANY   Great thing of us forgot!
  Speak, Edmund, where's the King? And where's
    Cordelia?
                Goneril and Regan's bodies brought out.
  Seest thou this object, Kent?   285
KENT Alack, why thus?
EDMUND Yet Edmund was beloved.
  The one the other poisoned for my sake,
  And after slew herself.
ALBANY Even so.—Cover their faces.   290
EDMUND
  I pant for life. Some good I mean to do

293–94. **my writ . . . life:** i.e., I have issued written orders commanding the death

306. **fordid:** destroyed

314. **stone:** i.e., mirror's surface

316. **promised end:** i.e., doomsday, the end of the world promised in the Bible

Despite of mine own nature. Quickly send—
Be brief in it—to th' castle, for my writ
Is on the life of Lear, and on Cordelia.
Nay, send in time.   295

ALBANY   Run, run, O, run!

EDGAR
To who, my lord? ⌐*To Edmund.*⌐ Who has the office?
    Send
Thy token of reprieve.

EDMUND
Well thought on. Take my sword. Give it the   300
    Captain.

EDGAR, ⌐*to a Soldier*⌐   Haste thee for thy life.
            ⌐*The Soldier exits with Edmund's sword.*⌐

EDMUND, ⌐*to Albany*⌐
He hath commission from thy wife and me
To hang Cordelia in the prison, and
To lay the blame upon her own despair,   305
That she fordid herself.

ALBANY
The gods defend her!—Bear him hence awhile.
                    ⌐*Edmund is carried off.*⌐

        Enter Lear with Cordelia in his arms,
            ⌐*followed by a Gentleman.*⌐

LEAR
Howl, howl, howl! O, ⟨you⟩ are men of stones!
Had I your tongues and eyes, I'd use them so
That heaven's vault should crack. She's gone   310
    forever.
I know when one is dead and when one lives.
She's dead as earth.—Lend me a looking glass.
If that her breath will mist or stain the stone,
Why, then she lives.   315

KENT   Is this the promised end?

EDGAR
Or image of that horror?

318. **Fall and cease:** probably addressed to the heavens or the universe

333. **falchion:** sword

335. **crosses:** troubles, adversities; **spoil:** impair, weaken

337. **tell:** recognize; **straight:** straightway, in a moment

338. **loved and hated:** i.e., first loved and then hated

340. **This . . . sight:** This may refer to Lear's own dull eyesight, or it perhaps refers to what he sees around him.

342. **Caius:** Kent's name when he was in disguise (This is the only time the name is used in the play.)

ALBANY   Fall and cease.
LEAR
  This feather stirs. She lives. If it be so,
  It is a chance which does redeem all sorrows   320
  That ever I have felt.
KENT   O, my good master—
LEAR
  Prithee, away.
EDGAR   'Tis noble Kent, your friend.
LEAR
  A plague upon you, murderers, traitors all!   325
  I might have saved her. Now she's gone forever.—
  Cordelia, Cordelia, stay a little. Ha!
  What is 't thou sayst?—Her voice was ever soft,
  Gentle, and low, an excellent thing in woman.
  I killed the slave that was a-hanging thee.   330
GENTLEMAN
  'Tis true, my lords, he did.
LEAR   Did I not, fellow?
  I have seen the day, with my good biting falchion
  I would have made him skip. I am old now,
  And these same crosses spoil me. ⌜*To Kent.*⌝ Who   335
    are you?
  Mine eyes are not o' th' best. I'll tell you straight.
KENT
  If Fortune brag of two she loved and hated,
  One of them we behold.
LEAR
  This is a dull sight. Are you not Kent?   340
KENT   The same,
  Your servant Kent. Where is your servant Caius?
LEAR
  He's a good fellow, I can tell you that.
  He'll strike and quickly too. He's dead and rotten.
KENT
  No, my good lord, I am the very man—   345

346. **see:** attend to

347. **your first . . . decay:** i.e., the beginning of the change and decline of your fortunes (**Difference** may also mean "quarrel" and may refer to Lear's relations with his daughters.)

352. **fordone:** destroyed

353. **desperately:** in despair

356. **us:** i.e., ourselves

357. **bootless:** useless

361. **What . . . come:** i.e., whatever opportunities that may become available for comforting (Lear in) this great decline

362. **For us, we:** i.e., as for myself, I

365. **boot:** advantage; **addition:** titles

369. **poor fool:** i.e., Cordelia (**Fool** can be a term of endearment.)

LEAR   I'll see that straight.

KENT
  That from your first of difference and decay
  Have followed your sad steps.

LEAR   ⌜You⌝ are welcome
  hither.   350

KENT
  Nor no man else. All's cheerless, dark, and deadly.
  Your eldest daughters have fordone themselves,
  And desperately are dead.

LEAR   Ay, so I think.

ALBANY
  He knows not what he says, and vain is it   355
  That we present us to him.

EDGAR   Very bootless.

                  Enter a Messenger.

MESSENGER   Edmund is dead, my lord.

ALBANY   That's but a trifle here.—
  You lords and noble friends, know our intent: 360
  What comfort to this great decay may come
  Shall be applied. For us, we will resign,
  During the life of this old Majesty,
  To him our absolute power; you to your rights,
  With boot and such addition as your Honors   365
  Have more than merited. All friends shall taste
  The wages of their virtue, and all foes
  The cup of their deservings. O, see, see!

LEAR
  And my poor fool is hanged. No, no, no life?
  Why should a dog, a horse, a rat have life,   370
  And thou no breath at all? Thou'lt come no more,
  Never, never, never, never, never.—
  Pray you undo this button. Thank you, sir.
  [Do you see this? Look on her, look, her lips,
  Look there, look there!   *He dies.*]   375

381. **rack:** instrument of torture on which a victim's limbs were stretched and torn apart
390. **journey:** i.e., to death

Victim tortured on a rack. (5.3.381)
From Girolamo Maggi, *De tintinnabulis liber . . . Accedit . . . De equulet liber . . .* (1689).

EDGAR   He faints. ⌜*To Lear.*⌝ My lord,
   my lord!
KENT
   Break, heart, I prithee, break!
EDGAR   Look up, my lord.
KENT
   Vex not his ghost. O, let him pass! He hates him   380
   That would upon the rack of this tough world
   Stretch him out longer.
EDGAR   He is gone indeed.
KENT
   The wonder is he hath endured so long.
   He but usurped his life.   385
ALBANY
   Bear them from hence. Our present business
   Is general woe. ⌜*To Edgar and Kent.*⌝ Friends of my
     soul, you twain
   Rule in this realm, and the gored state sustain.
KENT
   I have a journey, sir, shortly to go;   390
   My master calls me. I must not say no.
EDGAR
   The weight of this sad time we must obey,
   Speak what we feel, not what we ought to say.
   The oldest hath borne most; we that are young
   Shall never see so much nor live so long.   395
                   They exit with a dead march.

Textual Notes

The reading of the present text appears to the left of the square bracket. Unless otherwise noted, the reading to the left of the bracket is from **F,** the First Folio text (upon which this edition is based). The earliest sources of readings not in F are indicated as follows: **Q1** is the First Quarto of 1608; **Q2** is the Second Quarto of 1619; **Ed.** is an earlier editor of Shakespeare, beginning with the anonymous editor of the Second Folio of 1632. No sources are given for emendations of punctuation or for corrections of obvious typographical errors, like turned letters that produce no known word. **SD** means stage direction; **SP** means speech prefix; **uncorr.** means the first or uncorrected state of the First Folio; **corr.** means the second or corrected state of the First Folio. ~ stands in place of a word already quoted before the square bracket. ʌ indicates the omission of a punctuation mark. There is no division into acts and scenes in Q1, only in F. Not all Q2 readings are included in these notes.

1.1. 0. SD *Edmund*] *Bastard* Q1   2 *and often hereafter.* Cornwall] *Cornwell* Q1   4. kingdom] kingdomes Q1   5. equalities] Q1; qualities F   19. a son, sir] sir a sonne Q1   22. to] into Q1   26 *and hereafter.* SP ED- MUND] *Bast.* Q1   33. SD *Sennet . . . Attendants.*] *Sound a Sennet. Enter one bearing a Coronet, then Lear, then the Dukes of Albany, and Cornwell, next Gonorill, Regan, Cordelia, with followers.* Q1   34. the] my Q1   36. lord] Leige Q1   36. SD *He exits.*] F *only*   37. shall . . . purpose] will . . . purposes Q1   38. Give me] F *only*   39. that] F *only*   40. fast] first Q1   41. from our age] of our state Q1   42. Conferring . . . strengths] Confirming . . . yeares Q1   42–48. while . . . now] F *only*   49. two

263

great] Q1 *only*   54–55. Since . . . state] F *only*   58.
nature doth with merit challenge] merit doth most
challenge it Q1   60. I love . . . word] I do loue . . .
words Q1   62. and] or Q1   65. as . . . found] a . . .
friend Q1   68. speak] F; doe Q1   70. shadowy] shady
Q1   70–71. and with champains . . . rivers] F *only*   72.
Albany's] *Albaines* Q1   72. issue] Q1; issues F   75. of] to
Q1   75. Speak] Q1 *only*   76. I . . . that self . . . as my
sister] Sir, I . . . the selfe same . . . that my sister is
Q1   77. worth. In] ~ ، ~Q1   79. comes too] came Q1
82. possesses] Q1; professes F   87. ponderous] richer
Q1   91. conferred . . . Goneril.—Now] confirmed . . .
Gonorill, but now Q1   92. Although . . . love] Although
the last, not least in our deere loue Q1   93–94. The . . .
interessed] F (interest); F *only*   94. draw] win Q1   95.
Speak] F *only*   97–98. F *only*   99. Nothing will] How,
nothing can Q1   102. no] nor Q1   103. How . . .
Cordelia] Goe to, goe to Q1   103. speech a little] F *corr.*,
Q1; speec ah little F *uncorr.*   104. you] it Q1   110.
Haply] F (Happily)   115. Q1 *only*   116. thy . . . this]
this with thy heart Q1   117. my good lord] good my
Lord Q1   120. Let] Well let Q1   122. mysteries] F2;
miseries F; mistresse Q1   122. night] might Q1   131. to
my bosom] F *only*   144. dowers . . . the] dower . . . this
Q1   146. with] in Q1   151. turn] turnes Q1   151. shall]
still Q1   152. th' addition] the additions Q1   163. mad]
Q2, F; man Q1   163. wouldst] F (wouldest); wilt Q1
167. falls] stoops Q1   167. Reserve thy state] Reuerse
thy doome Q1   172–73. sounds / Reverb] sound /
Reuerbs Q1   175. a] Q1 *only*   176. nor] Q1; nere F
178. being motive] being the motiue Q1   182. SP LEAR]
Kear. F   183. SP KENT] *Lent.* F   185. O] F *only*   185.
Miscreant] recreant Q1   186. F *only*   186. SP CORN-
WALL] F (*Cor.*)   187. Kill . . . thy fee] Doe, kill . . . the
fee Q1   188. gift] doome Q1   191. recreant] F *only*
192. That . . . vows] Since . . . vow Q1   193. strained]

straied Q1   194. sentence] F *uncorr.*, Q1; sentences F
corr.   197. Five] Foure Q1   198. disasters] diseases
Q1   199. sixth] fift Q1   204. Fare] Why fare Q1   205.
Freedom] Friendship Q1   206–7. dear shelter . . . thee]
protection . . . the Q1   208. justly . . . rightly] rightly
. . . iustly Q1   213. SD *He exits. . . . Attendants.*] *Enter
France and Burgundie with Gloster.* Q1   214. SP GLOUCES-
TER] Q1; *Cor.* F   215. Burgundy] *Bugundie* F   216. this]
a Q1   220. Most] F *only*   221. hath] what Q1   228.
more] else Q1   231. Will] Sir will Q1   233. Dowered]
Couered Q1   237. in] on Q1   246. whom] that Q1
246. best] Q1 *only*   249. The . . . the] most . . . most
Q1   253. your . . . affection] you . . . affections   Q1
254. Fall] Falne Q1   256. Should] Could Q1   257. Majesty.] Ed.;~. F;~, Q1   259. well] Q1; will F   261. make
known] may know Q1   263. unchaste] vncleane Q1
265. richer] rich Q1   267. That] As Q1   268. Hath . . .
liking] F *corr.*, Q1; ath . . . lik ng F *uncorr.*   269. Better]
Goe to, goe to, better Q1   270. t' have] t haue F   272. it
but] it no more but Q1   273. Which] That Q1   276.
regards] respects Q1   278. a dowry] and dowre Q1
279. king] *Leir* Q1   283. I am firm] F *only*   288. respect
and fortunes] respects I Of fortune Q1   297. my] thy
Q1   299. of] in Q1   301. Can] Shall Q1   309. SD
Flourish . . . exit.] Ed.; *Flourish. Exeunt.* F; *Exit Lear and
Burgundie.* Q1   310. sisters] F *corr.* (Sisters), Q1; S sters
F *uncorr.*   314. Love] vse Q1   320. SP REGAN] *Gonorill*
Q1   320. duty] duties Q1   321. SP GONERIL] *Regan*
Q1   324. want] worth Q1   325. plighted] pleated Q1
326. with shame] shame them Q1   328. my] F *only*
329. not little] not a little Q1   335. not] Q1 *only*   338.
grossly] grosse Q1   342–43. from his age to receive] to
receiue from his age Q1   343. imperfections] imperfec-
tion Q1   344. the] F *only*   350. Pray you, let us sit] pray
lets hit Q1   352. disposition] dispositions Q1   354. of it]
on't Q1

1.2. 0. SD *Bastard*] *Bastard Solus.* Q1   1. SP ED-
MUND] Ed.; *Bast.* F (*and hereafter until line 173*), Q1
hereafter   4. me ˄] ~ ? F   6. base,] ~ ? F   10. bastardy]
Barstadie F   10-11. with "baseness," "bastardy,"
"base," "base"] base bastardie Q1   14. dull, stale, tired]
stale dull lyed Q1   15. creating a] creating of a Q1   16.
then] the Q1   18. father's] Q1; Farhers F   19. Fine . . .
"legitimate"] F *only*   22. top th'] Ed.; to' th' F; tooth'
Q1   25. prescribed] subscribd Q1   34. needed . . .
terrible] needes . . . terribe Q1   38. SP EDMUND] Ed.;
Bast. F; *Ba.* Q1 *corr.*; *omit* Q1 *uncorr.*   39. and] F
only   41. o'erlooking] liking Q1   49. SD *reads*] *A Letter.*
Q1 *after l. 48*   49. *and reverence*] F *only*   58. Sleep . . .
wake] slept . . . wakt Q1   61. you to this] this to you
Q1   70. his.] ~ ? Q1   73. before] heretofore Q1   75.
heard him oft] often heard him Q1   77. declined, the]
declining, his Q1   78. his] the Q1   81-82. sirrah . . .
I'll] sir . . . I Q1   84. lord] Ed.; L. F; Lord Q1   86. his]
this Q1   91. that] F *only*   92. writ] wrote Q1   93.
other] further Q1   100-2. EDMUND . . . earth] Q1 *only*   103. the] your Q1   106. will] shall Q1   107. find]
see Q1   111. it] F *only*   114. discord] discords Q1
114. in] F *only*   114. and] F *only*   115. 'twixt] betweene
Q1   115-21. This . . . graves] F *only*   123-24. honesty!
'Tis] honest, strange Q1   124. SD *He exits.*] F *only*   126.
surfeits] surfeit Q1   128-29. and stars . . . on] and the
Starres . . . by Q1   130. spherical] spirituall Q1   135.
on . . . a star] to . . . Starres Q1   138. Fut] Q1 *only*
139. maidenliest] F, Q1 (maidenlest)   139-40. in . . .
bastardizing] of . . . bastardy Q1   140. Edgar] Q1 *only*   141. and] Q1 *only*   141. pat] out Q1   142-43. My
cue . . . Tom] mine . . . them Q1   144. *Fa . . . mi*] F *only*   149. with] about Q1   150. writes] writ Q1   151-59.
as . . . come] Q1 *only*   160. The] Why, the Q1   162. Ay]
F *only*   164. nor] or Q1   168. until] till Q1   171.
scarcely] scarce Q1   173-79. I pray . . . brother] F *on-

ly   180. best. I] best, goe arm'd, I Q1   186. SD *Edgar exits.*] Q1 (*Fdgar*); F (*Exit.*) *1 line earlier*
1.3.   0. SD *Steward*] *Gentleman* Q1   3 *and hereafter in this scene.* SP OSWALD] Ed.; *Ste.* F; *Gent.* Q1   3. Ay] Yes Q1   8. trifle.] ~ ˰ Q1   14. fellows . . . to] fellow seruants, . . . in Q1   15. distaste . . . my] dislike . . . our Q1   17–22. Q1 *only*   23. have said] tell you Q1   24. Well] Very well Q1   27–28. I . . . speak] Q1 *only*   29. very] Q1 *only*   29. course. Prepare] course, goe prepare Q1   29. SD *They exit.*] *Exit.* Q1
1.4.   1. well] Q1; will F   7. So . . . come] F *only*   8. thee . . . labors] the . . . labour Q1   8. SD F; *Enter Lear.* Q1   32. canst do] Q1; canst thou do Q2, F   38. sir] F *only*   41–42. me—if . . . dinner. I] ~, ~ . . . ~, ~ F, Q1   44. SD *1 line later in* F *and* Q1   45. You] F *only*   46 *and hereafter to line 357.* SP OSWALD] Ed.; *Ste.* F; *Steward* Q1   46. *He exits*] F *only*   51. SP KNIGHT] *Kent* Q1   51. daughter] Q1; Daughters F   54, 57, 64, 73. SP KNIGHT] *seruant* Q1   60. of kindness] F *only*   70. purpose] purport Q1   72. my] this Q1   75. well] F *only*   77. SD *1 line later in* F; F *only*   78. come . . . hither, sir] sir, come you hither Q1   82–83. these . . . your pardon] this . . . you pardon me Q1   90. arise. Away] F *only*   92. lubber's length again,] F, Q1 *corr.*; ~, ~~ ˰ Q1 *uncorr.*   92. Go to] F *only*   92–93. Have you] you haue Q1   93. So] F *only*   94. my] F *only*   101. LEAR . . . my boy] *Kent.* . . . Foole Q1   106. did] done Q1   111. all my] any Q1   115. dog must] dog that must Q1   116. the Lady] Ladie oth'e Q1   118. gall] gull Q1   121. nuncle] vncle Q1   132. SP KENT] *Lear* Q1   133. 'tis] F *only*   135. nuncle] vncle Q1   141. Dost know] Q1; Dost thou know Q2, F   142. one] foole Q1   144–59. That . . . snatching] Q1 *only*   158. ladies] Q1 *corr.* (Ladies); lodes Q1 *uncorr.*   159–60. Nuncle, give . . . egg] giue . . . egge Nuncle Q1   160. crowns] F, Q1 *uncorr.* (crownes); crown e s Q1 *corr.*   164. crown] Q1; Crownes F   165. on thy] at'h

Q1   170. grace] wit Q1   172. And . . . to] They . . . doe
Q1   177. mothers] mother Q1   182. fools] Q1; Foole
F   184. learn to lie] F, Q1 *corr.* (learneto lye); learne lye
Q1 *uncorr.*   185. sirrah] F *only*   191. thee, nuncle] F,
Q1 *corr.* (thee Nuncle); theeNuncle Q1 *uncorr.*   195.
Methinks] Q1 *only*   196. thou] F, Q1 *corr.*; tho u Q1
uncorr.   197. frowning] frowne Q1   197. Now] F, Q1
corr. (now); thou, Q1 *uncorr.*   199. Fool. Thou] F, Q1
corr. (foole, thou); foole,thou Q1 *uncorr.*   203. nor
crust] neither crust Q1   203. nor crumb] Q1; not crum
F   209. riots. Sir,] Ed.; ~ ⌃ ~. F; ~,) ~ ⌃ Q1   213. it] F
only   215. redresses] redresse Q1   218. Which] that
Q1   219. Will . . . proceeding] must . . . proceedings
Q1   220. know] trow Q1   222. it's . . . by it] it . . . beit
Q1   225. I . . . your] Come sir, I . . . that Q1   227.
which . . . transport]   that . . . transforme   Q1   231.
This] why this Q1   234. weakens] weaknes, or Q1   235.
lethargied—Ha! Waking? 'Tis] lethergie, sleeping, or
wakeing; ha! sure tis Q1   237. SP FOOL] F *only*   238–
242. I . . . father.] Q1 *only*   244. This admiration, sir]
Come sir, this admiration Q1   246. To] F *only*   252.
Makes it] make Q1   252. a brothel] brothell Q1   253.
graced] great Q1   254. then] thou Q1   257. remain-
ders] remainder Q1   259. Which] that Q1   266. SD
Albany] *Duke* Q1   267. Woe] We Q1   267–68. O . . .
come] Q1 *only*   269. will . . . horses] will that wee
prepare any horses Q1   273. F *only*   274. liest.] list ⌃
Q1   275. are] and Q1   280. Which] that Q1   283. Lear,
Lear, Lear] *Lear, Lear* Q1   286 *and hereafter.* SP ALBA-
NY] *Duke* Q1   287. F *only*   289. Hear . . . goddess,
hear] harke . . . Goddesse Q1   291. fruitful.] F (:); ~ ⌃
Q1   297. thwart disnatured] thourt disuetur'd Q1   299.
cadent] accent Q1   301. that . . . feel] that shee may
feele, that she may feele Q1   303. Away, away] goe, goe,
my people Q1   303. SD F *only*   305. more of it] the
cause Q1   307. As] that Q1   307. SD F *only*   314.

which] that Q1   315–17. thee worth them . . . upon
thee! / Th'] the worst⌃ . . . vpon the⌃ Q1   317–18.
untented . . . / Pierce] F, Q1 *corr.*; vntender . . . peruse
Q1 *uncorr.*   318. thee! Old] F (~.~); the old Q1   320.
cast you . . . loose] you cast . . . make Q1   321. Yea, is 't
come to this?] Q1 *only*   322. Ha! Let it be so.] F
only   322–23. I have another daughter / Who] yet haue
I left a daughter, whom Q1   327. forever.] for ever, thou
shalt I warrant thee Q1   327. SD Q2, F; *omit* Q1   328.
that] that my Lord Q1   331. Pray . . . ho] Come sir no
more Q1   332. sir] F *only*   333. tarry. Take] tary and
take Q1   334–35. with thee. / A] with a Q1   339. SD F
only   340–55. GONERIL . . . Oswald] *Gon.* What *Os-*
wald, ho. *Oswald.* Here Madam. I *Gon.* Q1   356. that]
this Q1   357. SP OSWALD] Q1; *Stew.* F   357. Ay] Yes
Q1   359. fear] feares Q1   362. And hasten] F, Q1 *corr.*
(& hasten); and after Q1 *uncorr.*   362. No, no] now
Q1   364. milky] F, Q1 *corr.* (milkie); mildie Q1 *un-*
corr.   365. condemn] dislike Q1   366. You are] F2;
Your are F; y'are Q1   366. at task for] attasked for Q1
corr.; alapt Q1 *uncorr.*   367. praised] praise Q1   369.
better, oft] better ought Q1
   1.5.   0. SD F; *Enter Lear.* Q1; *Enter Lear, Kent, and*
Foole. Q2   8. were] Q2, F; where Q1   11. not] nere
Q1   16. can tell what] con, what Q1   17. What . . . boy]
Why what canst thou tell my boy? Q1   19. canst . . .
stands] canst not . . . stande Q1; canst not . . . stands
Q2   22. one's . . . of] his . . . on Q1   31. daughters]
daughter Q1   38. indeed] F *only*   43. till] before Q1
45. not mad] F *only*   45–46. heaven! / Keep] heauen! I
would not be mad, keepe Q1   47. How now] F *only*   48.
SP GENTLEMAN] *Seruant* Q1   49. boy.] boy. *Exit.* Q1   50.
a] F *only*   51. unless] except Q1   52. SD *They exit.*] *Exit.*
Q1
   2.1.   0. SD *severally*] *meeting* Q1   1 *and hereafter.* SP
EDMUND] Ed.; *Bast.* Q1, F   2. you] Q1; your F   4.

Regan] F *only* 4. this] to Q1 7. they] there Q1 8.
kissing] bussing Q1 11. the dukes] the two Dukes
Q1 13. do] F *only* 13. SD Q2, F; *omit* Q1 18. Which I
must act . . . work] which must aske⌃ . . . helpe Q1
19. SD *1 line earlier in* F; *3–4 lines earlier in* Q1 20. sir]
F *only* 23. Cornwall] *Cornwall* ought Q1 27. yourself.] your—Q1 29–30. me. / In] F (~: ~); ~ ⌃ ~
Q1 30. cunning] crauing Q1 31. Draw] F *only* 33.
hoa] here Q1 34. brother] brother flie Q1 35. SD F
only 40. SD F; *Enter Glost.* Q1 44. Mumbling] war-
bling Q1 45. stand] stand's Q1 51. ho] F *only* 54.
revenging] reuengiue Q1 55. the thunder] their thun-
ders Q1 57. in fine] in a fine Q1 59. in] with Q1 61.
lanced] Q1; latch'd F 62. And] but Q1 63. right] Q2,
F; rights Q1 72. coward] caytife Q1 78. would . . .
reposal] could . . . reposure Q1 80. I should] Q1;
should I F 82. would, though] would, I, though Q1
84. practice] pretence Q1 87. spirits] spurres Q1 89.
O strange] Strong Q1 90. said he] F *only* 91. Q1
only 91. SD F *only, 3 lines earlier* 92. why] Q1; wher
F 97. due] F *only* 99. SD F; *Enter the Duke of Cornwall.* Q1 100. came] F *corr.,* Q1; csme F *uncorr.*
101–2. strange news] Q1; strangenesse F 106. O] F
only 106. it's] is Q1 109. O] I Q1 111. tended] tends
Q1 112. bad.] F *corr.,* Q1; ~, F *uncorr.* 113. of that
consort] F *only* 116. th' expense and waste of his]
these—and wast of this his Q1 *uncorr.*; the wast and
spoyle of his Q1 *corr.* 121 *and hereafter.* SP CORNWALL]
Duke Q1 122. hear] heard Q1 122. your] Q1; yout
F 125. bewray] betray Q1 134–35. need. You⌃] F (~:
~⌃); ~ ⌃ ~, Q1 136. sir] F *only* 140. threading]
threatning Q1 141. poise] Q1 *corr.*; prize F, Q1 *uncorr.*
(prise), Q2 143. father] F, Q1 *uncorr.* (Father); Fa th er
Q1 *corr.* 144. differences] F, Q1 *corr.* (diferences);
defences Q1 *uncorr.* 144. best] F, Q1 *uncorr.*; lest Q1
corr. 144. thought] Q1; though F 145. home] F, Q1

corr.; hand Q1 *uncorr.* 145. several] Q1 *corr.* (seueral);
F, Q1 *uncorr.* seuerall 148. businesses] busines Q1
151. SD *Exeunt. Flourish.* F; *Exeunt.* Q1
2.2. 0. SD *and*] Q1; *aad* F 0. SD *severally*] F *only* 1
and hereafter. SP OSWALD] Ed.; *Stew.* F; *Steward* Q1 1.
dawning] deuen Q1 *uncorr.*; euen Q1 *corr.* 1. this] the
Q1 5. KENT I'] F *corr.* (*Kent.* I'); *Kent.*I' F *uncorr.*; *Kent.*
It' Q1 15. suited] snyted Q1 *uncorr.*; shewted Q1
corr. 16. worsted] Q1 *corr.*; woosted F; wosted Q1
uncorr. 17. action-taking, whoreson] action taking
knaue, a whorson Q1 17–18. superserviceable, finical]
superfinicall Q1 22. bitch; one whom] bitch, whom
Q1 23. clamorous] Q1 *corr.*; clamarous Q1 *uncorr.*;
clamours F 24. thy] the Q1 25. Why] F *only* 29. ago]
Q1 *only* 29–30. since . . . before] since I beat thee, and
tript vp thy heeles before Q1 32. yet] F *only* 33. you,
you] you, draw you Q1 36. come with] bring Q1 43.
Strike!] Q1 *corr.* (~?); ~. F, Q1 *uncorr.* 44. Murder,
murder] murther, helpe Q1 44. SD *Cornwall . . .*
Servants.] *Gloster the Duke and Dutchesse* Q1 45. Part]
F *only* 49–50. that I strikes] F *corr.*, Q1; that; s strikes F
uncorr. 59. A tailor] I, a Tayler Q1 60. they] hee
Q1 61. years o'] houres at Q1 62. SP CORNWALL]
Glost. Q1 67. wall] walles Q1 70. sirrah] sir Q1 71.
know you] you haue Q1 75. Who] That Q1 77. the
holy . . . atwain] those . . . in twaine Q1 77. holy] F
corr.; holly F *uncorr.* 78. too intrinse] Ed.; t'intrince F;
to intrench Q1 78. unloose] inloose Q1 81. Being . . .
fire] Bring . . . stir Q1 81. the] their Q1 82. Renege]
Q1; Reuenge F 83. gale] Q1; gall F 84. dogs] dayes
Q1 86. Smile] Ed.; Smoile F, Q1 88. drive] send
Q1 93. fault] offence Q1 95. nor . . . nor] or . . . or
Q1 98. Than] Q2, F; That Q1 100. some] a Q1 102.
roughness] ruffines Q1 103. nature] F *corr.* (Nature),
Q1; Narure F *uncorr.* 104. An . . . plain] he must be
plaine Q1 111. faith, in] sooth, or in Q1 112. great]

graund Q1 114. On] In Q1 114. flick'ring] Ed.; flick-
ing F; flitkering Q1 115. mean'st by] mean'st thou by
Q1 116. dialect] dialogue Q1 121. What was] What's
Q1 126. compact] coniunct Q1 128–29. man / That]
man, that, / That Q1 130. self-subdued] F *corr.*, Q1;
selfe-s[inverted]ubdued F *uncorr.* 131. fleshment]
flechuent Q1 131. dread] Q1; dead F 135. Fetch . . .
stocks] Bring . . . stockes ho Q1 136. ancient] ausrent
Q1 *uncorr.*; miscreant Q1 *corr.* 138. Sir] F *only* 140.
employment] imployments Q1 141. shall] should Q1
141. respect] Q1 *corr.*; respcct Q1 *uncorr.*; respects
F 144. Stocking] Stobing Q1 *uncorr.*; Stopping Q1
corr. 146. sit till] F *corr.*, Q1 *corr.*; set till Q1 *uncorr.*; si
ttill F *uncorr.* 149. should] could Q1 151. color]
nature Q1 152. speaks] Q2, F; speake Q1 152. SD F
only, 2 lines earlier 154–58. His . . . with] Q1 *only*
155. correction ̬] Q1 *corr.*; ~, Q1 *uncorr.* 156. basest]
Q1 *corr.*; belest Q1 *uncorr.* 156. contemned'st] Ed.;
contaned Q1 *uncorr.*; temnest Q1 *corr.* 158. King
must] Q1; King his Master needs must F 159. he] hee's
Q1 163. gentleman] Q2, F; Gentlemen Q1 164. Q1
only 165. SP CORNWALL] Q1 *omit* 165. my good lord]
Q1; my lord Q2, F 165. SD Ed.; *Exit.* Q2, F; *omit*
Q1 166. Duke's] Q1; Duke F 170. Pray, do] Pray you
doe Q1 171. out] Q2, F; ont Q1 174. taken] tooke
Q1 174. SD Q2, F; *omit* Q1 175. saw] F, Q1 *corr.*; say
Q1 *uncorr.* 180. miracles] my rackles Q1 *uncorr.*; my
wracke Q1 *corr.* 182. most] F, Q1 *corr.*; not Q1 *un-*
corr. 182. been] F, Q1 *uncorr.* (beene); bin Q1 *corr.*
183. course,] Q1; ~. F 185. their] F, Q1 *corr.*; and Q1
uncorr. 185. o'erwatched] ouerwatch Q1 186. Take]
F, Q1 *corr.*; Late Q1 *uncorr.* 187. shameful] Q1; shame-
fnll F 189. SD Q1 *only*

2.3. 1. heard] heare Q1 4. unusual] Q1; vnusall
F 5. taking.] ~ ̬ Q1 10. elf . . . hairs in] else . . . haire
with Q1 12. winds and persecutions] wind and perse-

cution Q1   15. and] F, Q1 *corr.*; *omit* Q1 *uncorr.*   15.
mortifièd arms] mortified bare armes Q1   15. arms‸]
~, Q1; ~. F   16. Pins] F, Q1 *corr.*; Pies Q1 *uncorr.*   17.
from low farms] frame low seruice Q1 *uncorr.*; from low
seruice Q1 *corr.*   18. sheepcotes] Q1; Sheeps-Coates
F   19. Sometime] Q1; Sometimes F   20. Turlygod] F,
Q1 *corr.*; *Tuelygod* Q1 *uncorr.*   **2.4.** 0. SD F; *Enter King.* Q1   0. SD *Gentleman*] F
corr.; *Gentlemaa* F *uncorr.*   1. home] hence Q1   2.
messenger] Q1; Messengers F   3, 68. SP GENTLEMAN]
Knight Q1   4. in them] F *only*   5. this] his Q1   7. Ha]
How Q1   8. thy] Q1; ahy F   9. F *only*   10. Ha, ha, he]
ha, looke he Q1   10. garters.] Q1 (~,); ~ ‸ F   11. heads]
heeles Q1   12. man's] Q1; man F   22–23. yea. / LEAR
By] yea. / *Lear.* No no, they would not. / *Kent.* Yes they
haue. / *Lear.* By Q1   24. F *only*   24. Juno] *Iuuo* F   25.
SP F *only*   26. could . . . would] would . . . could Q1
30. might'st . . . impose] may'st . . . purpose Q1   36.
panting] Q1; painting F   39. whose] Q1; those F   40.
meiny] men Q1   46. which] that Q1   51. The] This
Q1   52–61. F *only*   63. *Hysterica*] Ed.; *Historica* Q1,
F   64. below.—] Q1 (~,); ~ ‸ F   65. With] Q1; Wirh
F   65. here] F *only*   67. here] there Q1   67. SD F
only   68. but] then Q1   69. None] No Q1   70. the] Q1;
the the F   70. number] traine Q1   77. twenty] a 100.
Q1   79–80. following] following it Q1   80. upward] vp
the hill Q1   81–82. gives . . . counsel,] F *corr.* (giues
. . . counsell,), Q1; giue . . . counsell‸F *uncorr.*   82.
have] Q1; hause F   84. which] that Q1   85. And seeks] F
only   87. begins] begin Q1   94. fool] F *only*   94. SD *2
lines earlier in* F   97. have] F *only*   97. all the] hard to
Q1   97. fetches,] F *corr.*; ~ ‸ F *uncorr.*; Iustice, Q1   98.
The] I the Q1   104. plague, death] death, plague Q1
105. "Fiery"? What "quality"?] what fierie quality Q1
108–10. F *only*   113. father‸] F, Q1 *corr.*; fate, Q1
uncorr.   114. his] F, Q1 *corr.*; the Q1 *uncorr.*   114.

commands, tends ˄] Ed.; ~, ~, F; come and tends ˄ Q1
uncorr.; commands her ˄ Q1 *corr.* 116–17. F *only*
118. "Fiery"? The] The Q1 *uncorr.*; *omit* Q1 *corr.* 118.
that—] that *Lear* Q1 119. No] F, Q1 *corr.*; Mo Q1
uncorr. 119. yet] F (~,); ~ ˄ Q1 122. commands] Q2,
F; Comand Q1 130. practice ˄ only.] ~, ~ ˄ Q1 131.
Go] F *only* 131. I'd] Ile Q1 131. them.] F (~:); ~ ˄
Q1 135. SD F *only* 136. me] my heart Q1 136. my
rising heart! But down] F *only* 137. cockney] F, Q1
corr. (Cokney); Coknay Q1 *uncorr.* 138. paste] F, Q1
corr. (pa[circumflex]st); past Q1 *uncorr.* 138.
knapped] rapt Q1 141. SD F; *Enter Duke and Regan.*
Q1 143. SD F *only* 145. you] Q1; your F 147. di-
vorce] F, Q1 *corr.* (diuorse); deuose Q1 *uncorr.* 147.
mother's] Q1; Mother F 147. tomb] F, Q1 *corr.*; fruit
Q1 *uncorr.* 148. O] yea Q1 153–54. believe ˄ / With
how depraved] beleeue, Of how deptoued Q1 *uncorr.*
(depriued Q1 *corr.*) 155. you] F *only* 157. scant]
slacke Q1 158–63. F *only* 166. in] on Q1 167. his]
her Q1 169. pray you] pray Q1 171. her] her, sir
Q1 173. but] F *only* 179. Never] No Q1 186. sir, fie]
fie sir Q1 187. SP Q2, F; *omit* Q1 190. blister] blast
her pride Q1 192. is on] F *only* 194. tender-hefted]
tender hested Q1 206. SD F *only, 1 line earlier* 209.
letter] letters Q1 210. SD *3 lines earlier in* F, *2 in*
Q1 213. fickle] Q1; fickly F 213. her ˄] F, Q1 *uncorr.*;
~, Q1 *corr.* 214. varlet] F, Q1 *corr.*; varlot Q1 *uncorr.*
216. SP LEAR] *Gon.* Q1 216. stocked] struck Q1 217.
SD *2 lines earlier in* Q1, F 218. Who] *Lear.* Who
Q1 219. your] you Q1 220. Allow] F, Q1 *corr.*; alow
Q1 *uncorr.* 220. you] F *only* 224. will you] wilt thou
Q1 245. hot-blooded] F *uncorr.*; hot-bloodied F *corr.*;
hot bloud in Q1 247. beg] Q2, F; bag Q1 252. I] Now I
Q1 256. that's in] that lies within Q1 258. or] an
Q1 260. call it] F, Q1 *corr.*; callit Q1 *uncorr.* 263.
when] F *corr.*, Q1; wheu F *uncorr.* 266. so] so sir

Q1   267. looked] looke Q1   270. you old] you are old
Q1   272. spoken] spoken now Q1   275. and danger] F
corr., Q1; anddanger F *uncorr.*   276. Speak . . . one]
Speakes . . . a Q1   294. look] seem Q1   304. need]
needes Q1   305. need] deed Q1   307. nature] F *corr.*
(Nature), Q1; Nattue F *uncorr.*   308. is] as Q1   311–12.
true need] F *corr.*, Q1; trueneed F *uncorr.*   314. man]
fellow Q1   316. daughters'] F *corr.* (Daughters), Q1;
Daughte s F *uncorr.*   317. so] to Q1   318. tamely]
lamely Q1   319. And] O Q1   324. I'll ⌃ weep] F *corr.*,
Q1; ~ , ~ F *uncorr.*   326. SD F *only*   327. into . . . flaws]
in . . . flowes Q1   328. mad] F *corr.*, Q1; mads F *un-*
corr.   328. SD *Gloucester*] Q2; *Leister* Q1 *only*   336. SP
GONERIL] *Duke.* Q1   336. purposed] puspos'd Q1   337.
CORNWALL] *Reg.* Q1   340–41. CORNWALL . . . horse] F
only   341. but] & Q1   342. CORNWALL] *Re.* Q1   342.
best] good Q1   344. high] bleak Q1   345. ruffle] russel
Q1   346. scarce] not Q1   354. Regan] *Reg.* Q1
   3.1.   0. SD F; *Enter Kent and a Gentleman at seuerall*
doores. Q1   1. Who's there] Whats here Q1   4. ele-
ments] element Q1   7–17. tears . . . all] Q1 *only*   16.
fur] Q1 *corr.* (furre); surre Q1 *uncorr.*   22. note] Arte
Q1   24. is] be Q1   26–33. F *only*   34–46. Q1 *only*   49.
am] F *only*   50. outwall] Q1 *uncorr.*; out-wall F, Q1
corr.   54. that] your Q1   59–61. in . . . this] Ile this
way, you that Q1
   3.2.   0. SD *Storm still.*] F *only*   1. winds] wind Q1   1.
blow!] ~ ⌃ F, Q1   3. our] the Q1   3. drowned] Q1;
drown F   6. of] to Q1   9. Strike] smite Q1   10. molds]
Mold Q1   11. makes] make Q1   12. holy] F, Q1 *corr.*;
holly Q1 *uncorr.*   14. in. Ask] in, and aske Q1   15. men
nor fools] man nor foole Q1   18. tax] taske Q1   20.
subscription. Then] subscription, why then Q1   24.
will . . . join] haue . . . ioin'd Q1   25. battles] battel
Q1   26. ho] F *only*   35. of] haue Q1   37. but] F, Q1
corr.; hut Q1 *uncorr.*   40. SD *2 lines earlier in F, 1 in*

Q1   44. are] sit Q1   46. wanderers] wanderer Q1   47.
make] makes Q1   51. fear] force Q1   57. simular of]
simular man of Q1   58. to] in Q1   61. concealing
continents] concealed centers Q1   63. than] their Q1
69. harder than the stones] hard then is the stone
Q1   70. you] me Q1   73. wits begin] wit begins Q1
77. And] that Q1   77. your] you Q1   78–79. hovel.—/
Poor∧] F (~; / ~ ∧); ~ ∧ ~, Q1   79. in] of Q1   80. That's
sorry] That sorrowes Q1   81. and] F *only*   84. *Though*]
for Q1   85. my good] Q1 *only*   85. SD F *only*   86–103.
SD F *only*   103. SD F *only*

3.3.   0. SD *Edmund*] *and the Bastard with lights* Q1
1–2. this   ∧ . . . dealing.]   F   (~ ∧ . . . ~;);   ~,   . . . ~ ∧
Q1   3. took from] Q2, F; tooke me from Q1   4. perpet-
ual] their Q1   6. or] nor Q1   8. There is division] ther's
a diuision Q1   13. footed] landed Q1   14. look] seeke
Q1   17. If] though Q1   19–20. strange things toward,
Edmund] ~ ~ ~ ∧ ~ F; Some strange thing toward, *Edmund* Q1   22. Instantly] instanly Q1   25. The] then Q1

3.4.   0. SD *Fool*] F *corr.* (*Foole*), Q1; *Fo le* F *uncorr.*   2.
The tyranny] F, Q1 *corr.* (the tyrranie); the the tyrannie
Q1 *uncorr.*   3. SD F *only*   5. here] F *only*   8. conten-
tious] crulentious Q1 *uncorr.*; tempestious Q1 *corr.*   9.
skin. So∧] F *uncorr.* (skin.so), Q1; skinso: F *corr.*   12.
thy] Q1; they F   12. roaring] F, Q1 *corr.* (roring); raging
Q1 *uncorr.*   15. This] Q1 *corr.* (this); The F, Q1 *uncorr.*,
Q2   17. beats] F, Q1 *corr.* (beates); beares Q1 *uncorr.*
17. there.] F *corr.* (~,); ~ ∧ F *uncorr.*; their∧ Q1   19.
home] sure Q1   20–21. In . . . endure] F *only*   23. gave
all] gaue you all Q1   24. lies. Let] F *corr.* (lies, let), Q1;
lie,slet F *uncorr.*   26. here] F *only*   30–31. F *only*   31.
SD F *only, 1 line earlier*   33. storm] night Q1   42–43.
SD F *only*, SD *reading "Enter Edgar, and Foole." 2 lines
earlier*   42. half, fathom and] F *corr.*; half, fathomand F
uncorr.   47. A spirit, a spirit] A spirit Q1   51. blows the
cold wind] Q1; blow the windes F   51. Hum!] F *only*

52. cold] Q1 *only* 53. Didst thou give] Hast thou giuen Q1 53. thy daughters] thy two daughters Q1 56. through] Q1; though F 56. through flame] F *only* 57. ford] Q1; Sword F 59. porridge] pottage Q1 63. O, do de, do de, do de] F *only* 64. star-blasting] star-blusting Q1 66. there—and] there, and and Q1 67. and there] F *only* 67. SD F *only* 68. Has] What Q1 69. Wouldst] didst Q1 74. light] fall Q1 82. Pillicock Hill] pelicocks hill Q1 82. Alow, alow] a lo Q1 87. justice] iustly Q1 97. deeply] Q1; deerely F 101. rustling] ruslngs Q1 102. woman] women Q1 103. brothels] brothell Q1 103. plackets] placket Q1 104. books] booke Q1 106. says . . . nonny] hay no on ny Q1 106. boy, sessa] my boy, caese Q1 107. SD F *only* 108. Thou] Why thou Q1 108. a] thy Q1 110. than] but Q1 110. this?] ~ ˄ Q1 112. Ha] F *only* 115. lendings] F, Q1 *corr.*; leadings Q1 *uncorr.* 116. unbutton here] on bee true Q1 *uncorr.*; on Q1 *corr.* 117. contented. 'Tis] content, this is Q1 120. on 's] in Q1 120. SD F *4 lines earlier; Enter Gloster.* Q1 *1 line later* 122. fiend] Q1 *only* 122. Flibbertigibbet] *Sriberdegibit* Q1 *uncorr.; fliberdegibek* Q1 *corr.* 123. till the] Q1; at F 124. gives the web and] F, Q1 *corr.* (giues the web, &); gins the web Q1 124–25. squints . . . harelip] queues . . . harte lip Q1 *uncorr.;* squemes . . . hare lip Q1 *corr.* 128. He met the nightmare] F, Q1 *corr.;* a nellthu night more Q1 *uncorr.* 129. alight] O light Q1 131. witch] F, Q1 *corr.;* with Q1 *uncorr.* 137. tadpole] F, Q1 *corr.* (tod pole), Q1 *uncorr.* (tode pold) 137. newt] F, Q1 *corr.;* wort Q1 *uncorr.* 142. stocked, punished] stock-punisht Q1 143. had] Q1 *only* 148. Smulkin] snulbug Q1 153–54. blood, my lord . . . vile / That] bloud is growne so vild my Lord, that Q1 161. fire and food] food and fire Q1 164. Good my] My good Q1 165. same] most Q1 169. once more] F *only* 171. SD F *only* 182. sir.]

F *only* (~:)   185. into th'] in't Q1   195. tower came]
towne come Q1   197. SD F *only*
    3.5.   0. SD *Edmund*] *Bastard* Q1   1. his] the Q1   11.
letter he] Q1; Letter which hee F   13. this] his Q1   14.
were not] were Q1   26. dearer] Q1; deere F   26. SD F;
Exit. Q1
    3.6.   0. SD F; *Enter Gloster and Lear, Kent, Foole, and
Tom.* Q1   4. to his] to Q1   5. reward] deserue Q1   5.
SD F *only* (*Exit*), *2 lines earlier*   7. and] F *only*   12–15.
FOOL . . . LEAR] F *only*   17–59. Q *only*   23. Now] Q2;
no Q1   26. trial] Q2; tral Q1   27. *burn*] Ed.; broome
Q1   38. robèd] Ed.; robbed Q1   64. They] Theile Q1
71–72. mongrel ^ grim, / Hound] Ed.; ~, ~, ~ F; ~, ~–~
Q1   72. lym] Ed.; Hym F; him Q1   73. Bobtail tike, or
trundle-tail] Q1; Or Bobtaile tight, or Troudle taile
F   74. him] them Q1   76. leapt] leape Q1   77. Do . . .
Sessa] loudla doodla Q1   82. make] makes Q1   82.
these hard hearts] this hardnes Q1   83. entertain for]
entertaine you for Q1   85. Persian] Persian attire Q1
86. and rest] F *only*   88–89. So, so . . . morning] so, so,
so . . . morning, so, so, so, Q1   90. F *only*   90. SD
placed as in Q1; *4 lines earlier in* F   101. Take up, take
up] Take vp to keepe Q1 *uncorr.*; Take vp the King Q1
corr.   102. me, that] F, Q1 *corr.*; ~ ^ ~ Q1 *uncorr.*   104–
10. KENT . . . GLOUCESTER] Q1 *only*   110. SD F *Exeunt.*;
Q1 *Exit.*   111–26. Q1 *only*
    3.7.   0. SD *and Servants.*] F *only*   2. husband. . . .
letter.] F (~, . . . ~,);~, . . . ~ ^ Q1   4. traitor] vilaine
Q1   8. company] F, Q1 *corr.*; company company Q1
uncorr.   8. revenges] reuenge Q1   11. festinate] Ed.;
festiuate F; festuant Q1   11. preparation;] F (~:); ~ ^
Q1   12–13. posts . . . intelligent] post . . . intelligence
Q1   14. SD *1 line later in* Q1   18. questrists] questrits
Q1   24. SD Ed.; *Exit.* F; *Exit Gon. and Bast.* Q1   27.
well] F *only*   30. SD F; *Enter Gloster brought in by two or
three*, Q1, *1 line later*   40. I'm none] I am true Q1   52.

answered] answerer Q1   66. him answer] him first
answere Q1   68. Dover] Dover sir Q1   71. anointed] F,
Q1 *corr.*; aurynted Q1 *uncorr.*   71. stick] rash Q1   72.
as . . . bare] of . . . lou'd Q1 *uncorr.*; on . . . lowd Q1
corr.   73. buoyed] layd Q1 *uncorr.*; bod Q1 *corr.*   74.
stellèd] F, Q1 *corr.* (stelled); steeled Q1 *uncorr.*   75.
holp . . . rain] holpt . . . rage Q1   76. howled] heard
Q1   76. stern] dearne Q1   79. subscribe] subscrib'd
Q1   82. these] those Q1   88, 94, 97, 99. SP FIRST
SERVANT] Ed.; *Seru.* F, Q1   90. you] Q2, F; *omit* Q1   97.
Nay] Why Q1   99. you have] yet haue you Q1   105.
enkindle] vnbridle Q1   107. treacherous] F *only*   114.
SD F *only*   119. SD *Exeunt.* F; *Exit.* Q1   120–29. Q1
only   120. SP SECOND SERVANT] Ed.; *Seruant* Q1   122,
128. SP THIRD SERVANT] Ed.; 2 *Seruant* Q1   125. SP
SECOND SERVANT] Ed.; I *Ser.* Q1   126. roguish] Q1
uncorr.; *omit* Q1 *corr.*   129. *They exit.*] Ed.; *Exit.* Q1
   4.1.   2. flattered.] F (~,); ~ ⌃ Q1   4. esperance] experience Q1   6–9. Welcome . . . blasts] F *only*   9. But
who comes] Who's Q1   9. SD F; *Enter Glost. led by an
old man* Q1, *3 lines later*   10. poorly led] Q2, F; poorlie,
leed Q1 *uncorr.*; parti,eyd Q1 *corr.*   14. these fourscore
years.] this forescore—Q1   18. You] Alack sir, you
Q1   31. So] As Q1   41. flies to] flies are toth' Q1   42.
kill] bitt Q1   44. play fool] play the foole Q1   48. Then,
prithee] Q1 *only*   48. away] F; gon Q1   49. hence] here
Q1   52. Which] Who Q1   58. SD F *only*   60. daub]
dance Q1   62. And yet I must] F *only*   65. scared] Q1
(scard); scarr'd F   66. thee, good man's son] the good
man Q1   67–72. Five . . . master] Q1 *only* 69–70.
Flibbertigibbet] Ed.; *Stiberdigebit* Q1   70. mopping and
mowing] Mobing, & *Mohing* Q1   78. slaves] stands
Q1   80. undo] vnder Q1   84. fearfully] firmely Q1   90.
SD F *only*
   4.2.   0. SD Q1; *Enter . . . Bastard, and Steward.* F   2.
SD *Enter Steward.*] Q1, *1 line later; omit* F   12. most he

should dislike] hee should most desire Q1 15. terror]
F, Q1 *corr.* (terrer); curre Q1 *uncorr.* 18. Edmund] Q2,
F; *Edgar* Q1 19. powers.] ~ ˄ Q1 20. names] armes
Q1 25. command] F, Q1 *corr.*; coward Q1 *uncorr.* 25.
this;] F, Q1 *corr.* (~,); ~ ˄ Q1 *uncorr.* 29. thee] you
Q1 30. SD F *only* 31. dear] F, Q1 *corr.* (deer), Q1
uncorr. (deere) 33. F *only* 34. a] F, Q1 *corr.*; omit Q1
uncorr. 35. My] F, Q1 *uncorr.*; A Q1 *corr.* 35. fool] F,
Q1 *corr.*; foote Q1 *uncorr.* 35. body] F, Q1 *uncorr.*; bed
Q1 *corr.* 36. SD *He exits.*] Q1 *only* (*Exit Stew.*); *Enter
Albany.*] F *only* 37. whistle] F, Q1 *uncorr.*; whistling Q1
corr. 40–61. I . . . deep] Q1 *only* 40. disposition.] ~ ˄
Q1 41. its] Q1 *uncorr.* (it); ith Q1 *corr.* 56. benefited]
Q1 *corr.*; beniflicted Q1 *uncorr.* 58. these] Ed.; this Q1
corr.; the Q1 *uncorr.* 60. Humanity] Q1 *corr.*; Humanly
Q1 *uncorr.* 60. itself] Q1 *corr.* (it self); it selfe Q1
uncorr. 64. discerning] deseruing Q1 65–72. that . . .
so] Q1 *only* 65–66. know'st ˄ / Fools ˄ do] ~ ˄ ~, ~ Q1
uncorr.; ~, ~ ˄ Q1 *corr.* (know'st, foolsdo) 69. noise-
less] Q1 *corr.* (noyseles); noystles Q1 *uncorr.* 70. state
begins to threat] Ed.; slayer begin threats Q1 *uncorr.*;
state begins thereat Q1 *corr.* 71. Whilst] Q1 *corr.*
(Whil'st); Whil's Q1 *uncorr.* 74. shows] Q1 *corr.*;
seemes Q2, F, Q1 *uncorr.* 75. horrid] F, Q1 *corr.*; horid
Q1 *uncorr.* 77–83. Q1 *only* 83. mew] Q1 *corr.*; now
Q1 *uncorr.* 83. SD F *1 line later; Enter a Gentleman* Q1
1 line later 84. Q1 *only* 84. SP ALBANY] Q1 *corr.* (*Alb.*),
Q1 *uncorr.* (*Alb.*) 85. SP MESSENGER] F; *Gent.* Q1 89.
thrilled] thrald Q1 91. thereat] Q1; threat F 96.
You] F, Q1 *corr.* (you); your Q1 *uncorr.* 96. justic-
ers] Q1 *corr.*; Iustices Q2, F, Q1 *uncorr.* 104. in] on
Q1 106. tart] tooke Q1 106. SD Q1 *only* 118. SD
F; *Exit.* Q1

4.3. 0–66. Q1 *only.* 12. sir] Ed.; say Q1 19. strove]
Ed.; streme Q1 23. seemed] Ed.; seeme Q1 36. mois-
tened] Ed.; moystened her Q1

4.4. 0. Scene 4] Ed.; *Scena Tertia* F   0. SD F; *Enter Cordelia, Doctor and others.* Q1   2. vexed] vent Q1   3. fumiter] Q1 (femiter); Fenitar F   6. send] is sent Q1 11. helps] can helpe Q1   12. SP DOCTOR] Q1; *Gent.* F   14. lacks.] F (~:); ~ ͜ Q1   20. distress] Q1; desires F   29. importuned] important Q1   30. incite] Q2, F; in sight Q1   32. SD F; *Exit.* Q1

4.5. 0. Scene 5] Ed.; *Scena Quarta* F   3. there] F *only*   6. lord] Lady Q1   8. letter] Q2, F; letters Q1   13. Edmund] and now Q1   16. enemy] army Q1   17. madam] F *only*   17. letter] letters Q1   18. troops set] troope sets Q1   24. things] thing Q1   32. Y' are] for Q1   36. more.] F (~:); ~ ͜ Q1   40. you] F *only*   43. him] Q1 *only*   43. should] would Q1   44. party] Lady Q1   45. SD F; *Exit.* Q1

4.6. 0. Scene 6] Ed.; *Scena Quinta* F   0. SD *Edgar*] *Edmund* Q1   1. I] we Q1   2. up it] it vp Q1   11. In] With Q1   17. low!] F (~,); ~ ͜ Q1   22. walk] Q1; walk'd F   24. buoy] boui Q1   27. heard so] heard, its so Q1   27. high.] ~ ͜ Q1   44. SD Q1 *only*   49. snuff] Q2, F; snurff Q1   50. him] F *only*   51. SD Q1 *only*   53. may] Q2, F; my Q1   57. Friend] F *only*   57. you.] Ed.; ~ ͜ F, Q1   70. no] no 1 Q1   71. summit] Ed.; Somnet F; sommons Q1   74. eyes.] F (~:); ~ ͜ Q1   76. death?] ~ ͜ Q1   77. tyrant's] Q1; Tyranrs F   80. is 't] F *only*   82. strangeness.] F (~,); ~ ͜ Q1   85. beggar] Q2, F; bagger Q1   88. enragèd] enridged Q1   90. make them] made their Q1   95. die.] ~ ͜ Q1   96. 'twould] would it Q1 98. SD F; *Enter Lear mad.* Q1 *3 lines later*   100. ne'er] Q2, F; neare Q1   102. coining] Q1; crying F   108. piece of] F *only*   111. clout, i' th' clout! Hewgh] ayre, hagh Q1   115. with a white beard] ha *Regan* Q1   116. the] F *only*   118. that] F *only*   124. ague-proof] argue-proofe Q1   127. every] Q2, F; euer Q1   127. king.] ~ ͜ Q1 130. die. Die] die Q1   131. does] doe Q1   137. does] do Q1   138. to] F *only*   138. name. The] name ͜ to Q1

143. sulphurous] sulphury Q1   144. consumption]
consumation Q1   146. sweeten] to sweeten Q1   148.
Let me] Here Q1   150. Shall] should Q1   150. Dost
thou] Do you Q1   152. at] on Q1   153. this] that
Q1   153. but] F *only*   155. thy] the Q1   155. see] see
one Q1   165. this] the Q1   168. ear.] F (~:); ~ ᴧ Q1
168. Change places and] F *only*   169. justice . . . thief]
theefe . . . Iustice Q1   174. dog's obeyed] dogge, so
bade Q1   177. Thou] thy bloud Q1   179. cozener] Q2,
F; cosioner Q1   180. clothes] raggs Q1   180. small] Q1;
great F   181. hide] hides Q1   181–87. Plate . . . lips] F
only   181. Plate sin] Ed.; Place sinnes F   189–90. Now,
now, now] no Q1   192. mixed,] ~ ᴧ Q1   194. fortunes]
fortune Q1   195. enough;] F (~,); ~ ᴧ Q1   198. wawl]
wayl Q1   198. Mark] marke me Q1   202. shoe] shoot
Q1   203. felt] fell Q1   203. I'll . . . proof] F *only*   205.
SD *a Gentleman*] *three Gentlemen* Q1   206. hand] hands
Q1   207. him.—Sir] him, Sir F; him sirs Q1   208.
daughter] F *only*   211. surgeons] a churgion Q1   215. a
man] F *only*   217. Ay . . . dust] Q1 *only*   218. I] *Lear.* I
Q1   218. smug] F *only*   219–20. king, / Masters] King
my maisters Q1   222. Come] nay Q1   223. by] with
Q1   223. Sa . . . sa] F *only*   223. SD Q1; *Exit.* F   225. a]
one Q1   227. have] hath Q1   230. sir] F *only*   231.
vulgar.] F (~:); ~ ᴧ Q1   232. Which] That Q1   232.
sound] sence Q1   235. speedy foot.] F (~ ~:); speed
fort ᴧ Q1   235. descry] descryes Q1   236. thought]
thoughts Q1   240. SD *here in* Q1; *1 line earlier in*
F   246. tame to] lame by Q1   251. bounty and the
benison] F, Q1 *corr.* (benizon); bornet and beniz Q1
uncorr.   252. To boot, and boot] to saue thee Q1 *uncorr.*; to boot, to boot Q1 *corr.*   254. first] F, Q1 *corr.*;
omit Q1 *uncorr.*   255. old] most Q1   262. that] F *only*
264. vurther] F *only*   266. and] F *only*   268. as 'tis] F
only   268–69. vortnight] F, Q1 *corr.*; fortnight Q1 *uncorr.*   269. out,] Q1 *corr.*; ~ ᴧ F, Q1 *uncorr.*   270. cos-

tard] F, Q1 *corr.* (Costerd); coster Q1 *uncorr.* 271.
ballow] battero Q1 *uncorr.*; bat Q1 *corr.* 274. SD Q1
only, 1 line earlier 278. out ʌ] F, Q1 *uncorr.*; ~, Q1
corr. 279. English] *British* Q1 *uncorr.*; *Brittish* Q1
corr. 279. SD Q1 *only* 284. rest you.] ~ ~, Q1 *corr.*;
~ ~ ʌ Q1 *uncorr.* 285. these] his Q1 285. The] These
Q1 285. of ʌ] F, Q1 *uncorr.*; ~, Q1 *corr.* 286. sorry]
Q2, F; sorrow Q1 288. not.] ~ ʌ F, Q1 289. minds, we]
minds wee'd Q1 *uncorr.*; minds wee d Q1 *corr.* 290. SD
F; *A letter.* Q1 *corr.*; *omit* Q1 *uncorr.* 291. our] your
Q1 294. done ʌ] Ed.; ~. F; ~, Q1 295. jail] F (*Gaole*),
Q1 *corr.* (iayle); gayle Q1 *uncorr.* 298. *affectionate*]
your affectionate Q1 299. *and, for you, her own for
venture*] Q1; *omit* Q2, F 300. indistinguished] Q1; in-
dinguish'd F 300. will] wit Q1 302. brother.—] F
(~:); ~ ʌ Q1 302. the sands] rhe sands F 311. severed]
fenced Q1 313. SD F, *2 lines earlier;* Q1 (*A drum a farre
off.*) 314. hand.] F (~:); ~ ʌ Q1 316. SD F; *Exit.* Q1
4.7. 0. SD *Doctor*] Q1 *only* 0. and] F *corr.*; *omit* F
uncorr. 0. *Gentleman*] F *only* 7. suited.] F (~,); ~ ʌ
Q1 10. Pardon] Pardon me Q1 15 *and hereafter in this
scene.* SP DOCTOR] Q1; *Gent.* F 18. jarring] hurrying
Q1 24. will.] F (~:); ~ ʌ Q1 24. SD F *only* 25. SP
GENTLEMAN] *Doct.* Q1 25. of sleep] of his sleep Q1 27.
SP DOCTOR] Ed.; *omit* F; *Gent.* Q1 27. Be by, good
madam] Good madam be by Q1 27. him.] F (~,); ~ ʌ
Q1 28. not] Q1 *only* 29–30. Q1 *only* 35. Kind] Klnd
Q1 37. Did challenge] Had challengd Q1 38. op-
posed] exposd Q1 38. jarring] warring Q1 39–42.
To . . . helm] Q1 *only* 42. helm?] ~ ʌ Q1 42. enemy's]
iniurious Q1 55. do you] F *only* 59. I?] ~ ʌ Q1 66.
your] F *corr.*, Q1; yours F *uncorr.* 66. hand] hands
Q1 67. No, sir] Q1 *only* 68. mock] Q1; mocke me Q2,
F 70. not . . . less] F *only* 80. am; I am] am Q1 92.
killed] cured Q1 92–93. and . . . lost] Q1 *only* 98.
you] F *only* 99. SD Q1; *Exeunt.* F 100–12. Q1 *only*

5.1. 0. SD F; *Enter Edmund, Regan, and their powers.*
Q1   3. He's] F, Q1 *uncorr.* (he's); hee's Q1 *corr.*   3.
alteration] F, Q1 *corr.*; abdication Q1 *uncorr.*   11. In] I,
Q1   14–16. Q1 *only*   20. me] Q1 *only*   20. SD F; *Enter*
Albany and Gonorill with troupes. Q1   21–22. Q1 *only*
22. and] Q1 *corr.*; nd Q1 *uncorr.*   23. bemet.—] F (~:);
~ ͺ Q1   24. Sir . . . heard] For . . . hear Q1   26–31.
Where . . . nobly] Q1 *only*   34. and particular broils]
and particurlar broiles F; dore particulars Q1   35. the]
to Q1   37. proceeding] proceedings Q1   38. Q1 *only*
41. Pray, go] pray you goe Q1   45. SD F *3 lines earlier;*
Exeunt. Q1 *1 line earlier*   52. And . . . ceases] F *only*
52. love] Q1; loues F   55. the] Q1; t[inverted]he F   57.
thy] the Q1   58. view] F, Q1 *corr.*; vew Q1 *uncorr.*   59.
Here . . . guess . . . true]   Hard . . . quesse . . . great
Q1   63. sisters] Q2, F; sister Q1   64. stung] sting Q1
71. countenance] countenadce Q1   72. who] that Q1
73. the] his Q1
5.2. 0. SD F; *Alarum. Enter the powers of France ouer*
the stage, Cordelia with her father in her hand. Enter Edgar
and Gloster. Q1   1. tree] bush Q1   5. 1st SD *Exit.* F; Q1
(*1 line earlier*)   5. 2nd SD *within*] F *only*   5. 3rd SD Q2,
F; *omit* Q1   6. SP EDGAR] *Egdar* F; *Edg.* Q1   10. again?]
~ ͺ Q1   12. all.] ~ ͺ F, Q1   13. F *only*
5.3. 0. SD F; *Enter Edmund, with Lear and Cordelia*
prisoners. Q1   2. first] F; best Q1   6. I am] am I Q1   9.
No . . . no] No, no Q1   9. prison.] F (~,); ~ ͺ Q1   14.
hear ͺ poor rogues ͺ] Q1; ~ (~~) F   27. years] F *only*
28. starved] starue Q1   30. SD Q2, F; *omit* Q1   33. One]
F, Q1 *corr.*; And Q1 *uncorr.*   44–45. Q1 *only*   45. 1st SD
F *only*   45. 2nd SD F; *Enter Duke, the two Ladies, and*
others. Q1   47. well. You] F (~:~), Q1 *corr.* (~,~); ~ ͺ ~
Q1 *uncorr.*   48. Who] That Q1   49. I . . . them] We . . .
then Q1   53. send] F, Q1 *corr.*; saue Q1 *uncorr.*   54.
and appointed guard] Q1 *corr.*; *omit* Q1 *uncorr.*, F   55.
had] F; has Q1   55. more,] F, Q1 *corr.*; ~ ͺ Q1 *uncorr.*

56. common] F, Q1 *corr.*; coren Q1 *uncorr.* 56. bosom]
F (bosome); bossom Q1 *uncorr.*; bossome Q1 *corr.* 56.
on] of Q1 59. Queen,] ~ ^ Q1 62. session.] ~ ^ Q1 62–
67. At . . . place] Q1 *only* 63. We] Q1 *corr.* (wee); mee
Q1 *uncorr.* 65. sharpness] Q1 *corr.* (sharpnes); sharpes
Q1 *uncorr.* 72. might] should Q1 75. immediacy]
imediate Q1 79. addition] aduancement Q1 80.
rights] right Q1 82. SP GONERIL] Q1; *Alb.* F 90. F
only 93. him] him then Q1 97. SP REGAN] *Bast.* Q1
97. thine] good Q1 99. thine attaint] Q1; thy arrest
F 101. sister] Q1; Sisters F 104. your] the Q1 105.
loves] loue Q1 107. F *only* 108. SP F *only* 108.
Let . . . sound.] F *only* 108. trumpet] Trmpet F 109.
person] head Q1 112. make] proue Q1 116. medi-
cine] poyson Q1 118. he is] Q1; hes F 120. the] thy
Q1 124. Q1 *only* 125. SP Q1 *only* 128. My] This
Q1 129. SD F *only, 6 lines earlier* 130. trumpet]
Trumper F 132. Q1 *only* 132. SD F *only; trumpet*]
Tumpet F 133. *reads*] F *only* 133. *within*] in Q1 133.
lists] hoast Q1 136. *by*] at Q1 137. SD-139 SD F
only 138. HERALD Again] *Bast.* Sound? Againe? Q1
139. SD armed] *at the third sound, a trumpet before him.*
Q1 143. your quality] and qualitie Q1 145. Know] O
know Q1 145–46. lost, . . . tooth ^] ~ ^ . . . ~: F;
~ ^ . . . ~. Q1 147. am . . . as] are I mou't / Where is
Q1 148. cope] cope with all Q1 156–57. my privilege
. . . honors] the priuiledge of my tongue Q1 159. place,
youth] youth, place Q1 160. Despite] Q1; Despise F
160. victor-sword] victor, sword Q1 160. fortune]
fortun'd Q1 163. Conspirant] Conspicuate Q1 163.
illustrious] Q1; illustirous F 165. below thy foot] beneath thy feet Q1 166. traitor. Say] ~ ^ ~ Q1 167. are]
As Q1 170. should] sholud Q1 172. tongue] being
Q1 173. F *only* 174. rule] right Q1 175. Back] Heere
Q1 175. these] those Q1 176. hell-hated lie] hell
hatedly Q1 176. o'erwhelm] oreturnd Q1 177.

scarcely] Q1; scarely F   179. SD F *only, 1 line later*
181. practice] meere practise Q1   182. war] armes
Q1   182. wast] art Q1   185. Shut] Stop Q1   186. stop-
ple] Q1; stop Q2, F   186. Hold, sir] F *only*   187. name]
thing Q1   188. No] nay no Q1   190. can] shal Q1   191.
O] F *only*   193. SP GONERIL] Q1; *Bast.* F   193. SD *2 lines
earlier in* F; *Exit. Gonorill.* Q1 *here*   198. thou 'rt] thou
bee'st Q1   204. vices∧] vertues. Q1   205. plague]
scourge Q1   205–6. us. / The] F (~: / ~); ~ ∧ ~ Q1   208.
right] truth Q1   208. 'Tis true] F *only*   209. circle;] F
(~,); circled∧ Q1   211. nobleness.] F (~:) ~ ∧ Q1   212–
13. ever I / Did] I did euer Q1   218–19. burst! / The] F
(~.~); ~ ∧ ~ Q1   221. we] with Q1   226. Their] The
Q1   226. lost; became] F (~: ~); ~ ∧ ~ Q1   228. fault]
Father Q1   232. our] my Q1   242–60. Q1 *only*   245.
extremity.] Ed.; ~ ∧ Q1   251. him] Ed.; me Q1   255.
crack. Twice then] ~ ∧ ~, ~ Q1   258. disguise] diguise
Q1   260. SD F; *Enter one with a bloudie knife.* Q1   261.
O, help] F *only*   262. SP EDGAR] *Alb.* Q1   263. F *only*
264. SP EDGAR] F *only; in* Q1 *this speech is Albany's*   264.
this] that Q1   266. O, she's dead] F *only*   267. F; Who
man, speake? Q1   269. confesses] hath confest Q1
271. instant] intant Q1   272–272. SD F *only*   273. the]
their Q1   274. judgment] Iustice Q1   275. tremble,]
Q1; ~. F   276. pity. O] F; pity. *Edg.* Here comes *Kent* sir.
I *Alb.* O Q1   276. is this] tis Q1   277. allow the] allow
Enter Kent I The Q1   278. Which] that Q1   282 *and
hereafter.* SP ALBANY] *Duke.* Q1   284. Cordelia?] ~ ∧
Q1   284. SD F, *10 lines earlier; The bodies of Gonorill
and Regan are brought in.* Q1   300. sword. Give] sword
the Captaine, I Giue Q1   302. SP EDGAR] *Duke.* Q1   308.
howl! O] howle, howle, O Q1   308. you] Q1; your
F   319. stirs. She] F (~, ~); ~ ∧ ~ Q1   325. you, murder-
ers, traitors] F (Murderors); your murderous traytors
Q1   329. woman] women Q1   331. SP GENTLEMAN]
Cap. Q1   334. him] them Q1   338. brag] bragd Q1

338. and] or Q1   340. This . . . sight] F *only*   340. you
not] F; not you Q1   343. you] F *only*   347. first] life
Q1   349. You are] Ed.; Your are F; You'r Q1   352.
fordone] foredoome Q1   354. Ay . . . think] So thinke I
to. Q1   355. says] sees Q1   355. is it] it is Q1   357. SD
F, *1 line earlier; Enter Captaine.* Q1, *1 line earlier*   358.
SP MESSENGER] *Capt.* Q1   361. great] F *only*   365. Hon-
ors] Q2, F; honor Q1   369. No, no, no life] no, no life
Q1   370. have] Q2, F; of Q1   371. thou no] F *corr.*, Q1;
thouno F *uncorr.*   371. all?] all, O Q1   372. never,
never] F *only*   374–75. SD F *only*; O, o, o, o. Q1   374.
this? Look] F *corr.* (Looke); this, looke F *uncorr.*   378.
SP KENT] *Lear.* Q1   383. He] O he Q1   387. Is] Is to
Q1   389. realm] kingdome Q1   391. me. I] and I Q1
392. SP EDGAR] *Duke.* Q1   394. hath] haue Q1   395. SD
F *only*

King Lear:
A Modern Perspective

Susan Snyder

Each of Shakespeare's plays creates through language
its distinctive geography. In the mental map generated
by *King Lear*, the action occurs largely in this or that
house, as opposed to this or that town. "The kingdom" is
important, but not designated places in it. Even when
Lear is outlining to his daughters their shares in that
kingdom, he talks of natural features rather than named
sites. The striking exception to this pattern is Dover: this
place is first introduced in 3.1, and named ten times
thereafter, underlining its status in the action as a kind
of magnet-site to which every major character except
the Fool is drawn in the latter half of the play. Regan and
Cornwall harp on the place-name obsessively as they
interrogate the captive Gloucester:

CORNWALL   Where hast thou sent the King?
GLOUCESTER   To Dover.
REGAN
  Wherefore to Dover? Wast thou not charged at
    peril—
CORNWALL
  Wherefore to Dover? Let him answer that.
GLOUCESTER
  I am tied to th' stake, and I must stand the course.
REGAN   Wherefore to Dover?   (3.7.62–68)

The repeated questions have an immediate dramatic
point, certainly: Regan and Cornwall are trying to make
Gloucester admit his complicity with the French force

289

that Cordelia is leading into Britain to rescue her father. Nor is there any question why most of the characters go to Dover. That is where Cordelia will land: from her and her army, the Lear party can expect "welcome and protection" (3.6.98), and against this French expedition- ary force Goneril, Regan, Edmund, and the reluctant Albany must rally on the shore to fight. But repeating and insisting on the apparently simple question "Where- fore to Dover?" generates a certain excess of meaning, and suggests that Dover has significance beyond literal location.

And indeed, when we turn our attention to Lear and Gloucester at the very center of the dramatic action, the forces that propel these characters to Dover seem more fated than comprehensible and willed. While others may wish him to seek comfort from Cordelia, the mad Lear is on his own journey of self-discovery and cannot bear the shame of such a meeting with the daughter he wronged. Gloucester, blind and despairing, seeks only death at Dover. One place is as good as another for suicide, one might think. But Gloucester takes great trouble to get to Dover cliff, as if there were some peculiar rightness about this one spot as the stage for his exhausted exit from the world. The place again assumes special meaning in his insistent "Know'st thou the way to Dover? . . . Dost thou know Dover?" (4.1.63, 81).

Paying attention to these questions—"Wherefore to Dover?" "Dost thou know Dover?"—can focus for us several kinds of dynamic that work themselves out in *King Lear*. In Gloucester's mind, the reality of Dover is a cliff, where the land ends abruptly and the sea begins: a sharp demarcation between the familiar and the un- known. After he has first caused harm by being easy- going and credulous ("I stumbled when I saw") and then suffered shocking mutilation, Gloucester's awak- ened self-knowledge has brought him to a physical and spiritual low point. He goes to Dover, the boundary site, to cast off the burden of his life: "From that place / I shall no leading need" (4.1.87–88). But this edge of nothingness becomes for Gloucester a place of radically new vision. Even in his own anticipating imagination, the cliff's high head "Looks fearfully in the confinèd deep" (4.1.84), as if it is gazing into the alien element. When they arrive at Dover, the words of Edgar as Poor Tom spread out the disorienting new perspective:

> How fearful
> And dizzy 'tis to cast one's eyes so low!
> The crows and choughs that wing the midway air
> Show scarce so gross as beetles. Halfway down
> Hangs one that gathers samphire—dreadful trade;
> Methinks he seems no bigger than his head.
> The fishermen that walk upon the beach
> Appear like mice. . . .
> I'll look no more
> Lest my brain turn and the deficient sight
> Topple down headlong.   (4.6.15–29)

In fact, they are nowhere near the cliff. Edgar is deceiving his father, leading him through an elaborate enactment of his despair and remorse, in order that he may put these behind him and move into a totally different posture of acceptance. This speech that so sharply images the unseen precipice brings home to us Gloucester's inner crisis and the revolution of vision he undergoes at the extremity of life.

King Lear goes through his own psychological extremities in Dover. Brought there by his adherents to be put under Cordelia's protection, he is plunged by the very prospect of that reunion into greater anguish. Lear retreats from facing the daughter he once cast off:

> A sovereign shame so elbows him—his own
>   unkindness,
> That stripped her from his benediction, turned her
> To foreign casualties, gave her dear rights
> To his dog-hearted daughters—these things sting
> His mind so venomously that burning shame
> Detains him from Cordelia.   (4.3.51–57)

At the play's opening, Lear in his rage tried to erase this unaccommodating, plain-speaking daughter, to negate both her and the filial tie between them. "Better thou / Hadst not been born"; "we / Have no such daughter, nor shall ever see / That face of hers again" (1.1.269–70, 304–6). He has struggled in the meantime to keep Cordelia and his bond to her *banished*: from his sight, from his conscious mind. Her reappearance now, asserting that bond, is like Freud's return of the repressed that stings while it clarifies. Before he can encounter her, Lear at Dover plumbs the depths of madness even more deeply (4.6). Still acting the autocratic monarch and magistrate as he reviews his archers, pardons and condemns wrongdoers, he lays hold through these fantasized scenes on truths about himself, his limitations, his participation in grimy human nature. When brought together at last with Cordelia, the shattered old man marks his own extremity by insisting he must be dead— "You do me wrong to take me out o' th' grave" (4.7.51) —but the reconciliation that follows is on very human terms: "Pray you now, forget, and forgive. I am old and foolish" (98–99).

Lear and Gloucester both go to the edge at Dover, and both come up against death (Gloucester wants to die, Lear thinks he is dead). What they achieve instead is a kind of reorientation, a transformed perspective that could not come about except by the radical revaluation that such extremities force upon them. We should recall that Dover is not just the edge of Britain but the place in that island country that is closest to foreign lands. At this farthest limit of the familiar, Lear and Gloucester confront the unknown—which is, paradoxically, their own selves. And, like the French army that pushes in at Dover, this alien force brings both great fear and deliverance.

Dover plays its part in other movements that inform *King Lear*. One of these dynamics we might call "beyond the end." It has been operating in a way since the play's opening, when Lear formally signals an end to his power through abdication but then keeps right on acting like a king, as he banishes Kent and Cordelia and travels from daughter to daughter with a royal retinue of a hundred knights. Mainly, though, it is an end to *suffering* that is repeatedly sought after, promised—and then denied. On what he believes to be Dover cliff, Gloucester thinks to shake off the world's affliction because he cannot "bear it longer" (4.6.47). But when Edgar negates this closure of self-willed death, his father is pushed to endure yet more: "Henceforth I'll bear / Affliction . . ." (93–94). Edgar himself, in his outcast state, has already experienced personally this rhythm of being pushed yet further. After the miseries of the storm, he feels himself at the lowest point of Fortune's wheel, which must therefore turn him upward again; but then his father enters with bleeding holes instead of eyes, a sight to mock any balanced prediction of Fortune's unpredictable ways. Edgar's comforting conventional image of the course of events as a wheel guided by Fortune, which dictates that "The worst returns to laughter" (4.1.6), yields at this new, overwhelming pain to something much more like the wheel that the Fool has earlier shown us, something careening downhill out of control (2.4.78–79). "Who is 't can say 'I am at the worst'?" wonders a stunned Edgar, pushed to his own new extremity; "I am worse than e'er I was" (4.1.27–28). Lear, as we have seen, avoids the closure of suffering offered by Cordelia and runs on to endure more laceration in his madness. After father and daughter are at last reconciled, the comfortable end they promise each other is foreclosed again when her forces lose the battle and they are both taken prisoner. Even in the appalling finality of Cordelia's death, Lear's own end is postponed, so that he can suffer yet further agonies over her body before exhaustion at last takes him. What the awestruck survivors record at the play's close for both Gloucester and Lear is this endurance of repeated blows, beyond the end:

> The wonder is he hath endured so long. . . .
> The oldest hath borne most.   (5.3.384, 394)

The special emotional force that many feel in *King Lear* has much to do with this peculiar strategy of repeatedly suggesting a limit to pain and then frustrating the expectation; the dashed hopes of audience as well as characters intensify the suffering that follows.

Both of the dynamics so far discussed display kinds of pattern: the redemptive one of descending into the depths to be rewarded with new vision, the intensifying one of promising a stop to suffering only to bring on yet more. A third dynamic is akin to that of expectations denied, but is in its very nature more random and erratic. The Fool is its chief exponent. Through scene after scene, as the tormented king suffers one blow after another, the capering Fool by his side responds with jokes and reductive nonsense. The following short sequence may stand for many moments where heroic pathos is suddenly jarred by slapstick comedy:

LEAR
    O me, my heart, my rising heart! But down!
FOOL   Cry to it, nuncle, as the cockney did to the
    eels when she put 'em i' th' paste alive. She
    knapped 'em o' th' coxcombs with a stick and
    cried "Down, wantons, down." (2.4.136–40)

On Lear's towering rage and pain, the Fool superimposes a ludicrous kitchen scene with a foolish woman struggling to slap down live eels into a pastry. The degrading image complicates our sympathetic identification with Lear's royal pathos, enables simultaneously a more distanced and critical view which finds the king as foolish as that cockney and his imperious commands as ineffective as if they were addressed to a bunch of wriggling eels. With such dislocating effects, the Fool's patter again and again threatens Lear's heroic status—reduces him momentarily from his royal uniqueness to any ordinary, foolish old man, reduces his experience from world-shattering cataclysm to the commonplace, predictable fate of any father silly enough to give away his property and become dependent on his heirs. When Lear in the storm hails thunder, lightning, and torrents of rain in language of cosmic power and commands them to destroy the world that has so devastated him, the Fool thinks more prosaically that, even if it must be shared with hypocrites, "a dry house is better than this rainwater out o' door" (3.2.12–13). They are wet and unsheltered. Cosmic concerns shrink suddenly to homely needs. However titanic a figure Lear presents in the storm, we cannot shut out the other image opened by the Fool's down-to-earth practicality: that of an old man comically at odds with reality, giving orders to the universe.

    The Fool disappears from the play in Act 3, but his syncopated rhythm continues, grotesque comedy re-

peatedly threatening tragic dignity. To some extent the
Fool's role of nonsensical deflation is taken over by Lear
himself. Already his early tantrums have been open to
interpretation as overreactions to slights that are less
than earth-shaking, bringing him close to comic self-
parody. In later scenes the very language of wayward
association and non sequitur that manifests his madness
keeps him hovering between tragic grandeur and absurdity. The Fool is still with him when he arraigns his
absent daughters in the mock trial of 3.6, but Lear is now
himself a source of grotesque comedy, addressing his
real grievance against Goneril to a joint-stool and
couching it in an absurd image: she "kicked the poor
king her father" (3.6.51–52).

If Gloucester's sufferings at first seem exempt from
these grace notes of absurdity, he is nevertheless exposed at "Dover cliff" to the extreme of comic degrada-
tion. After the long buildup to a dramatic suicide leap
(matching his "climb" in the script), the old man simply
topples over. That which, as an idea of an action, arouses
not a smile (i.e., Edgar leading his father to a nonexis-
tent cliff and allowing him to go through the motions of
throwing himself over), when physically acted out becomes something like a clown's pratfall. At his most
serious moral climax, Gloucester enacts the supreme
indignity of falling on his nose. And when he intersects
with Lear later in this scene, the pain of these two
human ruins is punctuated by further absurdity. The
mad Lear finds in his former friend only grotesque
similitudes: Goneril with a white beard, a superannu-
ated blind Cupid (4.6.115, 152).

The final absurdity, the most shattering non sequitur,
is Cordelia's death. It is hard to see any dramatic logic
that prepares for this death or makes it an inevitable
consequence of previous action, especially when the
strong redemptive movement seems to point us in just

the opposite direction, i.e., to the refounded relation of an enlightened Lear to his newly valued youngest daughter. Edmund does indeed tell us that if Lear and Cordelia are captured they will be shown no mercy, and we see him sending off a captain with orders that we suspect are to be fatal for the king and his daughter, but Edmund is soon defeated by Edgar and in his dying repentance rescinds the order. He is, for no discernible reason, too late. The entrance of Lear with the dead Cordelia in his arms unites absurdity at its most cosmic with the second dynamic, expectations of better times frustrated by the blow that makes things worse than before. At the same time, this unexpected disaster violently contradicts the pronounced movement toward new wisdom through suffering.

As we live through the action of the play and experience its conclusion, how do we weight these dynamics that are similarly persistent but so radically different from each other in impact and import? Individual readers and viewers may well differ in their reactions. Does the persistent strain of reductive grotesquerie make Lear and Gloucester ironic figures rather than tragic, their actions pathetic gropings in a senseless universe? Or can they be felt as all the more heroic in triumphing over the forces of absurdity and random cruelty to arrive at an ethic of love and social obligation, an ethic no less necessary to the human community even if the larger universe is amoral? If wayward comedy attends their presentation, does the resultant laughter distance or intensify participation in their pain? Does Cordelia's death render Lear's painful progress meaningless, or does it force us to reevaluate in less sentimental terms the limits placed on any such progress by the human condition itself? At the very end, as Albany and Edgar look to a future beyond Lear, is the final stress on reordering more humanely the "gored state" (5.3.389), or rather on slogging stoically on, beyond the "promised end" which has once more been denied?

When we look away from Lear and Gloucester, the careers of other characters also defy easy moral and psychological assessment. Edgar's course is perhaps morally comprehensible in outline as he falls from high position to the condition of a destitute beggar and then wins his way back to his rightful estate, expanding his wisdom and sympathy in the process. Yet as Edgar at the play's beginning is hardly a blind, selfish Lear, we may wonder if his suffering is not more gratuitous than redemptive. Through Edgar's long engagement with the blind Gloucester, in his various disguises as beggar or countryman, the reader or viewer may well be anticipating the climactic moment when this devoted son reveals his true identity to the father who cast him off. But when it finally comes, that revelation is not shown to us but is only narrated. More unexpectedly, even shockingly, the revelation kills Gloucester. Does Gloucester's death in extremes of joy and grief fittingly conclude his long painful spiritual odyssey, or is it yet another indication that random absurdity governs events, making nonsense of Edgar's redemptive agenda? When Lear in defeat cares nothing for loss of royal power and serenely invites Cordelia to an idyllic life in prison where each will be totally absorbed in the other ("Come, let's away to prison," 5.3.9), Cordelia says nothing in response. Does Lear too unthinkingly accept the congealing of her young life with his old one, and look forward to a symbiosis that blots out her separate identity? So it could seem from the perspective of this daughter, who so firmly resisted Lear's initial wish to have all her love himself. From this point of view, in fact—the need of any child to break away from a demanding, all-engrossing parent—even the actions of Goneril and Regan escape neat categorization as unfounded pure evil. So, from another angle, does the course of Edmund, their ally in the play's oppositions of good children against bad. Even while these oppositions seem so stark as to invite a semiallegorical interpretation, Edmund can also be understood sociologically, as produced by the glaring social inequities of which this play recurrently reminds us. His malevolent ambition takes appropriate revenge on a society that has marginalized him as a bastard, automatically denying him the secure social position that otherwise his parentage and his talents would ensure.

Stark moral oppositions, then, are crossed in this complex play by trajectories of sociological and psychological questioning, just as the unexpected supplement and the random absurdity complicate Lear's and Gloucester's journeys toward insight. Like Dover, *King Lear* should act to open up vision, not close it down.

Further Reading

King Lear

Booth, Stephen. *King Lear, Macbeth, Indefinition and Tragedy*, pp. 5–57. New Haven and London: Yale University Press, 1983.

For Booth, *King Lear* is Shakespeare's greatest achievement because it is the audience's greatest achievement. *Lear* forces its audience to confront cruelty the way the characters of the play experience it, as a constant disappointment of the persistent promise of order and resolution. If we wish the ending otherwise, writes Booth, it would be to invite more discomfort. For every alternative to the ending of *Lear* "turns out to be in some way less acceptable." Thus the "greatness" of *Lear* derives in part from its great duration, its extended confrontation with inconclusiveness.

Delany, Paul. "*Lear* and the Decline of Feudalism." *PMLA: Publications of the Modern Language Association* 12 (1977): 429–40.

Delany considers the moral problems of *Lear* in the light of Shakespeare's history plays and the social problems of the period. The argument over Lear's train of knights reflects the struggle between the feudal aristocracy and the bourgeois class. The Tudor "crisis of aristocracy" is thus represented in the figure of Lear and in other figures of the old regime in Shakespeare's later plays. Although consistent with Marx's view of tragedy, Shakespeare's humanism, Delany argues, represents a nostalgic rather than forward-looking sensibility.

301

Everett, Barbara. "The New *King Lear*." *Critical Quarterly* 2 (1960): 325–39.

Everett reviews several "Christian" and allegorical interpretations of *Lear* before performing a more metaphysical reading of the tragedy. The play's presentation of startling disparity within a single imaginative world resists conformity with the symbolic clarity of a morality or mystery play, according to Everett. The play's continual relation of "the world" and "the soul" allows the expression of extreme malice and extreme good in the commonest of ways. Ultimately for Everett, the play exhilarates by allowing an audience to endure and understand great suffering, and thus to master it.

Goldberg, S. L. *An Essay on King Lear*. Cambridge: Cambridge University Press, 1974.

Goldberg argues that while *Lear* possesses some "integral meaning," it does not exist in any easily formulable "philosophy" or "moral vantage-point." The play's presentation to both characters and audience of "realities" that resist comprehension and any confident understanding reveals humanity's vulnerability to violence and chaos. In the end, the audience is forced to attempt an understanding of the "heightened vitality" to which the play brings them and an articulation of its own human existence.

Hawkes, Terence. "Lear's Maps: A General Survey." *Shakespeare Jahrbuch 1989:* 134–47.

Hawkes illustrates the symbolic force of the passage in *Lear* which features Britain's map by placing it in various con:exts: the play's material history, Harley Granville-Barker's 1940 Old Vic production, and contemporary literary criticism. Examining how cultural meanings are generated to produce different readings of the play—and texts in general—Hawkes explains the consequences of modern critical approaches and offers new perspectives to show that the play cannot be reduced to a single message.

Kozintsev, Grigori. *King Lear: The Space of Tragedy.* Translated by Mary Mackintosh. London: Heinemann, 1977.

Kozintsev's diary, kept by the Russian film director before and during the making of his notable version of *King Lear*, tracks his efforts to explore everything he encounters as a clue to a space in which Shakespeare's tragedy can find its being. The book treats diverse subjects, from the search for a landscape that can contain the dimensions of the play to the problems of directing a Lear with an Estonian accent.

Linville, Susan E. "'Truth is the daughter of Time': Formalism and Realism in *Lear*'s Last Scene." *Shakespeare Quarterly* 41 (1990): 309–18.

Linville examines the interpretive responses to Lear's "prison speech" at the beginning of the play's final act. Focusing specifically upon formalist and realist readings of the speech, she traces how each mode inevitably "generates its opposite" and therefore undermines cohesive ideas of the relationship between modes. Through an exploration of the supposed differences between readings, Linville comes to a conclusion that warns against any position that bars the intrusion of oppositional elements.

Long, Michael. *The Unnatural Scene: A Study in Shakespearean Tragedy*, pp. 158–219. London: Methuen, 1976.

Long views Lear as the only one of Shakespeare's tragic protagonists to achieve, if only momentarily, the Apollonian dream, in which contradictions between law and nature are fused. Long further argues that the final scene resists an allegorical or absurdist reading, and while he acknowledges Schopenhauer's and Nietzsche's responses to the tragedy (resignation and metaphysical solace or joy respectively), he adds his own sense of Shakespeare's "compassion" that makes the play "more humane" than either critic believes.

Mack, Maynard. *King Lear: In Our Time.* Berkeley: University of California Press, 1965.

Mack traces *Lear*'s stage history, its literary and imaginative sources, and what in the play "speaks most immediately to us" in our own time. Refuting both Christian readings that sentimentalize the play and nihilist readings that find only absurdity in the play's world, Mack submits that tragedy never "tells us what to think" but "shows us what we are and may be." Although *Lear* shows death to be "miscellaneous and commonplace," it shows life to be "noble and distinctive."

McEachern, Claire. "Fathering Himself: A Source Study of Shakespeare's Feminism." *Shakespeare Quarterly* 39 (1988): 269–90.

McEachern investigates Renaissance patriarchy through a study of fathers and daughters as presented in Shakespeare's plays, with special emphasis on *Much Ado About Nothing* and *King Lear*. She considers Shakespeare's transformation of *Lear*'s literary sources in terms of his reaction to ideologies of dominant male authority. By letting us see Lear abuse his authority over Cordelia, Shakespeare undermines our confidence "in the power that we invest in kings and fathers" and exposes the coercive pressures of patriarchy.

Orkin, Martin. "Cruelty, *King Lear*, and the South African Land Act of 1913." *Shakespeare Survey* 40 (1987): 135–44.

Orkin explores how the ramifications of the South African Land Act of 1913, which was crucial to the formation of apartheid, can illuminate the central issues of *Lear*: a ruthless ruling class and the relationship of land, power, and property. The image of Lear coming to realize—if confusedly—the nature of power's operation only after he has been deprived of power has special resonance for South Africans. For Orkin, the play acknowledges that only after loss do rulers learn anything; those in power never do.

Snyder, Susan. "*King Lear* and the Psychology of Dying." *Shakespeare Quarterly* 33 (1982): 449–60.

Snyder proposes that tragedy embodies two reactions to death. The first is that death is right and natural, since man is governed by nature's laws of growth and decay. Against this reaction, however, is set our implicit protest that death is wrong, unfairly imposed upon us by some external enemy. Our ambivalence toward death, the psychological process of protest, struggle, denial, and resignation, is enacted in *Lear*. Together, "Cordelia's death and Lear's act out the paradox of mortality."

Taylor, Gary, and Michael Warren, eds. *The Division of the Kingdoms: Shakespeare's Two Texts of "King Lear."* Oxford: Clarendon Press, 1983.

King Lear was originally published in two versions: a quarto of 1608 (Q1) reprinted in 1619 (Q2); and the version in the First Folio of 1623. The wide discrepancies between these versions (the Folio, for instance, is missing about 300 lines present in the quarto) is the subject of this collection of essays. The volume argues that the tradition of conflated texts has now died and that the play(s) must be thought of as distinct and must be issued today in separate editions. Although there is not total consensus among the volume's contributors, Gary Taylor's essay attempts to prove that the First Folio text is a Shakespearean revision of the quarto text, and that this revision dates from 1609–10.

Young, David. *The Heart's Forest: A Study of Shakespeare's Pastoral Plays*, pp. 73–103. New Haven and London: Yale University Press, 1972.

Young outlines *Lear*'s relation to the pastoral tradition, finding that the tragedy follows the pattern of pastoral romance as developed in Spain and Italy. *Lear*, like the pastoral, deals with characters forced to leave society and undergo a sojourn in a natural setting. But *Lear* employs the pastoral pattern in order ultimately to negate it. The characters are denied the consolations supposed to accompany "poverty, isolation, and humiliation." Having challenged the conventions of the pastoral tradition, *Lear* "drives on to challenge basic assumptions about the essential harmony of man and nature."

Shakespeare's Language

Abbott, E. A. *A Shakespearian Grammar*. New York: Haskell House, 1972.

This compact reference book, first published in 1870, helps with many difficulties in Shakespeare's language. It systematically accounts for a host of differences between Shakespeare's usage and sentence structure and our own.

Blake, Norman. *Shakespeare's Language: An Introduction*. New York: St. Martin's Press, 1983.

This general introduction to Elizabethan English discusses various aspects of the language of Shakespeare and his contemporaries, offering possible meanings for hundreds of ambiguous constructions.

Dobson, E. J. *English Pronunciation, 1500–1700.* 2 vols. Oxford: Clarendon Press, 1968.
This long and technical work includes chapters on spelling (and its reformation), phonetics, stressed vowels, and consonants in early modern English.

Houston, John. *Shakespearean Sentences: A Study in Style and Syntax.* Baton Rouge: Louisiana State University Press, 1988.
Houston studies Shakespeare's stylistic choices, considering matters such as sentence length and the relative positions of subject, verb, and direct object. Examining plays throughout the canon in a roughly chronological, developmental order, he analyzes how sentence structure is used in setting tone, in characterization, and for other dramatic purposes.

Onions, C. T. *A Shakespeare Glossary.* Oxford: Clarendon Press, 1986.
This revised edition updates Onions's standard, selective glossary of words and phrases in Shakespeare's plays that are now obsolete, archaic, or obscure.

Partridge, Eric. *Shakespeare's Bawdy.* London: Routledge & Kegan Paul, 1955.
After an introductory essay, "The Sexual, the Homosexual, and Non-Sexual Bawdy in Shakespeare," Partridge provides a comprehensive glossary of "bawdy" phrases and words from the plays.

Robinson, Randal. *Unlocking Shakespeare's Language: Help for the Teacher and Student.* Urbana, Ill.: National

Council of Teachers of English and the ERIC Clearing-house on Reading and Communication Skills, 1989.

Specifically designed for the high-school and under-graduate college teacher and student, Robinson's book addresses the problems that most often hinder present-day readers of Shakespeare. Through work with his own students, Robinson found that many readers today are particularly puzzled by such stylistic characteristics as subject-verb inversion, interrupted structures, and compression. He shows how our own colloquial language contains comparable structures, and thus helps students recognize such structures when they find them in Shakespeare's plays. This book supplies worksheets—with examples from major plays—to illuminate and remedy such problems as unusual sequences of words and the separation of related parts of sentences.

Shakespeare's Life

Baldwin, T. W. *William Shakspere's Petty School.* Urbana: University of Illinois Press, 1943.

Baldwin here investigates the theory and practice of the petty school, the first level of education in Elizabethan England. He focuses on that educational system primarily as it is reflected in Shakespeare's art.

Baldwin, T. W. *William Shakspere's Small Latine and Lesse Greeke.* 2 vols. Urbana: University of Illinois Press, 1944.

Baldwin attacks the view that Shakespeare was an uneducated genius—a view that had been dominant among Shakespeareans since the eighteenth century. Instead, Baldwin shows, the educational system of Shakespeare's time would have given the playwright a strong background in the classics, and there is much in the plays that shows how Shakespeare benefited from such an education.

Beier, A. L., and Roger Finlay, eds. *London 1500–1800: The Making of the Metropolis.* New York: Longman, 1986. Focusing on the economic and social history of early modern London, these collected essays probe aspects of metropolitan life, including "Population and Disease," "Commerce and Manufacture," and "Society and Change."

Bentley, G. E. *Shakespeare's Life: A Biographical Handbook.* New Haven: Yale University Press, 1961. This "just-the-facts" account presents the surviving documents of Shakespeare's life against an Elizabethan background.

Chambers, E. K. *William Shakespeare: A Study of Facts and Problems.* 2 vols. Oxford: Clarendon Press, 1930. Analyzing in great detail the scant historical data, Chambers's complex, scholarly study considers the nature of the texts in which Shakespeare's work is preserved.

Cressy, David. *Education in Tudor and Stuart England.* London: Edward Arnold, 1975. This volume collects sixteenth-, seventeenth-, and early-eighteenth-century documents detailing aspects of formal education in England, such as the curriculum, the control and organization of education, and the education of women.

Dutton, Richard. *William Shakespeare: A Literary Life.* New York: St. Martin's Press, 1989. Not a biography in the traditional sense, Dutton's very readable work nevertheless "follows the contours of

Shakespeare's life" as he examines Shakespeare's career as playwright and poet, with consideration of his patrons, theatrical associations, and audience.

Fraser, Russell. *Young Shakespeare*. New York: Columbia University Press, 1988.

Fraser focuses on Shakespeare's first thirty years, paying attention simultaneously to his life and art.

De Grazia, Margreta. *Shakespeare Verbatim: The Reproduction of Authenticity and the Apparatus of 1790*. Oxford: Clarendon Press, 1991.

De Grazia traces and discusses the development of such editorial criteria as authenticity, historical periodization, factual biography, chronological developments, and close reading, locating as the point of origin Edmond Malone's 1790 edition of Shakespeare's works. There are interesting chapters on the First Folio and on the "legendary" versus the "documented" Shakespeare.

Schoenbaum, S. *William Shakespeare: A Compact Documentary Life*. New York: Oxford University Press, 1977.

This standard biography economically presents the essential documents from Shakespeare's time in an accessible narrative account of the playwright's life.

Shakespeare's Theater

Bentley, G. E. *The Profession of Player in Shakespeare's Time, 1590–1642*. Princeton: Princeton University Press, 1984.

Bentley readably sets forth a wealth of evidence about performance in Shakespeare's time, with special